# Reform Judaism and Modernity

## Jonathan Romain

Born in 1954, Jonathan Romain is rabbi, writer and broadcaster. He took his first degree at University College, London, and then gained his PhD in Anglo-Jewish history. He studied for the rabbinate at Leo Baeck College and was ordained in 1980. He is minister of Maidenhead Synagogue in Berkshire. His seven publications include *The Jews of England* (Jewish Chronicle Publications) and *Renewing the Vision* (SCM Press). His book on mixed-faith marriages, *Till Faith Us Do Part* (Harper Collins), has helped pioneer a more welcoming attitude to couples who fall in love across the religious divide. He recently wrote *Your God Shall be My God* (SCM Press) on religious conversion in modern Britain. He also appears regularly on the radio and television, and was awarded the MBE for services to community relations. He is married with four sons.

# Reform Judaism and Modernity:

## A Reader

Jonathan A. Romain

scm press

For Benedict
(well named)

© Jonathan A. Romain 2004

British Library Cataloguing in Publication data

A catalogue record for this book is available
from the British Library

0 334 02948 1

First published in 2004 by SCM Press
9-17 St Albans Place, London N1 0NX

www.scm-canterburypress.co.uk

SCM Press is a division of
SCM-Canterbury Press Ltd

Printed and bound in Great Britain by
Biddles Ltd, www.biddles.co.uk

# CONTENTS

# LISTING OF EXTRACTS

## Chapter 4      Bible

## Chapter 5      Business Ethics

## Chapter 6      Charity

Chapter 17      Judaism

Chapter 18      The Messiah

Chapter 19      Mission

# PREFACE

Non-Jews are often confused by the variety of Jewish religious worship. Even the nomenclature can be confusing: it includes Ultra Orthodox, Hassidic, Orthodox, Reform, Liberal, Conservative, Reconstructionist, and even Secular. Many Jews cannot always appreciate, or enter sympathetically into the different strands of their religious diversity. Yet, despite being numerically a small people – less than fifteen million worldwide – they have always linked the Jewish ethic, as enshrined in the five Books of Moses, with the countries and cultures in which they lived, and both contributed to and drawn from the experiences of the nations that have accepted them.

The Reform movement entered the mainstream of Jewish religious life almost two hundred years ago. The first Reform synagogue was established in Germany in 1810. Eight years later the Reform synagogue in Hamburg used a prayer book specially revised to fit the community's perception of modern needs. In 1832 the revolutionary re-introduction of sermons in the vernacular began. As it spread throughout the Jewish world, with Britain and the United States in the forefront, Reform Judaism added to the immutability of the written law ideas and practices, reflecting contemporary outlooks and aspirations.

In this book, Rabbi Jonathan Romain presents the theological development of the Reform movement in Britain during the last 150 years, through the writings of a remarkable group of Reform thinkers and leaders. It is an instructive voyage of religious discovery. Some of the writers in these pages – among them Rabbi Lionel Blue and Rabbi Hugo Gryn – will be familiar to British Jews and non-Jews alike. Others, including Rabbi Leo Baeck, have long been at the centre of Jewish theological discussion and evolution. The writings of David Woolf Marks and Morris Joseph, two former Senior Ministers at the largest

Reform synagogue in Britain, the West London, make many thoughtful contributions.

Dr Romain has chosen twenty-six themes, which range, alphabetically, from Afterlife to Worship. He introduces each theme by placing it in the context of general Jewish thought, and ends each extract with a comment of his own. The Reform rabbis give us – through these extracts – their views and reflections. It is an instructive method that will quickly draw readers into the richness, modernity and spirituality of Reform theology.

My own introduction to the Reform movement came from Rabbi Hugo Gryn, whose congregant and friend I was for a quarter of a century. Among his contributions in this volume is one on the theme Jews in Society. Recalling his pre-war home town, from which he, his family and the whole Jewish community were deported to Auschwitz, and after noting that 'when the chips were down, I do not know of a single instance of a Jew from Berehovo being saved or hidden by a non-Jew', he went on to write: 'That I spend much of my time working for better understanding between religious groups and fighting racism as hard as I can, is partly because I know that you can only be safe and secure in a society that practises tolerance, cherishes harmony and can celebrate difference.'

Jonathan Romain celebrates difference with clarity, conviction and understanding.

Sir Martin Gilbert
Honorary Fellow, Merton College, Oxford

# INTRODUCTION

Reform Judaism is one of the most dynamic forces in the Jewish world. It dominates American Jewry, where it is not only the largest synagogue movement, but is at the forefront of outreach projects, both to those nominally involved in Jewish life and to those totally unaffiliated. It is instrumental in the rejuvenation of Jews within the former Soviet Union who are slowly reclaiming their Jewish heritage after seventy years of Communist suppression of religion in general and Judaism in particular. In Europe it has helped rekindle the flickering embers of Jewish communities devastated by the Holocaust. In Israel it is small but very much on the increase, forming a unique bridge between the largely secular Jewish population and the religious legacy it has previously rejected but is now beginning to rediscover.

Reform Judaism also occupies a leading place within the religious life of Britain today. Despite two negative trends – a decline in religious affiliation in the country at large and a decrease in the numerical size of British Jewry – Reform Judaism is bucking the trend and growing. Its communities are expanding and its rabbinic seminary is flourishing. On a wider front, its rabbis have been at the very forefront of inter-faith dialogue, both in Jewish–Christian and Jewish–Muslim relations. Moreover, two Reform rabbis in particular, Lionel Blue and the late Hugo Gryn, have contributed significantly to the religious life of the nation in recent decades through their high-profile roles on radio and television. In addition, they have helped shape (or, rather, re-shape) popular perception of what it means to be Jewish. The oft-heard quip that Rabbi Blue would have been a wonderful choice for Archbishop of Canterbury is testimony both to the high esteem in which he is held and to the form of Judaism he represents.

But what does Reform Judaism stand for? What does it believe? As is seen in the Historical Overview, Reform Judaism did not start from either the teachings of one charismatic individual, or from a declaration of new principles of faith by a group inspired to break away from tradition. Its birth in 1840 and progress thereafter was much more prosaic and incremental, and it underwent several theological lurches before a distinctive and coherent position emerged over a hundred years later. A detailed history of British Reform has already been written,[1] as has a practical guide to the day-to-day practices of the faith.[2] This book – the third in the trilogy – is concerned with the theology of Reform Judaism and the stance it takes on a variety of religious themes that will be of interest both to its own membership and far beyond. However, a word of warning is needed for those seeking definitive answers or doctrinal certainties. The movement's name is 'Reform Judaism' – not 'Reformed Judaism'. It did not depart from Orthodoxy only to form another Orthodoxy, merely exchanging one Mount Sinai for another fixed point, parts of which would eventually become obsolete too. Instead it adheres to the notion of Progressive Revelation, in which the human understanding of the will of God is constantly evolving, an on-going process that challenges every succeeding generation to find its own responses. It means, therefore, that many aspects of Judaism are subject to changes in perception or definition as greater knowledge or new insights emerge. This can be seen especially in the notion of suffering after the Holocaust, or the importance of the Land of Israel after the establishment of the State of Israel, as well as the changing role of women in Jewish life. Thus in many instances, this book traces developments in religious thinking and offers 'the story so far' rather than provide final conclusions.

Two criteria have guided the selection of material for the book. First, it is taken only from rabbis. This is not to ignore the fact that Reform Judaism was founded by laity and has involved a strong level of lay leadership ever since then, as well as some notable cases of lay scholarship. However, its religious direction has largely been shaped by rabbis. The fact that a person has gained rabbinic ordination does not make their views representative of the movement as a whole, but it does mean that they speak with at least some authority based on years of study. Second, the material chosen has been restricted to printed works, be it books, pamphlets and articles, as well as sermons and lectures that have later been published. If certain names emerge as regular features in the book,

---

1 Anne Kershen and Jonathan Romain, 1995, *Tradition and Change: A History of Reform Judaism in Britain 1840–1995*, London: Vallentine Mitchell.
2 Jonathan Romain, 1991, *Faith and Practice: A Guide to Reform Judaism Today*, London: RSGB.

it is indicative of the fact that, as a generalization, the Reform rabbinate over the last century and a half has been much more concerned with congregational work than with literary endeavours. Only a handful have become full-time academics and a relatively small number have published books. It has become very clear during the research for this book that – from the perspective of history – rabbis who do not write do not survive. Sadly, the impact of sermons that stirred and inspired in their day are limited to the lifetime of the hearers and does not continued beyond them. The only exceptions are if those rabbis have disciples who not only quote them but also record those quotes, although this is fairly rare. Moreover, of those who have written, pressure of space has meant that many extracts that were worthy of inclusion have had to be set aside. There are also those who have written extensively but not on the subjects covered in this book. The choice of a passage was never dictated by the author (neither to select leading figures, nor to include those not already mentioned) but solely by the intrinsic value of the passage itself, either because it contained an original viewpoint or articulated attitudes that were in general circulation at the time. Thus there has been no attempt to equalize the number of times different people have been quoted, or to balance male and female rabbis, or to enlarge the list of those cited. The significance of the extract was the only criterion.

The fact that the majority of the writers are men reflects the history of the rabbinate until recent times; if this book were to be written fifty years hence, a different picture would emerge. The omission of any rabbis whose material is not quoted does not carry any implication as to their contribution to Reform Judaism in general or to their own congregation in particular. Their absence reflects only my word-count, not on their merit. A series of essays by a wide list of contemporary rabbis is available for those interested in becoming familiar with other modern figures.[3] Constraints of space have also meant that certain topics could not be addressed. It was decided to omit those that had been at least partially tackled elsewhere, such as Sexual or Medical Ethics.[4] Others omitted were subjects that had not been addressed until modern times and there was little historical development to record. This applies to Islam: for geographical reasons, Reform Judaism has only just started having meaningful contact with its world, but although it has no separate section, attitudes to Islam are mentioned in the chapter on 'Dialogue'.

3 Jonathan Romain (ed.), 1996, *Renewing the Vision: Rabbis Speak Out on Modern Jewish Issues*, London: SCM Press.
4 See note 2.

If one of the objects of this book has been to present the essence of Reform Judaism, another has been to reclaim the past. Until now much of the material left by even those rabbis who did write has been lost from sight. Books can easily be forgotten once out of print, while articles can disappear even more quickly. The seminal figures of the past may be known by name – a David Woolf Marks or a Morris Joseph – but few are familiar with what they actually wrote. One of the religious giants of the last century, Leo Baeck, would probably be unknown to all but a handful had not a rabbinic college been named after him. Several generations have grown up sensing that such characters are important, but not knowing why. In some cases, their writings are significant because of the stages they represent in the development of Reform theology; in other cases, their thoughts are as relevant today as when they were first set down. It is noticeable that, with some exceptions, Reform publications today rarely quote works by Reform rabbis, past or present. In part this is because Reform Judaism sees itself as heir to Judaism in general and is happy to quote Jewish teachers from a wide range of traditions, but it also reflects the lack of availability of Reform source material. This book attempts to rectify that gaping hole. It is also to be hoped that those who have enjoyed reading the extracts of particular rabbis will obtain their books and delve further into their writings.

Thanks are due to Raymond Goldman, Rabbi Professor Jonathan Magonet and Rabbi Sybil Sheridan for their helpful comments on my first draft; to Rabbi Tony Bayfield for encouraging me to go ahead with the project when we discussed it during a late-night walk in Boston; and to Rabbi Dr Albert Friedlander for his useful advice whenever I requested some background information. On the production side, I am grateful to Alex Wright for his support during the initial stages of the book and to Catherine Marshall for always being there for me. A final word of appreciation goes to those who were my own teachers in Judaism – an extraordinary succession of individuals at Middlesex New Synagogue – thanks to whom I decided to enter the rabbinate: Gordon Smith, Sid Fenton, Abe Simons, Rabbi Michael Goulston and Rabbi Ady Assabi. Apart from Gordon, they have all passed away, but their influence remains.

Jonathan A. Romain
Maidenhead, 2004

# HISTORICAL OVERVIEW

It is astonishing that the British version of Reform Judaism, established in 1840, should have waited over 160 years for a comprehensive survey of its beliefs and theology to emerge. This lengthy gap is no accident but reflects the curious birth-pangs and peculiar development of the movement since then.

Judaism has been evolving ever since it began. It is evident within the Pentateuch itself, while the Prophets added a radical edge to the Law of Moses. This was followed by a period when different strands co-existed, with Pharisees, Sadducees, Essenes and others all promoting different versions of Jewish life. The dominance of rabbinic interpretation after the first century led to a more monolithic form of Judaism, although it also engineered major changes in the beliefs, practices and development of the faith. New movements arose over the centuries, with some falling away, such as the Karaites, but others assimilating into mainstream Judaism and adding their influence to it, such as Hasidism. It means that although Reform Judaism is described in some circles as a breakaway movement, it sees itself as merely part of the long tradition of change within Judaism.

Reform Judaism began in Germany, where the need for religious change had been heightened by the sudden emergence of the Jewish community into society at large after years of isolation. Jews had been cut off from wider social and intellectual life both by the confines of the ghetto and by numerous discriminatory laws preventing them from playing a meaningful role in European life. The collapse of the ghetto following the upheavals of the Napoleonic Wars brought a rush of new knowledge and opportunities. While some Jews reacted by hiding themselves away from this new world, others by converting to Christianity, and others by abandoning all faith, a large number sought to harmonize tradition and modernity through Reform Judaism. The first synagogue was established in 1810 in Seesen.

British Jewry, by contrast, had experienced no such isolation. Since the resettlement in 1656 Jews were free to reside wherever they wished and able to engage in most occupations. The primary prohibition they faced was from holding civil office. They did not experience any sudden social and cultural leap from the Middle Ages to the Enlightenment, and hence Reform's start in Britain was almost a generation later than in Germany. However, it should be noted that those Jews who were pressing for political reforms were also among those most interested in religious reform – such as Isaac Goldsmid – and there is undoubtedly a connection between their impatience with civil disabilities and their frustration with religious anachronisms.

It is also significant that Reform Judaism in Britain started before the impact of various scholarly developments, which had a major effect on religious thinking in Europe. These included Darwin's *On the Origin of Species* (published in 1859), and the growth of Biblical Criticism headed by Wellhausen's *Prolegomena zur geschichte Israels* (published 1882). While the religious debate they unleashed certainly helped the cause of Reform Judaism and gave it greater intellectual respectability, it had not been responsible for Reform's birth; nor had there been in England any equivalent of the historical study and scientific analysis of Judaism that had arisen in Germany in 1819 with the establishment of *Wissenschaft des Judentums*. Neither is there any evidence that British Reform was particularly knowledgeable of such initiatives in Germany, unlike Reform Judaism in America, which was heavily influenced both by trends in Germany and by German rabbis who emigrated to the United States. It is clear that British Reform did not have a strong intellectual or theological genesis, and its real parents, as seen below, were communal discord and individual dissension.

Unlike many religious groups both inside and outside Judaism, Reform Judaism was started not by a charismatic individual but by a committee. What is more, it was exclusively a lay committee, consisting of twenty-four individuals who were motivated not by any passionate religious principles but by practical concerns over the establishment of a branch synagogue nearer to where they lived. They belonged largely to the Spanish and Portuguese Congregation of Bevis Marks in the City of London, but resided some distance away in the West End of London and requested permission to hold prayers there. Had the Bevis Marks elders acceded to their petition, the new synagogue would have been Orthodox and the birth of Reform Judaism would have been considerably delayed. However, the authorities objected – fearing the loss of wealthy members, which would cause financial difficulties for the main synagogue. The result was that the committee of twenty-four decided to act independently and establish what became known as the West London Synagogue of British Jews. It was only at this point that they also decided to take advantage of their new freedom to exercise changes in religious matters also. They therefore introduced a few minor liturgical reforms and some calendrical alterations. There was no attempt at establishing a new theological system or proposing new articles of faith. They were guided by pragmatism rather than a new vision, and regarded themselves merely as making a few overdue prunings to an otherwise healthy tree. What they failed to appreciate – although their opponents realized it clearly enough – was that the right to make changes unilaterally and without reference to rabbinic authority was in itself an important new development. It was only after their secession that the committee sought to employ rabbinic leadership. Thus although the first Reform minister, David Woolf Marks, was subsequently to exert great influence, his role was to give shape and expression to a movement that was lay-led and founded on moderate change.

As the first non-Orthodox synagogue in the country, the establishment of the West London Synagogue was greeted with considerable excitement and debate within British Jewry. The 'Reformers' had issued a public defence of their principles, while the Ashkenazi and Sephardi ecclesiastical authorities had joined together to issue a *herem* (ban), and excommunicated them. For its part, the lay Jewish representative organization, the Board of Deputies, refused to acknowledge the validity of West London and denied it the right to send any deputies to the Board's meetings. In due course, these objections were quietly dropped, with the *herem* being lifted in 1849 and the Board admitting West

London to its membership some thirty years later. After this initial burst of activity, the next hundred years of Reform in Britain were relatively uneventful. Although West London grew in size, it did not make strenuous efforts to attract new members, nor to establish branch synagogues. Attempts by like-minded families to found a synagogue in South London failed. The birth of Manchester Reform Synagogue in 1856 was almost completely independent of West London, and, like West London's own genesis, was as much to do with disagreements among the local Orthodox community as with any reforming zeal.

The seeds of the subsequent growth of Reform did not occur until the 1930s, thanks to the immigration of refugees from Germany and elsewhere on the Continent, many of whom were Reform, and either swelled existing Reform congregations or led to the birth of new ones. Even more important was the arrival of a large number of Reform rabbis who were able to serve the new communities and provide a level of religious leadership to which the Reform movement could not otherwise have aspired. Prior to that point, the handful of Reform synagogues had been led by Reform rabbis trained in the United States, or by English ministers who had trained at the Orthodox seminary, Jews College, but later switched to the Reform.

Each of the Reform synagogues was independent and there was no formal contact between them until 1942. Here, too, it was practical problems rather than matters of principle that resulted in the formation of a national movement. In this instance, it arose over concerns surrounding the religious education of children who had been evacuated to non-Jewish areas during the Second World War. The committee charged with overseeing arrangements for them was controlled by the Chief Rabbi, who refused to make any separate provision for the education of Reform children, even though Reform teachers were available. Meeting on 4 January 1942, the six existing Reform congregations formed the Associated British Synagogues (ABS) to cater for the children's needs.[1] The benefits of joint action quickly became obvious, and the ABS began to tackle a wide range of other topics, from nurturing new communities to establishing a *Beth Din* to deal with status issues. In 1946 the organization changed its name to the Association of Synagogues in Great Britain

---

1 They were Bradford, Glasgow, Manchester, North Western, The Settlement, and West London. Edgware had been founded in 1935, but temporarily disbanded during the war.

(ASGB), reflecting a greater consciousness of being a national movement with a common purpose. As the constituent synagogues grew in number, size and confidence, there were calls for the name to be changed yet again to reflect their Reform character. Supporters of the proposals argued that ASGB was too anodyne a title and that the movement should be proud to show its true colours. Opponents claimed that to describe themselves as Reform would be an admission that they did not represent the main thrust of Judaism and would be condemning themselves to sectarianism. The debate over 'adjectival Judaism' was settled in 1958 when the movement became formally known as the Reform Synagogues of Great Britain (RSGB), by which time it had increased to sixteen congregations.

The continuous growth of the movement led to the need for the professionalization of its structure – until then conducted purely by voluntary leaders – both to support individual congregations and to develop central resources. In 1966 Raymond Goldman was appointed the General Secretary of the movement and heralded the successive arrival of other posts, including a Youth Development Officer and the Convener of the *Beth Din*. Another landmark came in 1980, when the RSGB moved out of the two rooms it had been renting at West London Synagogue and established its own premises, first in Swiss Cottage and then in the spacious grounds of the Manor House in Finchley, the Sternberg Centre, making it the largest Jewish community centre in Europe. The dramatic physical expansion of the Reform headquarters reflected its growth nationally, by then consisting of thirty communities stretching from Southend to Glasgow.

Developments during this period included the establishment of various national organizations to serve the membership – including a youth movement and association of guilds – as well as major revisions of the Prayer Book, foundation of a rabbinic seminary, Leo Baeck College, and the admission of women into the rabbinate. In 1981, the first Reform Jewish Day School was founded, Akiva, an unthinkable development for earlier generations, by whom it would have been regarded as separatist, but which marked a new stage in Reform's approach to Jewish education and lifestyle. Relations with the Orthodox became increasingly hostile from the 1960s onwards, largely in response to the growth of Reform, which previously had been dismissed as an irrelevance but which was now seen as a threat. However, the 'Stanmore Accords' of 1998 brought agreement among all the major sections of British Jewry not to engage in public vilification of each other and to work together in areas of common interest. Generally, cordial relations exist between Reform and the Liberals, the smaller, more radical movement established in 1902. Since then, the two have grown closer in approach and practice, and in the 1980s there were serious discussions over a merger, although this did not materialize. Today they share several institutions, including the Leo Baeck College-Centre for Jewish Education. The recent emergence of the Masorti movement, with a more enlightened traditional approach, could offer a challenge to Reform's appeal. However, it is too new to tell whether it might be a serious threat, while at present it consists of only a handful of congregations and is limited to London and the surrounding area. The appointment of a rabbi – Tony Bayfield – as Chief Executive, the Reform movement's professional head, in 1994 not only reflected his personal abilities but was also a signal of its commitment to make religious values and Jewish learning its core mission.

In 1840 West London was considered an interesting anomaly by some and a dangerous heresy by others. Today Reform is considered a respected part of the mainstream community, has a national presence and is the second largest movement in British Jewry. In the intervening years, it has experienced continuous growth, both in the number of synagogues and range of activities. It is especially prominent in the field of youth work and Jewish education, but also well known for its egalitarian stance in worship and in the rabbinate, as well as a leading light in social action and inter-faith dialogue. It also has a reputation for pioneering new approaches in difficult issues affecting modern Jewish life, such as mixed-faith marriage and gay rights. On the negative side, it has not grown as much as could have been expected, given the example of American Reform, which has become the largest Jewish movement in the United States. Moreover, there are a substantial number of British Jews who are affiliated to Orthodox synagogues but who think and practise Reform, yet have not transferred their membership.[2] In addition, the Reform movement's unwillingness (or lack of ability) to give

2 The factors behind this discrepancy are not the subject of this study but can be examined in Anne Kershen and Jonathan Romain, 1995, *Tradition and Change: A History of Reform Judaism in Britain 1840–1995*, Valentine Mitchell.

definite rulings on beliefs and observance, which is seen by some as a virtue, is regarded by others as a weakness and confusion. It reflects the lack of theological principles from which it has suffered from birth. The motto that used to appear on its letterhead for many years – 'rooted in tradition, responding to change' – is an apt summary of the ad hoc way in which it has developed, and the means by which it has achieved its place in modern Jewry.

It will quickly become evident to readers of this book that certain names dominate particular periods. David Woolf Marks and Morris Joseph feature heavily in the years 1840–1930 because of their influential position as Senior Ministers of the first and largest Reform synagogue, West London; moreover, although other ministers existed, it was Marks and Joseph alone who produced books through which they both addressed their contemporaries and handed down a legacy to future generations. They were the key influences in the development of British Reform, although their theology differed considerably. Marks had already displayed reforming tendencies while serving as an Orthodox minister and refusing to conduct services on the second days of festivals. His objection was that they were not sanctioned in the Bible but were merely later, rabbinic ordinances for communities outside the Land of Israel. For him, the Pentateuch was sacred and binding while rabbinic literature was man-made and lacked absolute authority. This radical viewpoint loosened his adherence to Orthodox Judaism and made him one of the few existing ministers who could be asked to lead the newly established Reform congregation. However, there were major inconsistencies in Marks' approach, as there were many commands within the Bible which he did not countenance, while there were also many rabbinic traditions that he did uphold. He never developed a coherent doctrine to resolve this conflict, nor even appeared to acknowledge its existence. Moreover, it could be argued that Marks was more concerned with challenging rabbinic authority than establishing new Reform principles. While he proved a vigorous voice for change, he did not provide guidelines by which this should be achieved. Joseph, who had also served as an Ortho-dox minister in the same town of Liverpool before joining West Lon-don, offered a less dramatic but more rounded approach. He sought to maintain the value of the Bible as well as acknowledge the importance of later traditions, but also to be open to new adaptations. His attempt to present Reform Judaism as (in the title of his major work) 'Creed and Life' offered a readable and reasonable account, but it still lacked a systematic theology that set out criteria by which traditions were judged and changes introduced. In many respects, the somewhat subjective step-by-step approach adopted by both Marks and Joseph has suited the practical development of Reform synagogues in Britain, but it did leave a theological vacuum that become apparent whenever intellectual chal-lenges are made to it from either side of the religious spectrum.[3]

In the years after 1930, the arrival of many refugee Reform rabbis from the Continent led to a much wider variety of Reform voices here, but two in particular stand out. Leo Baeck is quoted frequently because of his enormous personal stature. Even though the majority of his life had been spent in Germany, his scholarship and moral influence made him a significant figure in British Jewry too. Ignaz Maybaum was one of several much younger rabbis whose rabbinic careers were interrupted by the Nazi persecutions. Their names include Charles Berg, Curtis Cassell, Michael Curtis, Gerhard Graf, Bruno Italiener, Arthur Katz, Ernest Sawady, and Werner van Der Zyl. They all held pulpits on the Continent before the war and then, after experiencing a hiatus often fraught with per-sonal danger, continued their ministries in Britain. However, Maybaum alone had a prodigious literary output. Both Baeck and Maybaum were highly influential among fellow rabbis and rabbinical students, and brought with them a much greater emphasis on theological issues. However, the decidedly non-theological course of Reform Judaism in Britain was too set for their writings to make a substantial impact on the character of the movement at large, even if their own personal ministries had great effect. The establishment of the Leo Baeck College in 1956 for the training of Progressive rabbis in Britain resulted in a large increase in the rabbinate, producing a continuous stream of largely British-born

---

3 For a fuller discussion of Marks and Joseph, see Michael Goulston, 'The theology of Reform Judaism in Great Britain – a survey', in Dow Marmur (ed.), 1973, *Reform Judaism*, London: RSGB, pp. 53 ff.

graduates, who became the new leaders and moulders of Reform Judaism. A series of anthologies containing essays by such rabbis – edited by Dow Marmur (1973 and 1979), Jonathan Romain (1996), Sybil Sheridan (1994 and, with Sylvia Rothschild, in 2000), was indicative of the rabbinate's leap in size, diversity and confidence. From the 1990s, a growing number of individual rabbis published works of their own, building up a wide range of literary endeavour. However, these were virtually all with non-Jewish publishers, as the Reform Synagogues of Great Britain had no publishing arm, while the only specifically Jewish publishing house in Britain, Vallentine Mitchell, had a relatively small output. A special relationship grew up between several rabbis and SCM Press, originally a Christian publisher but which had developed an interest in Jewish themes. There were also rabbis who limited themselves to articles, which generally appeared in Reform journals, such as *The Synagogue Review*, or *Manna*.

It should be borne in mind that Reform Judaism in Britain is based on a highly democratic structure. There is no Chief Rabbi or other figure who imposes absolute authority or utters infallible statements. Instead, policy is debated by the Assembly of Rabbis, which consists of all the rabbis serving Reform congregations and institutions. Its decisions are usually the result of consensus based on research and discussion. When unanimity is impossible to achieve, matters are resolved by majority vote. However, the ultimate decision-making authority for the Reform movement is its annual conference, which is dominated by lay members, and any rabbinic decisions of far-reaching consequence have to be ratified by it. It is extremely rare for the lay body to turn down rabbinic decisions, but that is largely because any such decisions have been based on wide consultation within the movement beforehand and potential objections have been taken into account in shaping the final recommendation. The result is that definitive pronouncements are only made if they have wide support, which can be particularly difficult in the realm of theology. This is all the more challenging because of Judaism's long history of being concerned with the exact detail of rituals and practices, but being much more sanguine in the realm of beliefs. While many Jewish scholars have written extensively on theological issues, their writings have been ancillary to the primary thrust of the commandments obligatory on all Jews, which surround actions rather than ideas. As a generalization – with all the usual caveats – it is broadly true to say that in Christianity, the heretic is usually defined as someone who believes the wrong thing, whereas in Judaism, the heretic is someone who does the wrong thing. The paucity of theology also reflects a certain religious diffidence characteristic of British Jewry as a whole, which is wary of making grandiose statements of faith. This is distinct from the Reform movements in both Germany and America, which have produced a series of 'platforms' delineating their beliefs. Instead, British Reform has concentrated on practical issues it feels need to be mandatory, such as forms of liturgy and procedures in matters of conversion and divorce. Indeed, the first attempt to articulate a Reform theological position – 'the Manna platform' – had to wait until 1990 and, despite its usefulness, has not influenced the movement as a whole. It is because of the theological reticence that has characterized Reform Judaism until now that this book seeks to draw together the sporadic efforts of those individuals who have sought to address key issues in their time.

# NOTES ON THE TEXT

Each chapter is based around a separate theme. Some brief background information is given as to the development of the theme in Jewish thinking, or raising questions about the issue. This is followed by various passages on the subject by Reform rabbis, each of which has a number for ease of identity and to enable cross-referencing. The date given refers to when the piece was published, except in the case of D. W. Marks' published sermons, where the date of delivery is used. Each passage is preceded by a short paragraph setting it in context and followed by a comment on it. The object of the latter is to encourage the reader not only to peruse the material but to enter into the debate and interact with the texts. In some chapters there may be a time-gap of several decades between passages quoted, either because the general position on that theme had not changed radically during the intervening period or because, while attitudes may have altered, no one had addressed it formally until then. Most chapters end with 'A Final Thought' – a more anecdotal or personal piece which illustrates the theme from a different perspective. Biographical notes of authors quoted can be found at the back of the book.

The term Reform Judaism is used throughout the book to refer to the beliefs and practices of Reform synagogues. However, some writers in the passages quoted use the term Progressive Judaism as an alternative description. It should also be noted that in the nineteenth and early twentieth centuries, congregational ministers tended to be known as Reverend, whereas later they reverted to the more traditional title of Rabbi. However, no difference in role or scholarship is implied by the change in title. The full titles of authors are given in the introduction to each passage, but thereafter just surnames are used.

When quoting authors it has sometimes been necessary to curtail material, both for the sake of brevity and to preserve the main thrust of their argument. A substantial jump has been shown by a succession of dots, although omission of a few sentences has not been indicated unless there is a change of theme.

The passages quoted have been listed in chronological order of their original publication, even if the editions used are from a later date.

The differences in spellings and transliterations used by the individual writers have been allowed to remain, and so some variations will be noted. Hebrew terms are given in italics and can be found in the Glossary.

When a particular reference in the passages quoted needs explanation, or a word added to clarify a sentence, this has been given in square brackets [ ].

This book can be read in chronological order. However, the different chapters have been written as self-contained units so as to facilitate those readers who wish to consult a particular one independently.

# 1

# AFTERLIFE

In contrast to some religions, Judaism has never had a clear map of the hereafter. There are a few mentions of what happens after death in the Bible, but they are disconnected and inconclusive. When Enoch died 'God took him' (Genesis 5.24), while Korach and his followers went down into an undefined Sheol (Numbers 16.33) and Samuel was somehow summoned from the dead (1 Samuel 28.11). From these and other references, it seems that two different doctrines appear to co-exist within the Bible. First, the notion of the immortality of the soul, according to which, from the time of the death the soul lives on separately from the body and has a continued existence (see Proverbs 12.28). Second, the idea of the resurrection of the dead, according to which a person dies at the time of death (both body and soul) but will revive and be resurrected bodily in the messianic era (see Daniel 12.2). In early rabbinic thinking the two concepts merged to form the belief that a person's soul survived the death of their body and lived on until the messianic age when it was reunited with its body and the person resurrected. Orthodoxy today still maintains this belief in a combination of immortality and resurrection, whereas Reform Judaism has made a sharp distinction between them, accepting the former but rejecting the latter.

## 1.1 David Woolf Marks on Future Judgements (1884)

*Ecclesiastes 11.9 warns young men that while they may enjoy their youth now in self-indulgent ways, eventually they will have to face God's judgement. No details are given as to what this entails, but Reverend Professor*

1

*Marks was concerned that contemporary Jews could be influenced by the
strong Christian emphasis on the perils of hell in their reading of the Bible.
He comments on the text to show how Judaism differs from such a view.*

No Scriptural teaching has been more abused than that which is un-
folded in the text passage and it has not infrequently been perverted into
an instrument of terror, and made to serve as a prop to ecclesiastical
domination . . . For Israelites, the primary religious idea is the one and
only God, bearing to His children the relation of a tender and beneficent
Father and made perceptible to our comprehension in the book of nature
and through the gracious perfections revealed by Him through Moses.
Next in importance to this religious idea is the relation of our spirits to
'the Lord God of the spirits of all flesh' (Numbers 27.16) in another stage
of being; for that there is a hereafter for man may be reasonably inferred
from the passage [in Ecclesiastes], and the inference is confirmed by a
mass of indirect evidence. The moral aspect of things here below may
well impress all, who conceive of the supreme being as the perfection
of goodness, with the belief that a future state will bring out a more
distinct exhibition of divine justice than is made manifest on our earthly
planet.

   . . . Our Scriptures teach us that when we appear before the Supreme
Being in judgement, a distinction will be made between the good and
the bad (Ezekiel 24.7) . . . a great reward for the God-fearing and the
right-doing is the confident belief of the Psalmist (Psalm 31.20; 16.10)
. . . Of the condition that will await the wicked who die impenitent the
Hebrew Scriptures, after telling us that they will be 'cut off', suffer the
curtain to fall. But, though the Bible be reticent with respect to the lot
of the wicked, conjecture has assumed great licence, and has indulged in
wild speculation, the outcome of which has been, that there is a bottom-
less pit, or hell, abounding in every torment and horror which a morbid
fancy can conjure up, and language portray in the blackest colouring;
and that over this revolting place Almighty God, whom a fearful superstition has transformed into a kind of insatiable demon, will glut his
vengeance throughout eternity on sinful mortals. According to orthodox Christianity, this is to be the fate not only of those whose lives have
been tainted by crime, but of those also who may have fallen into error
of opinion on matters of religious belief.

. . . Now there is not a single word to be found in the Hebrew Scriptures that furnishes an equivalent to the vulgar notion of hell. The true meaning of *Sheol*, translated 'hell' would be 'the grave'. . . . The immortality of the soul is a belief common to all Jews, some of whom insist on the belief in a resurrection of the body, while others lay no stress on the latter dogma, because it finds no absolute authorisation in the Hebrew Scriptures. The rabbins [rabbis] kept clear of the notion of eternity of punishment, because it militates against the supreme doctrine of God's infinite mercy . . . We unconditionally reject the idea of a hell on various grounds, one of the chief of which is that it is . . . a teaching as revolting as it is paradoxical, that God will torture a human soul throughout eternity.

. . . It does not follow, however, that there is nothing to be apprehended beyond the grave by the persistent and unrepentant transgressor. Though nothing be revealed touching the nature of the punishment that awaits those whose whole lives have been stained by iniquity, it is assuredly no slight retribution to know that sooner or later they will have to render an account unto Him who knoweth the thoughts of mankind and 'considereth all their deeds' (Psalm 33.15).

Source: David Woolf Marks, *Lectures & Sermons*, Vol. III, pp. 209–28.

COMMENT: *Marks finds it easier to describe aspects of the afterlife in which Judaism does not believe, rather than describe what it does hold true. However, this merely reflects the aversion of Judaism in general to committing itself to specific details on the subject and the way in which, as he puts it so elegantly, Judaism much prefers to 'suffer the curtain to fall'. Marks adheres to the traditional belief that there is an afterlife and that some form of judgement takes place there, although he does also introduce the notion that a certain degree of punishment occurs in this world, through the fear a sinner feels at what may lie ahead. It is an idea that later thinkers develop and even use as an alternative to any form of retribution in the hereafter.*

## 1.2 Morris Joseph on the Afterlife (1903)

*Reverend Joseph was less concerned with distinguishing the Jewish concept of the afterlife from that of Christianity; his main thrust was to differentiate between past beliefs within Judaism and the more modern ones of his own time, especially with regard to the question of literal resurrection of the dead.*

That the future life was a reality to these ancient poets and seers [of the Bible] is certain. All that can justly be said is that their allusions to it are more or less veiled. If the Israelite cherished the great truth of immortality it was in his inmost heart. It was part of his consciousness rather than of his life. The present claimed his thoughts and his energies; the future he left to God . . . Judaism, when at its best, has steadily kept before it this idea of the spirituality of the future recompense. Such notions as that of a Resurrection of the Body, of physical torments for the sinner, of a celestial playground, the scene of more or less sensuous pleasures, have found a place in certain phases of Jewish doctrine; but they have been rejected by one of the best Jewish teachers [Maimonides] . . . and such is the view generally adopted by the modern Jew. For him punishment in the future life affects the soul only. He thinks of it as akin to the remorse which tortures the guilty even in this existence . . . Spiritual too is the reward. If Hell is remorse, Heaven is the bliss of conscious communion with the Highest . . . With this general conception of eternal life we shall do well to content ourselves. There is an existence beyond the grave; there are larger possibilities of happiness for the soul than this life can offer. The simple conviction is surely enough; to know more is unnecessary. Why essay to fill in the details of the gracious picture? The attempt is but unprofitable guesswork.

Source: Morris Joseph, *Judaism as Creed and Life*, pp. 89, 144–8.

COMMENT: *Joseph is at pains to stress that thoughts of the afterlife do not play an active role in Jewish life. Jews know about them, but concentrate on this world. He is also much firmer than Marks in his rejection of the Resurrection of the Body and makes it clear that this is no longer part of modern Judaism (although it is highly questionable whether it is legitimate to cite Maimonides as backing his claim). Joseph's final verdict is essentially that enquirers should kindly leave the subject alone – a remarkable statement when compared to the attitude of many other faiths, but typical of Judaism.*

## 1.3  Morris Joseph on Immortality (1907)

*Despite the advice Reverend Joseph had given in the extract quoted above, that Jews should shy away from the subject of the afterlife, he finds it impossible not to allude to it himself when addressing the congregation on Yom Kippur. In part this reflects the character of the day and its solemn theme of spiritual self-examination, but it is also an indication of the natural human inclination to wonder about what happens after death, notwithstanding rabbinic reservations.*

The Soul, Immortality – to trust these great conceptions is to have Religion's choicest benedictions. What strength, what comfort do they not instil into us when we are face to face with life! All the sorrow that burdens us, all the ridicules that vex us, disappear before the illumination they bring, like the mists before the rising sun. What can trouble do to the soul that knows its own imperishableness – that knows itself – knows itself for the very breath and therefore the very proof of God? There is a Heart akin to ours, that throbs with us in our griefs, in our longings after the good. There is a life hereafter which shall redress all the inequalities, repair all the seeming injustice of this life. Nay, more, there is hope for those who have loved and lost, who yearn for 'the touch of a vanished hand and the sound of a voice that is still'. Surely God, the good, the merciful, the just, will not deny them their heart's desire. He will satisfy them, just as He will fully satisfy hereafter that desire for goodness which He has made part of our being . . . This soul within us God will one day require at our hands. One day we shall be asked for an account of our spiritual stewardship. But to us, whose beliefs carry us the great step onwards, who hold that the heavenly light within is not quenched at death, there comes an added appeal. The hereafter must bring awakening; in

God's 'light we shall see light'. Everything will be made clear to us that needs to be made clear.

Source: Morris Joseph, *The Message of Judaism*, pp. 138–44.

COMMENT: *Joseph's main thrust is that the injustices and heartaches of this world will be ameliorated in the next world. However, he is more concerned to portray it in soothing terms – as a future to be desired, not feared – rather than develop a theology of reward and punishment. The curtain has not been lifted very much more than before, even if some of his listeners go away comforted.*

## 1.4 Leo Baeck on Eternity (1949)

*Rabbi Dr Baeck was writing not long after the war, trying to reassure a Holocaust-scarred community that Judaism offered much more than mere survival.*

The road to eternity has been shown to us. It never vanishes, not even in death, and it never ceases to be our road. The direction of life and its depth stretch beyond the limits of human existence. At its beginning and at its end the nearness to God remains, the source from which we come and the goal to which we go. Our life means something more than our narrow existence in this world. With all its lacks and limitations, its pain and suffering, it is, as the Rabbis said, just a place of 'preparation', an 'ante-chamber', it is only the 'life of the moment'. True life is eternal life. We are created and destined to be different from this world, to be holy. Made in the image of God, we belong to that other life, that higher life. We are the child of the world to come. The spiritual and the good are planted within us as the strength and reality of our existence, and the truly real things of our life are exalted above death and destruction. Our life remains life even beyond death.

Source: Leo Baeck, in Lionel Blue and Jonathan Magonet (eds), *Forms of Prayer for Jewish Worship: Prayers for the High Holy Days*, p. 516.

COMMENT: *Baeck writes with a tone of great authority and asserts both the existence and the beneficial character of the afterlife. He ignores the notion of it serving as a place of reward and punishment, and instead posits the idea that eternity is the natural home of the soul; death is not to be viewed as a defeat but a homecoming.*

## 1.5 Ignaz Maybaum on Death (1962)

*Rabbi Dr Maybaum was well aware that rabbinic attempts to discourage speculation about the afterlife were at odds with several references to it in the main prayers in the daily and Sabbath liturgy. For many Jews they raised more questions than they answered, and he sought to tackle the problem.*

What do our rabbis teach us about death? We know nothing about what is beyond the grave, and surely, the rabbis were strict about those who wanted to know what no man is given to know. But they taught us to pray: Blessed are Thou, O Lord, who art a true friend to those who sleep in the dust. The rabbis taught us to pray: Blessed are Thou, O Lord, who quickenest the dead. We do not die into the grave, we die into the eternity of God. In the *Song of Songs* it says that love is as strong as death, and God's love for man is not defeated by death. We mortal creatures who live in the fear of death have nothing to fear. Death, according to rabbinic interpretation, is not a blemish on this world but belongs to it to make it a complete creation. On the sixth day of the creation it says: 'God saw what he created and behold, it was very good'. The rabbis ask why the word 'very' was used. Would not 'good' have been sufficient? This 'very', they say, includes death into the perfect world . . . God, the merciful Creator, created death. When in the last hour of our lives death will unmask itself, it will say to each of us: 'Don't you know me? I am your brother'.

Moses died, who would not die? Those who you mournfully remember died into the peace of a perfect Sabbath, into the peace of unsurpassed atonement. They rejoice in the forgiveness of the Lord, and in His holy everlasting peace.

Source: Ignaz Maybaum, *The Faith of the Jewish Diaspora*, pp. 61–2.

COMMENT: *Maybaum's response is to address the fear of death, although, like others, he does not deal with the details of what it will involve. He is wonderfully reassuring in presenting death as a close companion, whose true identity had not been recognized beforehand and whose arrival, far from being unpleasant, will be a blessed occasion.*

## 1.6 Collective Theological Essay on the Afterlife (1990)

*The essay was the result of various informal discussions within the Reform Movement over several years that were then committed to writing by Rabbi Tony Bayfield, both to present current thinking and to stimulate further discussion. It dealt with a wide range of disparate issues, including the afterlife.*

We believe that there is part of each human being – personality, spirit, soul – which is unique and indestructible. It comes from God and it returns to God. Our tradition uses the term 'the world to come' to speak of existence beyond death. There is a wide range of imagery reflecting the very personal and individual nature of such speculation. We believe that, after our deaths, judgement is passed upon our lives. Death, which is the natural end to human life, has an unavoidable finality and is a source of pain and anguish for the bereaved. Nevertheless, we face death with trust and hope, not least in the knowledge that love and goodness are mightier than the grave and leave an indelible mark on the face of God.

Source: Tony Bayfield, 'Progressive Judaism, a Collective Theological Essay and Discussion Paper', *Manna*, 27, Theology Supplement C.11.

COMMENT: *This brief passage largely restates existing thinking. However, it also raises the idea that the impact people make while they are alive will live on not only in the memory of those who survive them, but also 'on the face of God'. It is a powerful image, implying that our individual lifespan has significance for God too, and suggests that one way in which we attain immortality is through our impact on God.*

## 1.7 Jonathan Romain on the Afterlife (1991)

Faith and Practice *was a comprehensive guide to Reform Judaism, published by the movement itself. It sought to represent the Reform position at that time on both practical matters and theological issues.*

Among Reform Jews the belief in the literal resurrection of the body is no longer maintained and only the belief in the immortality of the soul is accepted. The difference between the Reform position and that of the Orthodox is reflected in their respective translations of the blessing in the second paragraph of the *Amidah*: according to the Orthodox, it is 'Blessed are You, Lord, who revives the dead' but the Reform render it as 'Blessed are You, Lord, who renews life beyond death' – referring to immortality but not resurrection. The exact nature of the state of the soul after bodily death has never been defined in Jewish tradition, and this attitude is shared by Reform on the grounds that such existence is beyond our comprehension, and any comments can only be in the nature of speculation. It is not necessarily more desirable and to be valued above this life, but rather a different stage. The doctrine of reward and punishment, whereby one's merits or faults are recompensed accordingly in the world to come is essential to Orthodoxy. In the Reform it is neither denied nor enlarged upon, and is left a matter of individual belief. Some find it a helpful notion, through which many of the apparent injustices of this world are redressed in the next world. Others see it as operating in this world, albeit not necessarily in material terms, but in the sense of integrity that a righteous person has, and the guilt and foreboding felt by those who have committed wrongs.

Source: Jonathan Romain, *Faith and Practice: A Guide to Reform Judaism Today*, p. 36.

COMMENT: *The passage repeats the rejection of physical resurrection, but much more uncompromisingly than before, and emphasizes instead a belief in the immortality of the soul. This is based on the new Reform liturgy issued in 1977 and changes made within it. Moreover, the passage noticeably refrains from echoing descriptions of the next world as better than the current one. It is seen as a different stage, but not necessarily more blissful. This is more logical if it is accepted that the nature of the afterlife is unknown, but it departs from the traditional assumption. The extract also questions whether the problems of this world will indeed be resolved in the hereafter and gives emphasis to the thought already mooted by Marks that reward and punishment are mental states in this world. However, it offers the possibility that this more materialistic interpretation could be an alternative to an afterlife, rather than just a foretaste of it.*

## 1.8  Lionel Blue on What Happens Next (2001)

*The following passage was written when Rabbi Blue reached the age of seventy years. Having survived various medical scares, he considers death and what lies beyond in terms of his own demise rather than as a theological abstract.*

You can die any time, anywhere. But when you are ageing the horizon comes steadily closer and you either decide to grapple with death or just shrug it off. I have met secular people who have died considerately and confidently with no great fuss. And I have met spiritual types who have tried to flee reality and made a mess of it. There are no rules about something so personal.

For me it has been important to work out my attitudes to death and life which involve some reading, discussion with hospital chaplains and retreats with silence, when I try to stand aside from this world and anticipate death as I do on *Yom Kippur*. I have come to the conclusion that this world is not my home. It is more like the departure lounge of an airport – I enjoy the excitement of departure lounges. I make myself as comfortable as I can, I make friends but it remains a *prozdor*, a corridor to something beyond. I use the word 'beyond' not 'after' because when we die, time and space die with us. We are in between creations, living in an in-between world and the perfection we crave is not here. People's lives go wrong because they expect what this world cannot give.

What they seek, what I seek, is in another dimension. I label that dimension Heaven because that is how it feels to me. Most of us, perhaps all of us, have a toehold in it. It comes close and pulls us towards it like gravity when we do something for its sake – for heaven's sake. Then heaven happens and bits of bliss and exaltation of spirit remain with us. Sometimes it draws us quite unexpectedly and that is an instant of grace.

In such moments many of us are 'foolish' for the sake of heaven; we give things away, we are more generous, more understanding, more loving than is our wont. It is as simple as that. This is a foretaste of the life to come. Go over in your mind the times that this heaven dimension has happened. Don't throw them away or shrug them off. For a few seconds or minutes the soul is more real than our body or mind.

Source: Lionel Blue, 'Changing Gear but not Direction', *Manna*, 70, p. 9.

COMMENT: *Blue makes the important point that being religious does not necessarily mean being able to face death better than anyone else. This is not only realistic but very reassuring for those whose worries over death needlessly make them feel that their faith is inadequate. Typically, he uses a mundane image with which everyone can identify – in this case, an airport lounge – to express the idea of being in a state of temporary abode. However, like most other rabbis, he ends up describing how best to live rather than what happens upon death.*

## 1.9 Alexandra Wright on the World to Come (2002)

*Rabbi Wright was making a pastoral visit to someone who had lost a parent a year earlier. During lunch he suddenly asked her if she believed in an afterlife. Although she was well aware of what Jewish tradition says on the subject, it led her to explore her own personal beliefs in the following article.*

Do I believe in an afterlife? The answer, which took me nearly two months to put together after that extraordinary experience is 'yes'. But not in a world of fluttering wings and clouds somewhere in an unknown heaven. Only in this: that the essence of an individual, the very person they are, their qualities, their deeds and words and thoughts do live on after they have gone. Perhaps the soul of a man or woman does have some otherworldly existence, does bask in God's light. We cannot know. But I do know that a person lives on in their children, and among those who knew them. How important it is to summon the memory of those we love, to talk about them, to emulate their better qualities, to keep alive the souls of those who are so precious to us. This is eternal life.

A belief in the world to come is worth nothing if it is only to reward ourselves with dangerous indulgence or as a prize for martyrdom. It must be connected with the way we live our lives in this world. Whenever we are called to cleanse ourselves from error and sin, when we remember those who came before us, who trusted in God and in their own good deeds, who stood up to evil and protected others from its consequences, who conquered anger and overcame bitterness, we cherish and honour the memories of those we love, when we use their examples for our own lives.

We must resolve to live with honesty and kindness, with integrity and good deeds in this world; and at the same time to re-affirm the ancient faith of our tradition, that when our bodies become frail and wear out, our souls will live on in everlasting life.

Source: Alexandra Wright, 'Do I Believe in Life after Death?', *Manna*, 75, p. 24.

COMMENT: *Wright dismisses the childish images of heaven which are surprisingly pervasive among adults. She also cautions against using the afterlife in a self-serving way. On a positive note, she emphasizes how we achieve eternity in our influence on others (although, except for notable individuals whose influence spans the generations, for most people this means it is only a short-term eternity). Ultimately, her own thesis is typically Jewish in using the afterlife to focus on this world and our conduct in it.*

## A Final Thought . . .

A hospital phoned. A lady was dying and would not survive more than a day or two. 'Does she know?' I asked. 'We have not told her' they said to me.

I entered the room wondering how to start the conversation. She began 'Rabbi, I am dying.' She was utterly miserable, because in her eyes her great sins made her unfit to be in the presence of God. She had never given much thought to God, and her so-called crimes were largely ancient matters to do with her family. I suggested that she might talk to her family and to God, and ask their forgiveness. This seemed to come to her as a revelation.

To the hospital's surprise she lasted three more weeks. She spent the time talking to her family – physically to those who were alive and visiting her, and mentally to those who had died. She also made her peace with God. It was a privilege to watch her and the family as they worked together. They all seemed to grow, to become more alive. When she died she was at peace. In her death she had become fully alive. Those three weeks have remained a precious source of wonder for her family and for me.

Source: Daniel Smith, 'Religious Life and Personal Growth', in Howard Cooper (ed.), *Soul Searching: Studies in Judaism and Psychotherapy*, p. 142.

# 2

# ANIMALS
# (AND THE ENVIRONMENT)

Concern over the correct treatment of animals originates in the Bible with a variety of laws, ranging from not yoking together animals of unequal strength to sparing the feelings of a mother bird by not letting her see her eggs being taken (Deuteronomy 25.4 and 22.6). They were also included in the exemption from work on the Sabbath day (Deuteronomy 5. 14). In rabbinic tradition, it was assumed that in the ideal world of the Garden of Eden Adam and Eve were vegetarian, and that humanity would return to this state in messianic times. Although the consumption of animals was permitted, thoughts of animal welfare were still part of the complex system of dietary laws, for animal life could only be taken in prescribed ways, while the act of slaughter had to be as quick and painless as possible.

## 2.1 Morris Joseph on Animal Experiments (1903)

*The advance of human civilization did not necessarily bring a universally heightened sense of responsibility towards animals. Increases in medical knowledge led to greater use of animals for the purpose of experimentation. For some, this was wholly justified by the potential saving of human life in which it resulted. Others were less certain that one form of life could be expended for the sake of another form of life. Reverend Joseph sought to address the issue from a Jewish perspective.*

A practical question that is much discussed in these days here suggests itself for brief consideration. It is the question of what is called vivisection. Are experiments on living animals, performed in the interests of medical science, justified? And if they are, under what conditions are they to be carried out? Judaism has no hesitation in answering this question. Evincing a tender consideration for the lower animals, it has a still deeper compassion for mankind. It would save the one from unnecessary suffering, but it is even more greatly concerned to save the other from it. And when the two aims come into conflict, it prefers what it firmly holds to be the higher. If it can be established that experiments on living animals are an indispensable means of understanding and mastering disease and so of saving human beings from needless pain and death, then the right to make such experiments is by that fact vindicated. They can be no more condemned than the slaughter of animals for food can be condemned.

But on the other hand, a clear distinction must be drawn between necessary and superfluous experiments. The infliction of suffering in these cases may at times be unavoidable; in may even be necessary in certain circumstances to take the animal's life. But all such acts must be performed under a profound and solemn sense of responsibility. There must be no needless killing, no wanton cruelty, no painful experimenting for experiment's sake. If the scientific investigator owes it to mankind to carry on some of his researches at the expense of the brute, he owes it to the whole world of sentient things to carry them on mercifully. This is at once Jewish doctrine and the teaching of common sense.

Source: Morris Joseph, *Judaism as Creed and Life*, pp. 476–7.

COMMENT: *Joseph recognizes that animals have a life-force that needs to be respected, but also makes a distinction between the value of animal life and human life. This leads him to permit experiments that can cause both pain and fatality to animals if it is in the vital interests of humans, although it would rule out experiments that were for non-essential purposes. It is a conclusion commonly expressed a century later, but stood out as a principled stand at the time of writing. However, Joseph does a potential disservice to his faith by declaring that it is both a matter of Judaism and common sense, when it is an attitude that first permeated secular consciousness because of biblical teachings on animal welfare. The same is true of many other ethical and practical matters, now regarded as 'obvious' whose Jewish foundations are forgotten. It might have been better for Joseph to argue that 'This is a Jewish doctrine that has now become recognized as common sense'.*

## 2.2 Morris Joseph on Unacceptable Usages of Animals (1907)

*In the previous extract, Reverend Joseph emphasized areas in which the needs of humans took precedence over those of animals. However, he was keen to uphold the principle that in matters that were not life-enhancing, animal welfare took priority. The distinction that he made between the two was clear enough, but he was aware of the danger that his permissive attitude in the one respect could lead to carelessness in the other.*

Most forms of cruelty are taboo today; but there are others – those, more particularly, which minister to personal comfort and pleasure – which too often escape the lash. There are fashions – fashions, I regret to say, upheld by woman, the sex that nature meant to be compassionate – which inevitably involve suffering for animals or human beings. One thinks of the feathers plucked from harmless and beautiful birds, under circumstances which cause them exquisite suffering, in order to adorn or please the human wearer. Can that be beauty which is rooted in wrong? Can that be pleasure which is bought with a fellow-creature's pain? And then again there is the more direct cruelty that is connoted by the word 'Sport', so awful in its grim irony. An animal hunted to death, or crawling away to die in slow agony – this is Sport. And it is permitted and applauded in the twentieth century!

Is it not time that men dragged out the old Levitical precepts from the lumber-room to which they have been ignorantly and disdainfully consigned, and used them as a protest against the statutes of the nations that sanction such enormities? To us Jews those precepts call with especial force. For compassion is one of our most elementary duties, and ages ago our law took the brute-beast under its all-embracing protection, anticipating the modern warning, 'Never to mix our pleasure or pride with anguish of the meanest thing that feels'.

Source: Morris Joseph, *The Message of Judaism*, pp. 76–8.

COMMENT: *Joseph has no doubt that cosmetics, fashion and sport fall into the sphere of non-vital pursuits and therefore should not be undertaken at the cost of animal suffering. This was a particularly forthright stance bearing in mind that the majority of his congregation came from a socio-economic class which valued them highly. Nevertheless, he regarded the issue as a litmus test of Judaism's stand on animal welfare. It is slightly puzzling that, whereas in the previous extract he had hailed Judaism's horror at inflicting avoidable pain on animals as common sense, here he refers to it as forgotten ancient lore. This could be explained as a polemical ploy, although perhaps it also indicates that in the second passage he feels more need to appeal to tradition as his readers are less sympathetic to his message.*

## 2.3 Leo Baeck on Understanding Animals (1929)

*Rabbi Dr Baeck's essay on God and man included a broad sweep of the social tasks that faced humanity that resulted from the encounter with the Divine. Among these was a brief but significant mention of the animal kingdom.*

It is from the Bible that the social commandment has again and again gone forth into the world. There is still another important aspect of it. This social order, this great community, includes the animal world. The help and support enjoined by all the commandments are claimed for the lowest creatures, for it is said: 'Man and beast thou preservest, O Lord (Psalm 36.7). The two are frequently mentioned together in this way. Still more remarkable is another peculiar phrase which occurs twice in the Bible: 'to know the heart'. On the first occasion it refers to the stranger: 'Ye know the heart of a stranger, seeing ye were strangers in the land of Egypt' (Exodus 23. 9). The second reference is to animals: 'The righteous man knoweth the heart of his beast' (Proverbs 12. 10). Luther's translation, otherwise so masterly, in this case comes short of the meaning. He renders it: 'The righteous man has mercy on his beast'. To understand the animal, not to neglect or overlook it, is included in the law of justice.

Source: Leo Baeck, *God and Man in Judaism*, pp. 58–9.

COMMENT: *Baeck is so often associated with high-flowing prose on theological conundrums, that it is almost startling to find him writing on such a commonplace matter as the treatment of animals. For Baeck, though, it is not a lowly topic but a mirror image of the moral imperatives that govern all other relationships. Moreover, he introduces a subtle element to the issue: that Judaism demands not only correct behaviour towards animals but empathy with them. This transforms the obligation humans have from one arising from mere duty to that arising from relationship. This not only strengthens the obligation, but also puts it on a par with duties towards fellow-humans.*

## 2.4 Hillel Avidan on Respecting the Environment (1989)

*By the 1980s, awareness of the need to respect animal life had long been widespread in society at large, but it was only at that point that it began to extend to the natural environment as a whole. It was becoming apparent that modern technology and economic growth not only brought many blessings, but also made heavy demands on the world's natural resources. Calls for 'sustainable growth' started to be heard by those concerned for the long-term future of the planet. Rabbi Avidan was among those who were critical of the way in which the earth's riches were being plundered, and he offered a Jewish perspective.*

'God took man and placed him in a garden . . . to work it and to preserve it.' This verse from Genesis 2. 15 expresses the view that man may work the earth and extract its wealth providing that he also guards and conserves it. 'The earth is the Lord's and the fullness thereof; the world and all who dwell in it'. In these words from Psalm 24 we are reminded of who is ruler. God is 'Master of the Universe' and man is His servant or, at most, His steward. Proper conservation of the earth's precious resources should follow naturally upon acceptance of God as master and man as servant, but where man dethrones God and sets himself up as the absolute ruler, chaos is bound to follow. We cannot force theocentricity, the idea that God rules, upon a reluctant public, but there is some comfort in the knowledge that even where anthropocentricity, the notion that man is master, reigns supreme, self-interest can eventually force the abandonment of destructive habits in favour of constructive modes of behaviour. It is in the interests of everyone who is sane, whether theist or humanist, to work for a world that is safer and more pleasant than the one we currently inhabit.

Jewish environmental legislation rests, in the main, upon a principle extracted from Deuteronomy 20. 19–20: 'When you besiege a city . . . you shall not destroy its trees . . . you may eat from them but not destroy them'. From this specific prohibition were drawn many others which in sum total serve to prevent wanton destruction of anything that might be useful to humanity. If something ceases to be of value or becomes a serious threat to humanity then its destruction, or replacement is permitted. In assessing the usefulness or value of something we must be guided by long-term considerations or effect upon the environment, for we know today that assaults against nature ultimately threaten the quality of human life. A contemporary Jewish *halachah* on ecology must prohibit all acts likely to damage or further damage our planet . . . Concern for the environment was evident in Judaism from the outset, so it is entirely appropriate for Jewry to immerse itself in the struggle to halt and reverse the models of behaviour which threaten the future of our planet.

Source: Hillel Avidan, 'Save Our Planet', *Manna*, 22, pp. 24–5.

COMMENT: *Avidan may be right that the best way to promote widespread adoption of an environmentally-sound policy is an appeal to self-interest. However, he himself has no doubt that, however strong its utilitarian value, it is primarily a religious obligation. Moreover, any attempt to ignore it is not just foolish but a denial of God, both as Source of the universe and as the One who gives humanity commands. It would be excessive to claim that Judaism has always made 'green' policies one of its central tenets, but it certainly contains teachings that correspond powerfully to modern concerns for the ecology.*

## 2.5  Hillel Avidan on Animal Rights (1995)

*Among the many aspects of the festival of Sukkot is its agricultural base. This was reflected in the Study Anthology in a new edition of the liturgy for use in Reform synagogues. It featured a variety of different readings on this theme, including one by Rabbi Avidan on preventing distress to living creatures.*

In Jewish post-biblical literature much is written about the need to spare animals from pain or stress. The Talmud forbids gladiatorial shows and hunting so that bull- or cock-fighting or big-game hunting are quite abhorrent to the observant Jew. So too is the trapping of animals for such luxury items as fur coats or the merciless hunting of whales for the production of perfumes or pet foods. None may purchase an animal till he has first purchased the food for an animal to eat. The Sabbath may be profaned to assist an animal in distress.

The abuse of animals desensitises the abuser and facilitates the abuse of fellow humans and the spoliation of soil, air and water and all that they support.

Source: Hillel Avidan, in Lionel Blue and Jonathan Magonet (eds), *Forms of Prayer for Jewish Worship: Prayers for the Pilgrim Festivals*, p. 778.

COMMENT: *Avidan largely repeats Jewish teachings on the subject, but adds the important gloss that maltreatment of animals not only harms them but can also have a brutalizing effect on the person concerned. In addition, it can spill over into their relationship with other people as well as the environment at large. The way one treats animals is not an isolated part of life, but a reflection of one's wider social conscience, or lack of it.*

# 3

# ANTI-SEMITISM

Anti-semitism is a term that was coined in 1879 by Wilhelm Marr, but the phenomenon of opposition to Jews because they are Jews dates back to earliest times. The two main incidents of it in the Bible highlight the variant forms that anti-semitism can take. The accusation that Jews are disloyal and a threat to the political equilibrium occurs when a new Pharaoh comes to the throne and declares that the Israelites – who had been resident in Egypt for a considerable period – might prove to be traitors who conspire with Egypt's enemies (Exodus 1.8–10). By contrast, Haman's opposition to the Jews is based on the fact that they have different customs to other people in the kingdom and therefore present an affront to the king's rule (Esther 3.8). This 'dislike of the unlike' was to become a feature of Jewish history because so much of it was spent in exile. It meant that Jews had a triple disadvantage: first, being in a minority wherever they lived and subject to the automatic prejudice of many in the majority culture; second, being available as a useful scapegoat for rulers who sought to divert their own unpopularity onto the Jews; third, often living in a climate in which religious differences were regarded as political deviation and liable for punishment. In Christian countries this was compounded by the villainous role Jews occupied within Church teaching, based on the central crime of rejecting the supposed Son of God and then being responsible for his death. The Enlightenment allowed Jews to escape from some of the opprobrium heaped upon them for religious reasons, but also saw the rise of a racial anti-semitism in which Jews were hated because of their very nature. It was to culminate in the Holocaust, a systematic attempt to destroy the Jews as a people that succeeded in murdering a third of world Jewry in only six years.

## 3.1 David Woolf Marks on the Ingratitude of the World (1848)

*The Jews in the England of Reverend Professor Marks' time enjoyed a high measure of integration in society at large. However, this did not include certain political rights, and the extract below was written in the midst of the struggle to allow Jews the ability to sit in Parliament – which was not won till 1858. Still, the situation of Jews virtually everywhere else was much worse, ranging from lack of civil rights to active persecution. The medieval Blood Libel had resurfaced in Damascus in 1840; many Jews in Central Europe were still living in ghettos and those in Eastern Europe suffered numerous discriminatory restrictions.*

It were much to be wished, that the Passover had been duly remembered by non-Israelites also, and that the claims of the Hebrews, whose ancestors instructed the world how to obtain and enjoy freedom, had been taken into account, in after times, by the several nations and states. If that festival had been remembered with gratitude, we should now be spared the pain of perusing many a page in the annals of history stained with persecution and blood; if it had been remembered, the anomalous spectacle would not today be offered to view, of the descendants of that race which gave freedom and light to the world, soliciting for themselves the very rights and privileges, which their ancestors first inspired men to demand, and instructed them how to employ, for their own benefit and for the common weal. If the Passover had been remembered, the title of the Jewish citizen to equal immunities with his fellow-subjects would long since have been recognised and decreed, not only on the broad basis of humanity, but also on the grounds of common gratitude. However selfishness and prejudice cloud men's minds and narrow their views, yet a little reflection would have convinced all those who had been adverse to our claims, that the event of the Passover is to be placed amongst the most powerful causes of all concessions to civil and political liberty.

Source: David Woolf Marks, *Lectures & Sermons*, Vol. I, p. 261.

COMMENT: *Marks not only blames non-Jews for the sufferings they have caused Jews over the centuries (anti-semitism was a term yet to be invented), but regards it as doubly heinous because they should be grateful to the Jews for sharing with them the social ethics that they received. The freedom-message of Passover – 'let my people go' – combined with the legislative system received at Mount Sinai shortly after the exodus from Egypt has benefited everyone but has been denied to the Jews, the very people who enlightened the world with it.*

## 3.2 Morris Joseph on Combating Anti-semitism (1907)

*Reverend Joseph was writing in the wake of two major developments within Jewish history. A vitriolic campaign of pogroms against Jews in Russia by the Czarist government resulted in a massive emigration of Jews to the West, including 100,000 who came to Britain. The sudden influx of so many impoverished foreigners led to some outbreaks of anti-semitism in England itself, on the grounds that they were transforming the character of certain areas as well as stealing jobs from local people. In addition, just across the channel, France was being traumatized by the Dreyfus Affair that dragged on throughout the 1890s and early 1900s.*

What, then, is our duty at such a crisis? To me, it seems, to consist in a careful revision of our personal conduct. Nothing, I freely admit, that the Jew can do, short of putting an end to his own existence, will ever stop this anti-Semitic fury. The real remedy lies far ahead in the remote future. It will come with the disappearance of religious animosity, with the triumph of humane feeling, with the universal recognition of the transcendent tie of brotherhood that binds all men together. The causes of the world's hostility towards us are beyond our control; all we can do is remove some of the pretexts for it. The Jew-hater prefers against us certain charges to justify his enmity. They may be frivolous; they may even be false. Our duty is to make our conduct of life a practical demonstration of their utter absurdity. We may have, in consequence, to impose severe restrictions upon our just liberty, to consider forbidden not a little that is permissible. But to these sacrifices we must cheerfully submit . . .

I think we have to strive more strenuously after simplicity of life. That the rich Jew is ostentatious and overbearing is an assertion that forms part of the stock-in-trade of every anti-Semite. Personally, I do not believe that, as a rule, those Jews whose conduct lends colour to the accusation, who load themselves with jewels in and out of season, who make themselves unpleasantly conspicuous at social gatherings, who choose Sundays for their noisiest entertainments, who seem bent on monopolizing the best that this material world affords, intend to flaunt their prosperity in the faces of their neighbours, or to hurt their feelings in the slightest degree. All that they are really guilty of is want of good taste and want of thought. But the results are unfortunate, nonetheless.

We are charged further with materialism, with being devoid of all ideals, save such as are sordid. We live, it is said, only for money and for what money can purchase. To this charge, likewise, we must give serious heed. The *tu quoque* argument will not avail us. It is useless to urge that, as regards love of money, the Jew is no worse than the Gentile. He must be better, or anti-Semitism, which lives on half-truths, will never want for specious arguments ... Another sin which is laid at the door of Jews is vulgarity. He is loud, it is said, not only in speech, but in dress and in manner. Whether the charge be true or false, let us treat it as true, and go out of our way to create scrupulously quiet demeanour ... Why are Jews charged with materialism? Is it not largely owing to their predilection for finance and the occupations connected with it? That we Jews should adopt the heroic remedy, and unanimously resolve to forswear such callings, is, no doubt, impossible. Let it not be forgotten, too, that these occupations are of the greatest value for the business community, and that the Jews, as leaders of finance, when they have been true to the old Levitical ideals of uprightness, have conferred solid benefits upon the world. But in future would it not be well, in order to prevent misunderstanding, if these occupations were more often left to the Gentile? Why should not the sons even of wealthy parents be trained, if not to do manual labour themselves, at any rate to associate themselves, as owners of factories, with such labour when done by others? What a magnificent thing it would be if they were to settle on the land as farmers, and so help, at one and the same time, to remove a reproach from the Jewish name, and to restore to English agriculture some of its waning prosperity!

The most plausible grounds for hostility towards the Jews are furnished by religious indifference. Those who are false to their faith, it is argued, cannot be true in anything; they cannot be loyal citizens, or staunch friends, or honest men of business. And this is the one argument of anti-Semitism that we may accept as true. Therefore, I say, let us be better Jews, if we would take a better place in the opinion of the world. The weak-kneed Jew, the Jew who plays fast and loose with his religion, who hides it when he can, and apologizes for it when he cannot, is rightly despised by Gentiles, and the whole race has wrongfully to pay, in distrust and contumely, the penalty of his wrong-doing . . . We are not going to commit religious suicide because our enemies recommend it to us as our only possible salvation. If we are to perish, it should be in the manner of the Jewish martyrs of old – with the law in our hands and its words on our hearts.

Source: Morris Joseph, *The Message of Judaism*, pp. 82–8.

COMMENT: *The final section makes clear Joseph's pride in the Jewish heritage and his determination to maintain it in the face of all detractors. However, everything that precedes it could lay him open to the charge of self-contradiction and cowardice. He begins by stating that there is no likelihood of any immediate cure for anti-semitism and he postpones it until the coming of the messianic age. Despite this admission, he calls for a number of measures with which to combat it. His suggestions, though, require no effort by the anti-semites themselves, nor even the attempt to educate them, but demand 'sacrifices' by Jews to whittle down any excuse others have to be hostile to them. The victims of hate must accommodate the perpetrators of it. Joseph then lists the perceived misdemeanours of Jews, but in such a detailed way ('who load themselves with jewels' etc.) as to virtually give them credence and provide an anti-semite's handbook. In all cases, his response is not to condemn the accusation or defend the majority of Jews from being tainted by less admirable co-religionists, but to collude with the criticism and advocate corrective behaviour. It is possible that Joseph was in fact not at all persuaded by the accusations, yet chose to use them as a sermonic device to urge greater ethical standards, but the overall impression he gives is one of cowed embarrassment.*

### 3.3 Morris Joseph on the Eventual End of Anti-semitism (1930)

*The 1920s saw the children of the East European immigrants begin to inte-grate gradually into British society. However, it also witnessed the humili-ation of Germany following the First World War and the subsequent rise of rabidly anti-semitic parties in the Weimar Republic.*

Detraction and calumny are the outstanding residue of the age-long persecution which has incessantly tortured our race. When we think of them as persisting in these days, marked by a deepening passion for justice, by a growing liberality of thought, by an increasing rejection of theology which divides, we are disappointed and sad. 'When', we ask, 'will these relics of dark ages disappear? When will Israel be free from his oppressor, fully cleared in the sight of mankind? What can we do to speed that consummation?' Patience – there is no better way, none half so good . . . Now and again anti-Semitism lifts is head even in this country. An individual or a newspaper breaks out into vile accusation of the Jew; he is a warmonger, a shirker, a bloated profiteer, a parasitical pauper. And straightway some well-meaning, but misguided people on our side launch into fiery objurgations and indignant arguments. All such efforts are either useless or superfluous. They are useless because anti-Semitism, if genuine, is an irrational prejudice which obviously can-not be reached by argument, and if artificial, is a mere crafty fraudulent pose not to be overcome by any appeal to truth or justice. Anti-Semitism is often a trade, and falsehoods are the goods it trades in. It deliberately aims at hurting us. So that when it is hurled out of one trench it estab-lishes itself in another, and the angrier we are, the more sensitive we show ourselves, the more clearly we are hurt; and that is just what the enemy desires. If there are to be protests and articulate vindications let them come from others; they will be far more telling because obviously unbiased and disinterested.

. . . No, the proper way to deal with an anti-Semite is to let him severely alone. Let him roll himself in the web he spins so cunningly. One day, perhaps, it will be a trap that he spins for himself. But whether it be so or not matters little; the main point is that we should trust for our justification to the force of truth and enlightenment, which one day will assuredly master the minds of men. It is a slow business, but let us not despair or grow weary. If the Light seems never to be coming, or to come too slowly, we may be sure that Eternal Wisdom has ordained it . . . Patience, then. But with the quietness must go a dogged persistence in rectitude. The inevitable victory of right and truth must be prepared by the integrity of those who would taste the blessedness of it. Nothing can withstand these world-forces any more than one can stop the march of dawn which slowly beats back the night. It is the powers of light arrayed against the powers of darkness. Can the issue be in doubt?

Source: Morris Joseph, *The Spirit of Judaism*, pp. 24–8.

COMMENT: *Joseph's remarks here are much less apologetic and defensive than his earlier statement on the subject – perhaps because he has come to the view that, as he alludes in his opening sentences, so little can be done to combat anti-semitism. This is both because it defies rational argument and because it is able to survive the passing of less civilized times. Joseph makes an interesting distinction between 'genuine' and 'artificial' anti-semitism – one being a matter of conviction, the other of opportunism – but in both cases his response is still a passive one: patience . It is based on an optimistic reading of history and a confidence that a new age of enlightenment will come and will bring an end to anti-semitism. It is, however, impossible to read his words without being chilled at the date they were published. Joseph's hope of a bright new dawn was to prove pathetically misplaced; far from being over, the worst was yet to come.*

## 3.4 Ignaz Maybaum: Anti-semitism is Anti-Christian (1960)

*Rabbi Dr Maybaum knew anti-semitism at first hand, having witnessed the increasingly murderous persecution of Jews by the Nazis and his own synagogue in Berlin go up in flames. He fled to England in 1939. The following is a short extract from a chapter on Jewish-Christian relations.*

In Jewish-Christian co-operation the Jew gives Judaism, the Christian Christianity. What they give is blessing. Jews and Christians are trustees of a blessing. The mystery surrounding blessing is this: although man can render blessing to his fellow-man, there is no human giver. God is the giver of blessing. With the blessing of God man prospers. Jew and Christian prosper together or suffer together. The anti-Semite is not only anti-Jewish, he is anti-Christian; the anti-Semite hates and opposes messianic man, man with messianic hope.

Source: Ignaz Maybaum, *Jewish Existence*, p. 164.

COMMENT: *Although Maybaum makes his point very succinctly, its implications are considerable: at a time when Jews and Christians meet together in religious dialogue and find common ground in their pursuit of the path of God, the enemy of the Jew is also the enemy of the Christian. It is a double message: to anti-semites, that they cannot attack Judaism without attacking the other partner in the new religious alliance; to Christians, that if they value their relationship with Jews, they must regard prejudice against Jews as an affront to themselves too.*

### 3.5 Ignaz Maybaum: Anti-semitism is Anti-God (1965)

*Five years after the book quoted above, Rabbi Dr Maybaum used another publication to develop his theme on the nature of anti-semitism. He focuses on Kristallnacht ('the night of breaking glass'), the widespread attack on Jewish homes, shops and synagogues throughout Germany and Austria on 9 November 1938.*

We do not commemorate the martyrdom of the six million Jews as a national catastrophe, which it certainly is. We commemorate the death of our six million brethren as a human tragedy, as an assault against man, as a crime against humanity. The fourteen million gentiles who were also murdered by the Nazis, and all the soldiers, sailors, and airmen, and all the civilians who died in the air raids in Great Britain, on the continent, and in Japan – they would not have died, if the Jews had not first been singled out for aggression. The attack against the Jew hits man. The Jew represents mankind. The pogrom of the Crystal Night twenty-five years ago was the prelude. From this prelude, disaster followed, which left its mark on the whole globe. Poland, Eastern Europe, and great parts of Russia which were devastated, German cities which lay in ruins, the cities of Great Britain which were bombed, Pearl Harbor and Hiroshima, all the battles on land, sea, and in the air, the whole apocalyptic holocaust began with the pogrom twenty-five years ago; then the Nazis openly showed the world their antisemitic hatred. This hatred led to Auschwitz. But mankind cannot afford to suffer antisemites. The antisemite does not only persecute the Jew, his hatred persecutes man and God. The Jew is defenceless and utterly exposed. The Jew, without the soldier's weapon and without the guarantee of political protection is utterly human in his helpless dependence on God. God is in His heaven, but man is on earth. When the Jew is persecuted, the persecutor persecutes God.

Source: Ignaz Maybaum, *The Face of God after Auschwitz*, pp. 57–8.

COMMENT: *Maybaum widens the definition of anti-semitism from antagonism towards Jews to rejection of humanity itself. He justifies this not philosophically or morally, but based on pragmatic considerations and the fact that Nazi hostility against Jews eventually engulfed the world at large. It could be objected that the Second World War was the result of political ambition, whereas the Holocaust was the result of ideological hatred – but Maybaum would assert that tolerance of the latter led to the former. A failure to resist attack on a religious minority inflamed a cult of racial superiority that culminated in attacks against nation states. As Jewish tradition regards humans as the creation of God, it is only logical that Maybaum should extend his definition of anti-semitism even further to being an attack on God.*

### 3.6 Ignaz Maybaum on Christian Responsibility for Anti-semitism (1969)

*After 30 years teaching and preaching as a communal rabbi in Britain, and being heavily involved in furthering relations between Judaism and Christianity, Rabbi Dr Maybaum felt able to be more critical of the historical defects that such rapprochement had to face if it was to be meaningful.*

The Jewish-Christian dialogue which is now in progress is, indeed, an epoch-making event. But this dialogue is idle talk if Auschwitz is excluded as a subject for dialogue. Who is responsible for Auschwitz? The Germans of course. But this answer will not satisfy an Asian who disregards the national varieties within Europe and sees Europe as the Christian realm different from the Buddhist unity of Asia. 'Surely', an Asian intellectual said to a missionary, 'Hitler was a Christian'. To explain to him that Hitler was a secularised Christian, a heathen, will not satisfy the Asian observer of European affairs. Only there can secularised Christians in their passion for a 'second creation' become guilty of demoniac destruction of the creation. It was in a Christian country, not in the lands of the Buddha, that Hitler and those that followed him were born and bred.

. . . Antisemitism is of Christian origin. Those who had once received the word of God from the Jews deserted the Jews. The two-thousand-year-old Jew-hatred led to modern antisemitism and eventually to Auschwitz. In the beginnings of Christianity Jewish sons tore themselves away from their Jewish fathers. When sons rebel against their fathers, the terrible sin of patricide looms over the divided family. Auschwitz was patricide. The guilt at the beginning of Christianity repeated itself at Auschwitz. Christian sons revolted against their Jewish fathers. Patricide was again committed. Auschwitz is the monument of a *judenrein* Christianity, of a de-judaised Christianity.

Source: Ignaz Maybaum, *Creation and Guilt*, pp. 93–5.

COMMENT: *Maybaum is unhesitatingly forthright is his view that Auschwitz was a direct result of Christian teaching and that the Church must admit its culpability. He freely admits that Hitler was not a Christian himself, but asserts that he and the millions of his supporters emerged from a society deeply imbued with Christian prejudices. The same point is also made by others, but what is unusual about Maybaum is that he is not an academic writing a theoretical critique from afar, but someone deeply involved in inter-faith dialogue who is not afraid to shirk from awkward truths. Moreover, he departs from merely repeating the conventional references to the villainous role ascribed to the Jews by the Gospels and subsequent Church teachings. Instead he presents a psychological analysis that explores why they arose in the first place. He depicts Judaism and Christianity in Freudian terms of a father-son relationship, with the guilt of the latter at rejecting the former becoming twisted into a murderous hatred which culminates in the Holocaust.*

## 3.7 Ignaz Maybaum on the Effects of the Culture of Suffering in Christian Europe (1973)

*Rabbi Dr Maybaum returns to the theme of Christian culpability for the Holocaust, but from a different angle, in which he seeks to explain why so many people from Christian countries either actively supported Hitler or at least acquiesced in his anti-semitic policies.*

For the pious Christian the Cross is a symbol of martyrdom. But we must ask whether the killing through burning, torture and sophisticated executions practised in the Middle Ages had its brutalizing cause in the image of the Cross. People came to watch an execution armed with food and drink. The men with their wives and children watched someone executed on the wheel – a very long drawn-out process. What steeled the nerves of these people? Was it perhaps the sadistic contemplation which any cross could throughout the years arouse in a primitive mind? In the churches, paintings drew attention to the saints with realistic illustrations of the forms of their martyrdom, their executions, showing their mutilation in stages, the ground strewn with severed limbs. An eyewitness tells us how long the strongly built Jan Hus battled with the flames and how hideously he screamed. The screams were ignored by the recorder of the *gesta sanctorum*. Thus rose a generation which tortured, burned, killed millions of Jews and non-Jews in the Nazi period.

They did so in countries where the Cross was exhibited everywhere. In Poland one could not walk down a country lane without encountering again and again the stern spectacle of the man dying in agony from his cruelly inflicted wounds. In the countryside where the Nazis built Auschwitz and Treblinka, the Cross was the distinctive characteristic. Vicarious suffering is holy. Cruelty is demonic. The Cross preaches about both.

Source: Ignaz Maybaum, *Trialogue between Jew, Christian and Muslim*, p. 67.

COMMENT: *Maybaum reminds his audience of the extraordinary degree to which suffering is not only central to Christianity but is constantly highlighted both inside and outside churches. No other faith makes such public display of horrendous human agony. This, he claims, has had a de-sensitizing effect over the centuries and resulted in such suffering being seen as almost normative and inevitable. It is little wonder, therefore, that it was so easily transferred onto the Jews. He also notes that although the Nazis arose in Lutheran Germany, the extermination camps were all situated else-where, in Catholic lands, where the cult of the Cross was most pronounced and where brutality was readily visible as a religious virtue.*

### 3.8  Dow Marmur on the Absence of Anti-semitism (1982)

*For Rabbi Marmur, the problem with life in late twentieth-century Britain was not so much the presence of anti-semitism but paradoxically its absence. While Jews were delighted not to face hostility, it was becoming increasingly obvious that the removal of any external threats could also pose negative consequences.*

Contemporary Judaism is the victim of a survival syndrome i.e. that it seems unable to offer a positive reason for staying Jewish but at the same time is neurotically pre-occupied with the danger of ceasing to be Jew-ish . . . It is as if we Jews could not cope with the success of our endeav-ours to assimilate. In the same way as persecution destroys us physically, tolerance tends to demoralize us psychologically. What we are looking for is a kind of compromise between the concentration camp and the public school, and we find it often enough in the latent and overt anti-Semitism in Western society. The only way, as it were, by which we can seek assimilation and survival at the same time is if the Western world sets limits on our integration and penalizes us for our Jewish origins. And as long as this is also felt by our children, their allegiance to Judaism can also be counted upon. The anti-Semitism that exists in countries where Jews live as equal citizens is ironically, a kind of safeguard for Jew-ish continuity. However neurotic and self-destructive we Jews may be about our Judaism, our foes make sure that we remain Jewish.

. . . A faith that is only expressed when the enemy attacks, and not when God calls man to prayer and atonement, is a faith forged by foes. There is much to suggest that the survival syndrome, which so strongly dominates contemporary Jewish life, is based on such faith. It is this that makes Jewish existence and Jewish faith so precarious in our time. A vision of the future must, therefore, begin with a radical understanding of the present condition and an almost ruthless determination to change it. If survival is not to be at the mercy of our adversaries, it must be based on a sense of Jewish purpose. Even in the concentration camps, where life and death were totally dependent on the camp commanders, to know that one's existence had meaning helped many an inmate to endure and to survive. How much more is this true in our generation!

Source: Dow Marmur, *Beyond Survival*, pp. 29–31.

COMMENT: *It has often been noted that persecution makes Jews more Jewish but tolerance makes them less so, and Marmur argues the point cogently. His response is not to decry the benefits of modernity nor to criticize Jews for embracing it, but to argue that Jewish leaders must provide positive reasons for remaining Jewish in this new climate. His final sentence may seem extreme – claiming that current needs are more urgent than during the Holocaust – but they highlight his concern at the prospect of the silent disappearance of almost as many Jews through the more benign but equally devastating effects of assimilation.*

### 3.9 Dow Marmur on Not Being Misled by Anti-semitism (1989)

*As a result of the Lebanon War in 1982, Israel became the subject of much criticism over civilian casualties in Beirut and deaths in the refugee camps. British Jews were among those concerned at Israel's actions, but they were also alarmed at the level of hostility directed at Israel. Another concern was the negative consequences upon themselves from non-Jews who saw them as public representatives of Israel. Rabbi Marmur sought to address those fears.*

Part of our critical apparatus has to be directed towards the question of anti-Semitism. We have to ask ourselves not only why we were once so naive as to believe that if only we made a good impression on gentiles, anti-Semitism would go away but also why we today have such a great need to exaggerate every anti-Semitic manifestation. Of course, there is anti-Semitism in our society and, of course, we have to take steps to expose it and to protect ourselves against it. But it is not the greatest threat to Jewish existence today. There are even cynics who would contend that it keeps us together, at least in the free world, more than it threatens us. Apathy – indifference to tradition and to matters of the spirit – is a much greater threat to our present and our future as Jews. By concentrating on anti-Semitism we are evading the real issues and thus damaging ourselves under the guise of protecting ourselves. We would be much wiser to recognise anti-Semitism for what it is, namely a gentile disease, rather than to see its eradication as exclusively our problem.

In order to cure anti-Semitism, we must seek to cure the society that breeds it and that means fighting every form of discrimination and championing every cause that promotes equality and social justice. We would probably diminish anti-Semitism greatly if we devoted some of the energies that now go into the Jewish organisations dedicated to its eradication, to causes that work for an overall better society. Solidarity with the disadvantaged will advance our cause more than our present communal insularity. Our desire to be accepted by society has – paradoxically again – driven us into an isolationism that defeats our purpose. We have contrived to build a ghetto in an effort to break down the ghetto. No wonder that our efforts manifest themselves more in neuroses than in successes, for we are fighting the wrong battles with the wrong weapons.

Source: Dow Marmur, 'Stop Fighting these Wrong Battles', *Manna*, 25, pp. 4–5.

COMMENT: *Marmur shows little patience with the idea of lessening anti-Semitism by appeasing critics of the Jews, as Joseph seemed to suggest at the beginning of the century. He is equally scathing of those who over-emphasize anti-semitic incidents and let them dominate communal thinking to the point of self-defeating introspection. Instead, he makes the important point that it is a Gentile problem rather than a Jewish one and shifts the responsibility for combating it onto the outside world (although some might argue that it is Jews who suffer the consequences and so it ends up becoming their problem too). Marmur's preferred response is to follow the wider ethical ideals of Prophetic Judaism and seek an overall solution for all who suffer from discrimination. Improving society at large would be right in itself and would also have a beneficial effect for Jews.*


## A Final Thought . . .

When teaching about Judaism in local schools I never came across anti-semitism but often encountered the ignorance or stereotyping that can lead to it. For instance, at virtually every school to which I went, I was asked whether Jews had birthdays. 'Yes, of course', I replied, 'they are jolly good fun' – but I could not understand why it was such a persistent question. Eventually the reason became clear: there were usually one or two Jehovah's Witnesses at each school, and they do not celebrate birthdays. The children made the simple but flawed deduction: Jehovah's Witnesses are different from us, Jews are different from us, so they must be similar to each other. My first task, therefore, was to get them to accept each minority faith in its own right and not lump them all together. Another puzzle was the question: 'Is it true that the Jewish religion does not allow you to shut your garage doors at night?' What on earth was this all about, I thought. But again there was a simple and revealing explanation that can apply to many adults too. It turned out that the child asking this question had Jewish neighbours who never closed their garage doors at night; and so the assumption was automatically made that all other Jews did likewise! So my second task was to stop them judging those who belong to a particular group as all being the same – be it religious or racial group – and instead treat them as individuals and judge them by their own characteristics.

Source: Jonathan Romain, 'Teaching Tolerance', *Common Ground*, 2, 1996, p. 16.

# 4

# BIBLE

The Bible occupies a curiously ill-defined place within Judaism. The term itself is problematic because it is prone to being used inaccurately. The first five books within it, the *Torah*, are of much greater importance in Jewish tradition than the other books. Thus what is stated about the Bible as a whole, may not apply to the *Torah* in particular, and vice-versa. There is also debate over the exact role of the Bible within Judaism. It is the centre of the faith, the foundation of its beliefs and laws, a major source for its liturgy, and the biography of the Jewish people. At the same time, it has been superseded by the vast compendium of rabbinic literature which has changed Judaism immeasurably from the biblical version of it. The course of Jewish history has also had a major effect on aspects of the Bible, such as the cessation of the sacrificial system, which accounts for much of the Book of Leviticus, following the destruction of the Temple. Thus some parts of the Bible are still crucial to Judaism, others are now obsolete. This in turn raises the question of what authority it holds today and what criteria – and whose – are used to determine the answer. Much depends on opinion as to the authorship of the Bible. It is this issue that is at the very heart of the differences between the two main groups within Judaism: Orthodox Judaism regards the Bible as the literal word of God, and so its teachings have lasting power and cannot be altered, even though they may be interpreted in different ways. Reform Judaism considers the Bible to be written by humans under divine inspiration, but subject to human limitations and errors, and open to change in the light of new conditions or superior knowledge.

## 4.1 Morris Joseph on the Authority of the Bible (1903)

*Reform Judaism is often described and judged by the changes it has made in Jewish rituals and observances, but in fact its defining characteristic is not the changes themselves but the right to make such changes. Opponents of Reform denied that this right existed and criticized Reform for usurping divine authority. Reverend Joseph sought to answer these accusations.*

That the real authority of the Bible is intrinsic rather than prescriptive becomes clear as soon as we think of the circumstances in which the Scriptural Canon was formed. The decision by which certain Books were included in the Bible and others excluded, was a purely human decision. The great teachers sat in judgement upon the claims of the various works, and decided upon those claims by the light of reason – in other words, by the internal merits of the works themselves . . . Assuming the right to say 'this is canonical, and that is not,' they necessarily implied that the final test of authority and inspiration of the Bible was the sufficiency of its appeal to human reason, in other words the value of its teaching for the religious life. And if that was their test, it may well be ours. Indeed, it must be ours. The formation of the Canon was an intellectual act and therefore the intellect has a right to judge it. That the Bible was declared divine centuries ago does not prove it possesses that character. It is a plea for tender and respectful treatment of the Scriptures, but nothing more. The mere words of any number of learned men, however learned or pious, cannot suffice to determine the character of the Bible, for they avowedly had but the same qualifications as other learned and pious men have for determining it. Possessing an *a priori* title to our reverence and obedience which no sober mind can contest, the Bible must, in the last resort, plead for itself – plead for itself with the intellect and conscience in every age.

. . . The Bible being the work of godly men, necessarily contains both a divine and a human element. But, since everything human is imperfect, we must not expect to find an absolutely perfect representation of Divine truth even in God's book. We must be prepared to meet in the Bible with incomplete and even diverse representations of religious truth, and with allegories and legends . . . And if it be asked how we are to distinguish the legendary from the historical in the Bible, the answer is by the help of reason and study.

Source: Morris Joseph, *Judaism as Creed and Life*, pp. 17–23.

COMMENT: *Joseph regards it as perfectly obvious that if one group of humans could decide what constituted the Bible and what was sacrosanct, a later group could differ from that decision. Moreover, as human debate was the determining factor for the sages of old, it can equally be the tool of modern rabbis. Thus he seeks to show that reason, far from being antithetical to Judaism, always has to be part of it and should continue to be a guiding factor. It is noticeable, though, that Joseph makes no distinction between the entire Bible and the first five books, whereas Orthodox authorities would regard the latter as completely divine in origin but admit human involvement in other books.*

## 4.2 Morris Joseph on the Bible and Science (1903)

*One of the most frequently challenged aspects of the Bible was its account of Creation. Biblical Criticism highlighted discrepancies within the Book of Genesis itself, while Darwin's* On the Origin of Species, *published in 1859, suggested a radically different process from the biblical version of events. The response of Orthodox Judaism was to maintain its belief in the inerrancy of the Bible, but Reverend Joseph sought to harmonize the Bible and scientific findings.*

The Bible is, above everything, a book about religion; it is not a book about science or any other brand of profane [secular] knowledge. In regard to scientific matters it reflects only the knowledge of the age in which each writer lived. It is as an authority on Faith and Duty only that the Bible stands above all books. If we bear this truth in mind we shall cease to find any difficulty in passages like the first chapter of Genesis. Whether the universe was formed in six days, or is the product of ages of evolution, as men of science now affirm it to be, is a question that need not enter our minds when we try to determine the value of that great opening paragraph of Holy Writ. The grand truths to be learned from it are not scientific but religious.

. . . In former days it was thought that the heavens and the earth and all that is in them were the result of special creative acts. But in modern times, the doctrine of evolution, largely as a result of Darwin's momentous researches, has found wide acceptance, and has revolutionized men's ideas on this question . . . [but this does] not weaken in the smallest degree the credibility of the fundamental proposition laid down by Religion – that which affirms the existence of God. The idea of evolution does not deliver us from the necessity of postulating Divine intelligence as the cause of the universe. On the contrary, it intensifies that necessity. If transcendent wisdom was required to create each type of animal life separately, how much more so was it needed to endow a few simple organisms with the capacity for gradual development into a vast multitude of highly complex forms, and to think out and will the appropriate conditions for that capacity to come into play. Man's remote ancestor may possibly have been a jellyfish; but only infinite intelligence could have made a jellyfish a potential man, and have planned and ordained the long series of changes that would have to take place before the potential became the actual, before the jellyfish developed into an Isaiah or a Shakespeare.

Source: Morris Joseph, *Judaism as Creed and Life*, pp. 23, 54–5.

COMMENT: *Joseph's response is neither to deny the results of scientific findings, nor to claim that the Bible is really in consonance with it if interpreted correctly. Instead, he simply sidesteps any confrontation between the Bible and Science by freely admitting that evolution is not an area of authority of the Bible and happily accepting Darwin's research. At the same time he points out that the notions of evolution and of God are not incompatible by citing the argument of First Cause: that God was still responsible for the sequence of events that led to the world as it is today. Human understanding of the methods God used may now be altered, but that God exists is not under debate.*

## 4.3  Leo Baeck on the Enduring Value of the Bible (1905)

*Following the publication of Adolf Harnack's* The Essence of Christianity, *which implied that Judaism had little religious validity, Rabbi Dr Baeck wrote* The Essence of Judaism *as a refutation of such claims and to prove the continuing vitality of the Jewish faith.*

All the features of the Jewish religion show it to be a prophetic creation stressing not abstract conceptions but rather man, his life and his conscience. The books of the Bible, however much their authors retire behind the lines, are not really books; they are confessions of individual religious quests behind which there stand most definite personalities. We are seldom given an inkling of who that man may have been, but wherever distinct personality can make itself felt, it shines forth boldly. That is why the Bible is so fragmentary, so undogmatic; it has no chain of conclusions, no formulas; it is as unsystematic as man himself. And that is also why it is so full of questions, and so full of things only half-said: it is as incomplete as man himself.

But the Bible contains an unanalyzable residue of its own, which cannot be enclosed in mere sentences but which can only be felt in a state of holy awe. That residue goes beyond all wit and wisdom; it is the source of the personality of every true man. Hence the lasting youthfulness of the Bible which will never fade but will at all times provide a fresh revelation.

Source: Leo Baeck, *The Essence of Judaism*, pp. 41–2.

COMMENT: *Baeck's concern is neither to resist the new challenge of secular research nor to distance himself from the literal beliefs of Orthodox Judaism, but to re-engage in a much older struggle against Christian claims that their faith had superseded Judaism and nullified it. He sees the inconsistencies and repetitions within the Hebrew Bible not as evidence of its structural flaws but as proof of its religious sincerity, the product of a human quest for the Divine that is wonderfully expressive and continuously relevant. Baeck is not dismissive of literary criticism, but prefers to focus instead on the inspirational nature of the Bible, which he regards as still present.*

## 4.4 Vivian Simmons on the Relevance of the Bible (1931)

*Despite the calm and unperturbed reaction of Joseph earlier, many felt that Biblical Criticism and Darwinism had damaged the standing of the Bible, and regarded their findings as attacks. Reverend Simmons was exercised by the need to assert the continuing worth of the Bible.*

Our age is a sceptical one, not towards the realities of religion, but towards the forms which were the vehicles of those realities in bygone days. It is not to be deplored – this widespread doubt. Only doubt and enquiry produce true faith. Yet our generation has not fully recovered from the shock produced by the result of scientific Bible study. These great modern achievements are, even among many to-day, regarded as a real danger to religious belief. What kind of faith is it, we may well ask, which accepts as its permanent authority a doctrine of verbal and complete inspiration of the Scriptures, utterly incompatible with the light of reason and inconsistent with the evidence of history? There are those who still insist that reason and evidence are human, and therefore imperfect, while Scriptures are Divine. We do not seek to convert them. But their faith is not ours. He who can hold a blind faith, he who can reject unassailable evidence, he who fears the effect of the light of reason and the result of modern searching after truth, is definitely opposed to progressive religion.

. . . Progressive Judaism demands of us that we should, on the one hand, accept the standards of truth which our knowledge and intellect enable us to employ, and at the same time should admit the possibility of changes great or small, in future standards or future knowledge. For us, progress is a principle of life. We cannot imagine how it can ever come to be denied or set at nought. For us, knowledge of the Bible is, in fact, progressing fairly constantly. Its sanctity and power of appeal is thereby heightened, not diminished . . . [although] it is always requiring a fresh statement. Thirty years ago it was necessary to explain that the greatness of the Bible, and its authority for us, were by no means impaired by the conclusions of modern science. The then new theory of evolution and the findings of astronomical and geological research necessitated an altered conception of many biblical statements about the origins of life and the processes of the universe. That adjustment has not affected the value of the Bible for us. The present-day difficulty is rather how to retain the sacred character of the Bible as a whole, now that the inequality of its various revelations and of its literary and religious quality are manifest to every student of its pages. Our tendency is to repeat and to give due prominence to those parts of the Bible whose teaching is universal, or in other respects appeal to us, leave alone those parts which are definitely of poor quality or of temporary character. We have even established the principle, unheard of in the past, that nothing should be read or taught from the Hebrew Bible which cannot be fittingly read or taught in an English translation.

Here again there can be no finality. We reserve to ourselves the right to pick and choose those Psalms and prophecies and legal statements which seem to us to constitute the highest and most universal messages of the past . . . We see a grave danger to the enquiring child-mind of this generation in presenting to him the Bible as a whole, expecting him to regard all its parts as equally divine, and encouraging that perplexity about the moral and social conditions of Bible times, exhibiting as they do in so many cases a glaring contrast to the standards and usages of the child's own day . . . If the day comes when we progressive Jews shall decide to use a smaller Bible, one which shall contain only the great teachings and sources of inspiration for our religious life, I, for one, will be neither disappointed nor surprised. Such a decision, in spite of its inevitable drawbacks, would at least vindicate our belief in the actual mingling of human and divine elements in the Bible, which we see to be the case in most other forms of God's revelation to mankind.

Source: Vivian G. Simmons, 'Progressive Judaism and the Bible', *The West London Synagogue Magazine*, V, pp. 191–3; VI, p. 5.

COMMENT: *Simmons is not afraid of the new age that Jewish teaching faces. Instead, he is forthright in positively welcoming it, and regarding the new insights it has to offer as being thoroughly in keeping with the progressive spirit of Judaism. He is consistent enough to accept that the principle of progress may also mean that current truths may become outdated and have to be jettisoned to make way for new understandings. Simmons is particularly keen to emphasize that real change has to take place as a result of the new research, and that the findings of scholarship have to be translated into practical action. This means editing which parts of the Bible are used in synagogue and which taught to children. The guiding principle to which he refers – using nothing in Hebrew that is unacceptable in English – emphasizes the new supremacy of reason, with all of its subjectivity. His own radicalism is evident from his desire to shorten the Bible, whereas other Reform rabbis preferred to keep the existing text of the Bible intact for historical reasons, even if they used its material selectively.*

## 4.5 Ignaz Maybaum on Welcoming Biblical Criticism (1949)

*Rabbi Dr Maybaum was greatly concerned to combat what he regarded as alien concepts within Judaism. He asserted that they had crept into Judaism through the influence of the other faiths among whom Jews had lived and whose ideas Jews had erroneously assimilated. By pinpointing them and rejecting them, Maybaum hoped to restore the original purity of Jewish thinking, and one area to which this applied was the Bible.*

Biblical criticism is destructive in that it destroys inevitably the conception of the holiness of the Bible as held in the past. The holiness of the word of God spoken through his prophets in the Bible, its timeless validity, cannot be destroyed. But what has been destroyed is the conception that the Bible as a book – and a book is a human work – is holy. No human work is holy. God alone is holy.

Here is the point where Progressive Judaism has again to make a great contribution to modern Jewry. What, in fact, has been destroyed by Biblical criticism? The answer is: Something which should have no place in our faith. A misinterpretation, which sees the Bible as the Mohammedan sees the Koran, has been destroyed. Judaism is a religion without sacrament. A sacrament is earthly matter which can be seen, touched, felt and as such it is regarded as holy. The Kaaba, the stone in Mecca, is regarded not as a stone but as something holy; the pilgrims come to worship it. The wine given in the Roman Catholic Mass to the worshipper is a sacrament.

We Jews do not see the Bible as a sacrament. It is a book like every other book; this is proved by the critical analysis of the historian. He has by that not destroyed part of our faith, he has purged it from an alien conception. At no point must we stop Biblical criticism. The conception of the 'verbal inspiration', meaning that every word and comma is inspired by God and not written by the hand of a human writer, may have been held by Jewry in the past; it has to be discarded by us to-day. It is a Roman Catholic dogma and an Islamic idea.

As Jewish faith has no sacrament so it has no mediator. The rejection of a personal mediator is established in Jewry. But the orthodox conception of the holiness of the Bible makes a book a mediatory instrument. Whether the Christian believer says that he comes to God through Christ, whether the orthodox Jew says that the *Torah*, meaning a holy book or holy literature, is between him and God, in both instances prophetic Judaism has been given up.

A situation arises after the destructive work of Biblical criticism similar to the destruction of the Temple in Biblical times. Every people of antiquity connected God with a fixed place. In becoming emancipated from this belief the Jewish people became emancipated from the times of antiquity and progressed to a new age. In the same way the destructive work of Biblical criticism has undermined the mediaeval structure of Jewish religious life and it is the re-interpretation of the conception of *Torat Moshe*, of 'Mosiac law from Sinai' through Progressive Judaism which is leading the Jewish people into a new age.

After the critical work of the historians, the Bible has ceased to appear as the treasured piece of memorial, left to us in a miraculous way from Mount Sinai and proving that the events on Mount Sinai are historical events. There is no historic material proving the existence of God; there is no material proof for the historic reality of the Sinaitic revelation. God wanted it so. God did not want man to turn to Him under the pressure of a proof not arrived at by man himself. God wants man a free agent. It follows that every generation has to set out anew and wander through the desert of doubt and unbelief in order to arrive at the Sinai of their own time. Only when they themselves stand before Sinai, too, will the Sinai of the forefathers be proved as concerning a real event.

Source: Ignaz Maybaum, *The Jewish Mission*, pp. 107–9.

COMMENT: *There is nothing cautious about Maybaum. He admits more openly than most the destructive power of Biblical Criticism, but wel-*

*comes it unreservedly. He is adamant that all that is lost by it are aspects of Judaism that were not Jewish in the first place, only false additions derived from Islam and Catholicism. Whether the negative implications of his remarks would be accepted by members of those faiths is open to question, as is his linkage of Orthodox Judaism to them. What is beyond doubt, though, is the apocalyptic terms in which he sees Biblical Criticism, comparing its arrival to the destruction of Jerusalem, one of the definitive turning points in Jewish history. Moreover, far from regarding the new age with trepidation, he sees it as a wonderful opportunity to unshackle Judaism from the element of compulsion and to restore its spirit of religious freedom. It could be argued that, in terms of communal cohesion, the emphasis on individual quest is no compensation for the loss of former certainties, but Maybaum does not share such fears.*

### 4.6 Jonathan Magonet on Surviving the Death of the Bible (1979)

*The optimism of Rabbi Maybaum seen above proved to be unfounded. Biblical Criticism and its challenge to the authority of the Bible led not so much to individuals feeling free to explore their own relationship with God but contributed to a weakening in faith and a loss of confidence in Judaism. Rabbi Professor Magonet sought to address the problem of what place the Bible now occupied in modern Jewish thought.*

The Bible died in our part of the Jewish world, as it died in the Christian world, perhaps some time in the last century. It was one of the casualties of the Enlightenment and the secular revolution. For is not the Bible, after all, only a book or rather a library of books. So it can be analysed and dissected like any other piece of 'classical' literature. We can admire the ethical advance here, the aesthetic success there, the occasional legal breakthrough or 'progress' in the 'later' books, even 'prove' through archaeological evidence that there is some historical truth in certain Biblical claims. But should such things really intrude in our consciousness in this day and age?

    . . . But the shocks of the twentieth century have shattered the optimism which saw a splendid progress towards an imminent Messianic age.

Auschwitz has forced us to turn again to Job, and the emergence of the State of Israel seems to have thrown us back into the age of Joshua and Judges ; the sense of meaninglessness in contemporary society finds expression in Ecclesiastes and the figure of Jonah stumbling on unwillingly to fulfil some unwanted Jewish destiny uncomfortably describes another aspect of recent Jewish experience . . . Clearly we can no longer support a theory that the entire *Torah* was, word for word, dictated by God to Moses upon Mount Sinai. What we can nevertheless say is that the *Torah*, like the rest of the Bible, represents the attempt of men to record their experience of God in different times in Israelite history, expressed as law, legend, parable, prophecy, homily, court and folk wisdom, prayer, story, song or interpreted history, all modified by critical reassessment at subsequent stages in the people's development.

Why should we read the Bible? Because it is our book. It is the story of our journey in search of truth, justice, love and God; our birth as a people, our leap into freedom, the model for a just society which we brought to the world, the men of vision who carried this vision and moulded the people to live by it, our attempts to create that society, our partial success and tragic failures, the renewal of that vision when every rule of history predicted the end of our tiny nation, swallowed up in the empires of the world. It is also a picture of us as we are today, thinly disguised by different clothes and unfamiliar names and places, with the same ambitions, passions and stubbornness, the same pride and achievement, the same fatal flaws and blindness. Perhaps in a time like ours, when the encounter with God seems rare or is hardly recognised when it occurs, we can turn for help to the tales of those whose vision was clearer because their stories are our stories, their struggles to grow, to learn, are our struggles. In trying to clarify the meaning of their experience of the divine, as they recorded it, we clarify our own experience.

Source: Jonathan Magonet, 'The Bible in Our Synagogues', in Dow Marmur (ed.), *A Genuine Search*, pp. 99–102.

COMMENT: *Magonet begins with an honesty that is both arresting and refreshing. By announcing the death of the Bible so forthrightly, he grips our attention and – certainly for those who agree with him – gains our confidence and thereby makes his subsequent remarks more persuasive. He*

*asserts that the Bible is still vital for two reasons: first, the age of enlighten-
ment that so challenged the Bible has itself been replaced by an age in which
many biblical books have become startlingly relevant. Second, the Bible is
essentially a national autobiography, and therefore has a power that over-
rides its flaws and can be an inspiration to the present generation. It could
be argued that past truths are not necessarily pointers to future ones, or that
autobiography can be narcissistic, but Magonet considers that the spiritual
history available from the Bible makes it of great value to those floundering
today.*

## 4.7 Jonathan Magonet on the Subversive Nature of the Bible (1991ff.)

*Having argued above that the Bible still had much to offer, Rabbi Professor
Magonet sought to show in two of his subsequent books on the Bible why the
critical approach should not be allowed to hide great religious lessons still to
be found in its pages.*

My first studies were in medicine. Having a scientific discipline behind
me made me highly critical when I came into the field of biblical studies.
Too much of it was merely the repetition of what someone had posited
over a century ago and too many hypotheses had taken on the nature of
a dogma that could not be criticized. Too much of scholarship seemed
to be concerned with disinterring and dissecting a dead body rather
than engagement with the wonder of a living organism . . . The Bible is
always in dialogue with us, believers and non-believers alike – and what
seems to matter is less the 'truth' we discover than the integrity with
which we struggle with that 'truth' and try to assimilate it into our lives.
The Rabbis summed up this view very nicely when they pointed out that
at the burning bush, God introduced himself to Moses as 'the God of
Abraham, the God of Isaac and the God of Jacob' – but not as the 'God
of Abraham, Isaac and Jacob'. Why is this the case? Because each of the
patriarchs had to discover God for himself out of his own experience
in his own time, certain only that it was the same God. If the Rabbis
are right, then this process never stops, and the act of interpreting the
Bible is our own way, in each generation, of entering the same process

of discovery, but carrying with us as we do it, all the understanding and lessons of the past.

Source: Jonathan Magonet, *A Rabbi's Bible*, pp. 3, 8.

The very contrasts that lie within the Bible actually contribute to its subversive quality since the reader is forced to engage in the debate. The obsessive details of the cultic arrangements of Leviticus are questioned, if not actually undermined, by the repeated prophetic critique of injustice masking itself behind public piety. Spiritual certainties stand alongside equally spiritual doubts in the pages of the Psalms. Laws about proper sexual behaviour stand in stark contrast to the actual practice of the most pious patriarchs and heroic kings, let alone the erotic power of the Song of Songs. Despite the repeated quest for peace, the pages of the Bible are stained with blood, shed all too often in the name of the God of peace.

Nor can such paradoxes, or for that matter such violence, simply be dismissed as the result of a 'primitive' level of religiosity, either to be superseded by a new or better covenant or explained away and justified in terms of an uncultured ancient world. We have to start with the premise that the sophistication of the biblical writers then was no less than ours – otherwise we would not still be reading their literary remains with such fascination and personal commitment.

If there are things we reject because no amount of interpretation can really justify them, then there are others that we have to recognize have yet to be taken seriously or implemented in our own 'advanced' society. If debts were abolished as in the Jubilee year (Leviticus 25) so that people could periodically get a fresh start; if we did indeed love our neighbour as ourselves (Leviticus 19.18); if we did beat our swords into ploughshares and no longer trained for war (Isaiah 2.4); if we could be a blessing to all the families of the earth (Genesis 12.13) – then the world would be a better place, and we would not even need the Bible. To press the point further home – our duty to read the Bible 'critically', with open eyes, with questions, even with judgements on the values it is offering us, is itself one of its legacies, and perhaps the most subversive of all. We are pulled into valuing and evaluating everything between the covers of the books of this library, and by direct extension the private books of our lives.

... The stories of the patriarchs are still available as models of behaviour or as evocative ways of reflecting our own situations – domestic and national. The way the story is told reflects back to us as a mirror our own reality and suggests ways of coping with it. The problem today in society at large is that we tend to relegate story-telling of this sort to the nursery, and in Jewish terms have lost much of the direct line of contact we once had . . . But the need for such enrichment of our imagination still exists, except that we experience it in a secular form. In place of Abraham and Sarah, Isaac and Rebeccah, today's real heroes and heroines, our role models, no longer walk the streets of Jerusalem or Beersheba, but inhabit the ranchhouses of Dallas or the suburbs of Australia. The [television] soaps, which are watched with the attention, devotion and love that no contemporary religious stories can command, contain the images and values that actually shape our sense of reality. Whether one form of story-telling and mirroring is more profound than the other hardly matters . . . the effectiveness of the traditional stories lies in our personal engagement with them, with their resonances within us. Moreover they were meant for adults to make them more adult and not just for children. Instead the soaps render us passive. They infantilize us by doing it all for us and converting everything into the same undifferentiated fare.

Source: Jonathan Magonet, *The Subversive Bible*, pp. 7–8, 97–8.

COMMENT: *Magonet's position is that he fully accepts the notion of Biblical Criticism, but is equally sure that it is not the only approach possible. He is keen to suggest that the received text, however it may have been formed and through whatever sources, is also worth studying in its own right. Its true value lies in the personal engagement of the student with the text and the insights that can emerge. He gives powerful examples of its moral lessons, and claims that secular society needs such role-myths just as much, but simply uses different formats, such as the television series 'Dallas' and 'Neighbours'. For him, the glory of the Bible is its ability to challenge both individuals and society at large by offering a mirror to their own situation. However, this could be said to apply as much to many other literary collections of great merit, such as the works of Shakespeare or Dostoyevsky, and the way they too force us to examine our lives. The question remains: if the Bible has lost authority and just has relevance, is that enough to still be a guide to communal structures and social mores?*

## 4.8 Lionel Blue on the Scripture of our own Lives (1995)

*Rabbi Blue constantly advocated that religion be rooted in the reality of people's lives, and saw the need to bridge the gaps that sometimes occurred between official teachings and everyday practice. One example of this was the harsh attitude of the Bible towards homosexuality. For some people, if the Bible could be so badly wrong in this case, it raised doubts as to its worth in general. Blue argued otherwise.*

To guide us in this work of reconciliation the traditional scriptures in isolation are not sufficient, and indeed never have been. That is because they are external to us. Books stand still, experience does not. Every religion has required some device, such as an oral law, an adaptive tradition, a legal fiction, a far-reaching commentary which goes behind the text, to fit the truths which come from both scripture and experience together, for they are one. All books can only speak of God's redemption to other people at other times. We have to supplement them with our own experience, which tells us how the same God redeemed us from our own Egypt in our own time. It is these scriptures, signed by our lives, which are needed to connect the truth in the present to the truth in the past, the truth we have experienced to the truth of the community. The psalmist knew long ago that you met the same God in the Bible as you did in the late watches of the night. Saintliness can be found in a disco, and a blessing in a bar. We should not take fright at this abundance of grace, and lock God up in a historical cage, or reduce the cosmos to safe ecclesiastical proportions – parish size. The choice is always there, and always the same, between what is mean and what is generous, between what is expedient and what is true, and whether people can help each other or destroy each other. This is the plot. The Kleenex, the cosmetics, the furniture of piety, the dressing up, clerical or lay, only supply the incidental scenery to our own drama of salvation.

Source: Lionel Blue, 'Godly and Gay', in Jonathan Magonet (ed.), *Jewish Explorations of Sexuality*, pp. 120–1.

COMMENT: *Blue takes the post-Biblical Criticism thinking a stage further in terms of the relevance of the text. Whereas others had suggested that more important than the text itself was the encounter between the individual and the text, Blue argues that individuals need to supplement the biblical text with their own insights. In this way the Bible is saved from becoming dated and outdated, and lives on in the life of the reader. It could be argued that without such radical engagement, the Bible becomes instantly fossilized, and does not even have any life unless it is picked up, read and confronted in this way. However, this approach could also carry the danger of the Bible becoming the prey of every individual's interpretation and no longer a basis for communal traditions. The need for balancing individual perspectives and communal needs is still present.*

## A Final Thought . . .

In 1968 our Progressive Jewish youth movement hosted a group of young Czech Jews for a conference near Edinburgh. They stayed on for an additional week – and the Russians marched into Prague, cutting them off from their country and their families. Many of them became refugees overnight. They taught me something very special about the Bible in the time we were together. We studied some Bible texts and they were incredibly good at understanding them, picking up all the nuances very quickly. I was surprised as they had never studied the Bible before.

'It's easy, ' they explained. 'You see, in Czechoslovakia, when you read a newspaper, first you read what is written there. Then you say to yourself, "If that is what they have written, what really happened? And if that is what really happened, what are they trying to make us think? And if that is what they are trying to make us think, what should we be thinking instead?" You learn to read between the lines and behind the lines. You learn to read a newspaper as if your life depended upon understanding it – because it does!'

'You learn to read a newspaper as if your life depended upon understanding it.' Sometimes the same applies to the Bible, sometimes we just have to learn how to read.

Source: Jonathan Magonet, *A Rabbi's Bible*, p. 25.

# 5

# BUSINESS ETHICS

The term 'business ethics' may be a modern phrase, but its roots stretch back to the Bible and a variety of commands that made it clear that Judaism was as much concerned with what individuals did in the market place as they did in the house of prayer. Thus the Israelites were enjoined in the Book of Leviticus to ensure they paid the wages of employees promptly (19.13), had just weights and scales (19.36) and priced their goods fairly (25.14). Rabbinic literature continued this theme. Judaism applied as much midweek in everyday trading as it did on the Sabbath and for worship. There was no distinction between religious life and ordinary matters. Amid all their debates on rituals and observances, the rabbis emphasized that God needed to be served also through ethical practices during the working day. However, the need for rabbinic strictures against profiteering or selling faulty items can be taken as evidence that these were regular occurrences and required combating. It was much easier to be pious in prayer than in daily dealings, and hence the rabbinic homily that the first question one would be asked in order to gain entry to Heaven would not be if one had attended services regularly but whether one had been honest in one's business affairs. Nevertheless, honesty does not preclude the pursuit of wealth and it was never suggested that Jews should not seek material comforts.

## 5.1 Morris Joseph on Integrity in Business (1903)

*Before Reverend Joseph issued his* Judaism as Creed and Life *there had been several other books published in England summarizing the essential features of Judaism. However, one of the reasons that his was so notable was because of its emphasis on the ethical values of the Jewish faith. Divided into three sections – on Beliefs, Ceremonial, and Moral Duties – the last of these was by far the largest. Within that section, he devoted an entire chapter to business integrity.*

The good man will be upright abroad as well as at home. He will be strictly honest in his business life. Not only will he not commit the vulgar crime of stealing, but he will shrink with abhorrence from fraud and deceit of every kind. Significant is the warning 'Ye shall not steal, neither shall ye deal falsely, nor lie one to another', which puts the offences of false action and untruthful speech into the same category with the heinous crime denounced by the eighth Word of the Decalogue. Deception in business is robbery. The tricks of trade are not less dishonest because they are not punishable by the law of the land, or because the custom of the trade sanctions or condones them. Merely to imply, even without warranty, that spurious pictures are genuine, to say that an article is re-duced in price simply because the additional price has first been put on, to employ the misleading exaggerations of the conventional advertise-ment – all such devices are violations of the moral law as laid down by Judaism. Honesty and truthfulness are the first debts due from a man to his neighbour. If there is no certainty of that debt being discharged, there is an end to all mutual confidence, to all real intercourse between man and man – an end to society itself.

Source: Morris Joseph, *Judaism as Creed and Life*, p. 422.

COMMENT: *Joseph's statement is no bland repetition of traditional rabbinic thinking but seethes with passion. The detailed examples he gives of current business malpractices show how aware he is of moral lapses by Jews of his time. He is keen to assert that although in some quarters such acts are seen as part of normal business life, that is no excuse for a Jew to behave in this way. As a way of showing how serious he considers business fraud to be, he links it with the Ten Commandments and thereby attempts to change its status from a minor misdemeanour to a major crime.*

## 5.2 Morris Joseph on the Dangers of Moneylending (1903)

*One of the main occupations of Jews in the Middle Ages – although by no means the only one – had been moneylending. This was not because of any natural propensity for it, but simply because so many other trades were barred to them. In addition, Christians were not allowed to be money-lenders by Canon Law, and so there was a vacuum in society that needed filling. However, it was an occupation that attracted great unpopularity when debts had to be repaid or pledges forfeited. It severely tarnished the image of Jews for several centuries and was still of sufficient concern to be addressed as a specific evil by Reverend Joseph at the beginning of the twentieth century.*

The moneylender's vocation is objectionable, not because of any vice inherent in itself, but by reasons of its evil results. Carried on fairly, it may be a perfectly harmless and even useful trade. If it is denounced by social opinion, it is because it has too often degenerated into usury and become the source of the dire mischief which usury inevitably begets. This is the explanation of the odium which attaches even to respectable money-lending. For the good Jew that odium is its all-sufficient condemnation. It is not enough for him to say 'My hands are clean; the terms on which I lend my money are honest and fair; I need not trouble about anything else'. Public opinion is a force which no man may properly disregard. Least of all may the Jew defy it, for beside his own good name he has the reputation of his people to defend. And he compromises that reputation when he devotes himself, however innocently, to a calling which, because it has been so often prostituted for the vilest purposes, has become an object of universal distrust and repugnance. For the world is only too prone to judge the Jew harshly, and to include the race in the blame which, rightly or wrongly, it metes out to the individual. Therefore the Israelite will often deny himself a liberty which abstract considerations would permit. And he will be especially careful to do so in this particular instance, seeing that the world has come to regard usury as a Jewish practice, and thus to include a rapacious cupidity among Jewish characteristics. And so some of the motives which forbid him to practise usury will urge him to shun even the better sorts of money-lending. He will keep ever before him that wholesome horror of *Chillul*

*Hashem* – of profaning the Name of God – which is so powerful a factor in his ethical consciousness.

Source: Morris Joseph, *Judaism as Creed and Life*, p. 429.

COMMENT: *Whereas in the previous excerpt Joseph had condemned business malpractices as evil in their own right, his attack on moneylending is far more concerned with its effect on the public image of Jews. He reflects a British Jewry that is not only a minority, but a very nervous one and ever-anxious as to the opinions of the host population. Nevertheless, his underlying thesis is probably true, for an unscrupulous Christian would be seen as un-Christian and therefore not reflect on his co-religionists, whereas an unscrupulous Jew was often taken as representative of all Jews. Joseph's concern with usury is exacerbated by the historic unpleasantness connected with the trade. A Jewish florist who short-changed his customers, for instance, would not evoke the same associations. Joseph's congregation felt sufficiently strongly on the issue to bar Jewish usurers from membership.*

## 5.3 Morris Joseph on the Acquisition of Wealth (1907)

*As has been seen in the two extracts above, Reverend Joseph was concerned with the moral conduct of business as a tenet of Judaism and also the damage done to the reputation of Jews in general by any lapse in standards. There were also important political considerations that may have influenced his thinking, as the two decades after 1881 witnessed a massive migration of Jews from Eastern Europe to Britain. This provoked a degree of anti-semitism – fuelled by allegations of unfair competition and the horrors of sweat-shop labour – and led to calls to halt the unchecked flow of immigrants into the country, culminating in the 1905 Aliens Act. Many within established Jewry were embarrassed by the commotion that arose, and the need to maintain business probity became an important priority.*

The pursuit of wealth is not only defensible but even commendable. It is at once a necessary condition of the world's progress and a valuable builder of character. It is the parent of enterprise and discovery. It often calls out in the individual such sterling virtues as industry, sincerity and self-restraint. It may be, in short, a moral discipline. But, on the other hand, if these benefits are not to be neutralized, it must be engaged in for the sake of something better than the material prizes at which it aims. It must be carried on for moral ends, and under a deep sense of ethical responsibility. The higher welfare of the individual, the good of the race, the promotion of philanthropy – these are legitimate and laudable objects to set before one's self in the acquisition of wealth.

It is here that the modern temper is seen to be signally defective. Money, instead of being the stepping-stone to higher things, is made an end in itself. It is the one standard by which men measure their own happiness and gauge the worth of others. As so results that deterioration of character, that lowering of the tone of everyday life, which is so noticeable in these times. The consequent evils are not only moral, but physical. The Law-giver, in a sombre passage, speaks of the earth, exhausted by the people's greed, enjoying in the period of their exile the Sabbatical rest so long denied it (Leviticus 26.34). How often does the modern man break down in body or in mind under the strain of money-getting. And only then, in that time of physical collapse, does outraged nature come by its own.

Source: Morris Joseph, *The Message of Judaism*, pp. 73–4.

COMMENT: *Joseph – many of whose congregants could be classed as rich – seeks to steer a balanced course between approval of acquisition and denunciation of avarice. He raises no objections to wealth, but only to the way in which it is gained. Perhaps concerned that the moral case is not strong enough by itself, he seeks to bolster his argument by warning of the unfortunate personal consequences that unrestrained greed can produce. However, he spares the reader from too much lurid detail, either because he is unwilling to offend or because he is short of such evidence.*

## 5.4  Ignaz Maybaum on the Anguish of Poverty (1944)

*Rabbi Dr Maybaum's book* Synagogue and Society *was given the sub-title* Jewish-Christian Collaboration in the Defence of Western Civilisation *and was directed both at Jewish readers immersed in wider society and*

*Christians who wished to know more about Judaism. In writing this public presentation of Judaism, Maybaum was conscious of the different attitudes between the two faiths to wealth and poverty and sought to address the contrast.*

Jewish compassion makes us protest against the saying 'Blessed are the poor'. They are to be pitied. They cannot fully develop as human beings created in the image of God. Hunger and undernourishment will not let a man develop his mental and spiritual powers. Poverty means hunger and undernourishment. Poverty means dirt. It means freezing in winter, it means living and sleeping in badly ventilated houses, it means wearing rags. The child of God, man created in God's image, must not live in that unworthy state to which poverty condemns him. Jewish compassion does not understand such things as 'Blessed are the poor'.

Jewish understanding of this Christian message of the Sermon on the Mount, this 'Blessed are the poor' goes so far as to recognise the Christian heroism it reveals. Those who have been defeated by Fate, those chained to the unalterable, are like the dying, like those who facing death seek no further chance in life. This 'Blessed are the poor' may have something in it of the bliss of dying. But this is as far as we can go. For we know nothing of life after death. We only know of God, for whom death has no bounds. But we are not permitted to run towards death as bliss, even though we may in the knowledge of God die in peace.

Source: Ignaz Maybaum, *Synagogue and Society*, p. 102.

COMMENT: *Maybaum rejects the Christian notion that poverty has a redemptive quality to it or is even to be admired. He lists the brutal reality of those without means – cold, hunger and dirt – and punctures the idea that it is a natural state for the creatures of God or a religious ideal. The clear inference is that seeking material comfort is sanctioned by Judaism and regarded as religiously appropriate. This is not to say that the poor do not deserve pity or charity – a point dealt with elsewhere by Maybaum.*

# 6

# CHARITY

The importance of charity runs through both the Bible and Judaism in general as a constant theme. Attending to the needs of those disadvantaged in society – typified by the widow, the orphan and the stranger who is homeless – is a common refrain. In biblical times, this was more likely to take the form of hospitality rather than donations, and Abraham is credited as a prime exemplar of such virtues. In later times, when monetary gifts became a more common means of supporting others, Jacob's pledge to give a tenth of his possessions to God (Genesis 28.22) was taken to be the ideal amount one should give, although the rabbis reckoned that giving a sixtieth of one's income was a more realistic expectation for most people. The Hebrew word usually translated as charity – *tzedakah* – actually carries a wider sense of righteous behaviour. It implies that charity is not so much an out-of-the-ordinary act deserving of special praise, but is social justice, a basic duty that should be taken for granted. There still remain many questions as to how charity should be given, who is most deserving, whether anyone is exempt from the obligation to give, and the relationship between donor and recipient.

## 6.1 David Woolf Marks on the Necessity of Charity (1854)

*Reverend Professor Marks comments on Proverbs 3.27, which declares: 'Withhold not good from him to whom it is due, when it is in the power of your hand to do so.' The verse becomes a useful instrument by which he can expand on the importance of charity and the best way of approaching it.*

Man and Israelite! thou art God's appointed steward: and whatsoever thou dost possess is not absolutely thine own, to be used for thy exclusive or selfish ends, but is consigned to thee in sacred trust, that thou mayest dispense a portion thereof to thy suffering and afflicted brother. Harden not, then, thy heart, O thou who hast enough to spare, and let not thine anger be aroused, because thy path is so frequently crossed by the appeal of the widow and orphan, and of the houseless and the needy. Remember! He from whom comest all that thou dost possess, hath not only charged thee to do good, but also not to withhold from thy fellow man any benefit which thou hast the means to confer on him. Moreover thy God exhorteth thee not to sport with the feelings of a poor man, nor to put him off from day to day, saying 'Come tomorrow and I will give'. No, saith the holy and merciful God, seize the occasion whilst it offers itself, for discharging this moral obligation; since thou knowest not what change a single day may bring about in thy condition or in thy fortune; neither knowest thou how near the hour may be, which is to summon thee to another state, where thou must render an account, at the tribunal of thy God, of the uses to which thou hast put the several gifts and capacities with which thy Heavenly father hath invested thee. Let the text instruct us in two important things. First, that it is our essential vocation as Israelites, to be constantly employed in the promotion of our own improvement and of the comfort and well-being of our fellow creatures. Between mankind of every nation and of every faith a universal bond of brotherhood should be recognised. Secondly, that nothing can be more injurious to our moral nature than to miss the opportunities which are afforded us to do good, whilst it is in our power to take advantage of them and put them into practice. Inasmuch as the future is uncertain, time present is all that we can properly call our own.

Source: David Woolf Marks, *Lectures & Sermons*, Vol. II, pp. 152–4.

COMMENT: *Marks asserts that charity is not a meritorious act but a moral obligation. He is robust in emphasizing that any wealth that has been accrued is only a temporary loan from God, with the task of distributing it to others wisely rather than hoarding it for oneself. He also stresses how impermanent is our hold on wealth, either because our circumstances may change or because our life itself may end abruptly. However, Marks is sensitive enough to recognize the annoyance or weariness that can result from*

*constantly being implored to give to charity. But having given expression to*
*the feelings of those 'frequently crossed' by appeals, he does not hesitate to*
*remind that a positive response is still the only correct course.*

## 6.2  Morris Joseph on the Nature of Charity (1903)

*Reverend Joseph was as emphatic as Marks above on the duty incumbent*
*on all Jews to give charity. However, he was also keen to stress the need for*
*effective charity-giving. In an era when philanthropy was highly esteemed*
*in society at large – but was regarded by some as an easy source of kudos – he*
*emphasized the recipient's need to be helped (and in the best possible way)*
*rather than the donor's need to be seen to be giving.*

Charity must not be practised merely for its own sake, without reference
to its effects. It must not be thrown away. The improvident man who
refuses to live within his means and seeks to be supported by charity
must not be helped. On the other hand, the wholesome objections of a
poor man to gifts of money deserves the greatest consideration. For such
persons loans are recommended in order to preserve their self-respect.
'Greater,' a rabbi declares, 'is he that lends than he that gives, and greater
still is he that lends, and, with the loan, helps the poor man to help himself.' (Shabbat 63a). It is with this maxim in his mind that Maimonides
assigns the eighth and highest place in his scale of benevolent deeds to
assistance, such as gifts and loans of money or the procuring of employ-
ment, which will render the poor self-helpful and independent.

   In this, however, Maimonides is only fulfilling the spirit of the old
Mosaic Law. The Pentateuch commends not charity merely, but well-
considered charity, not almsgiving, which fosters pauperism and
encourages idleness and deception, but the generous and thoughtful
benevolence which 'upholds' the poor man when his hand begins to
'fail', and saves him from penury and demoralisation (Leviticus 25.35).
All charitable effort must be directed towards these ends. It must, as far
as possible, be curative, redemptive. Too many forget this truth. The
distress they are chiefly concerned to relieve is their own. The thought of
human misery causes them a certain discomfort, of which they cheaply
rid themselves by petty and more or less indiscriminate almsgiving. The

glow of self-satisfaction which rewards their so-called charity suffices them; and they are not at pains to consider whether their act has really benefited the person towards whom it has been performed. And yet it is in this effect that the real worth of benevolence chiefly resides.

For much charitable effort, indeed, no money whatever is needed. Many a falling man has been saved by wise advice or kindly interest. Some true friend has intervened in time and shown him a means of self-help which he had overlooked. Or work has been found for him when he was unable to get it for himself. Many a man, moreover, has been saved merely by an encouraging word which, because it told him that he was not alone, but that another heart was beating in sympathy with his, has nerved him to make another and a more effective bid for success. Such fruitful deeds of mercy are done every day, and done without money. Perhaps that is why the Rabbis urge the duty of charity even upon the poorest; for even the poorest can do such deeds (Gittin 7b).

Source: Morris Joseph, *Judaism as Creed and Life*, pp. 463–4.

COMMENT: *Joseph advances the cause of charity a step further: giving is not enough; it has to be done in a way that eradicates poverty permanently rather than alleviates it temporarily. Living in an age where the workhouse was infamous for offering some assistance to the impoverished but no long-term remedy, Joseph urges that Maimonides' principle of helping others to achieve self-sufficiency be considered the yardstick by which charity is judged, and not dismissed as the highest ideal that was least likely to happen. He also emphasizes that charity is the duty of all, whatever their financial status, and that as giving kindness can be as valuable as giving money, those who cannot offer the latter can provide the former.*

## 6.3 Morris Joseph on the Relationships Involved in Charity (1903)

*In the extract above, Reverend Joseph had addressed both the obligation to provide charity and the best method of doing so. However, he also considered the underlying relationship between donor and recipient to be an important feature of the command to be charitable. In addition, he was concerned that this relationship had deteriorated because of changes in society and feared that the very concept of charity was suffering as a result.*

In great cities like London or New York, where the struggle for life is especially keen and absorbing, and where the population is broken up into many sections, it is idle to look for that close and almost brotherly intercourse, between rich and poor which was one of the beautiful features of social life in former times, and which is to some extent possible even today in smaller communities. Once the stranger was not merely relieved with a dole at the door, but was invited into the house, and lodged in the guest chamber, or if he decided not to continue his journey, he might be taken into the service of his host. Among Jews, at any rate, the Rabbinic command 'Let the poor be members of thy household' (Pirke Avot 1.5) found many an obedient listener. And if dole were given, the donor would bestow it with his own hands, and with the gift draw the recipient nearer to him. The gap that separated the wealthy from the needy was bridged by countless personal kindnesses done every day.

Our modern social organisation affords little opportunity for such intercourse, full of blessings as it is, no less for the rich than for the poor. Personal service has frequently to be commuted nowadays for money payments. Instead of housing the wayfarer, or feeding the hungry, or nursing the sick, we perform these duties by proxy. We pay poor-rates, and we subscribe to benevolent societies. The change is the inevitable consequence of the altered conditions of modern social life. Still the old-fashioned system had advantages over and above the charity it dispensed. It assuaged the sufferings of the poor, but it also kept the stream of sympathy flowing in the hearts of the rich. It is one thing to relieve poverty vicariously through a society or through the machinery of the poor-law; it is quite another thing to relieve it with one's own hands. To hear of human misery is a far less powerful stimulus to compassion than to see it. And in these days of enforced egoism such emotional exercises are more than ever valuable as elements of moral hygiene.

Moreover, the ever-widening chasm that divides the classes is a serious social danger. It behoves us to keep steadily in view the urgent necessity of arresting this mutual alienation of rich and poor. The rich man must recognise once more that the poor are his brothers, with a right to something more than the crusts heedlessly thrown to him from his over-loaded table, and the poor must be able to feel once more that the rich man is no strange creature, to be regarded with suspicion and distrust. More generosity must mark their mutual relations. On the one side there must be more lavish bestowal of personal aid, more thoughtfulness, a greater disposition to 'take trouble' for the necessitous. On the other side there must be more responsiveness, more confidence, more goodwill. For the obligation is mutual. Both have to learn to open their hearts a little wider. Both have to remember that though they are superficially divided by worldly circumstances, the transcendent tie of their common humanity fundamentally unites them.

Source: Morris Joseph, *Judaism as Creed and Life*, pp. 465–7.

COMMENT: *Joseph presents an idealized view of charity in former times that may not have been so widespread as he likes to imagine. However, he still has a strong point that charity conducted through others from a distance is not as meaningful to either the giver or the receiver compared to when it is carried out personally face to face. It also increases the alienation between the rich and poor, even though Joseph glosses over the fact that the main divide is caused by wider factors operating in society at large and not by those trying to ameliorate the situation. He is undoubtedly correct in insisting that charity should not merely be a financial transaction but a personal investment of one's time and commitment. That way a relationship is established between the two parties, while there is much greater determination to solve the problem at hand.*

## A Final Thought . . .

My grandmother took me on expeditions. On Thursday night she woke me up and at the dead of night, when the gas lamps were turned down to a flicker, we went round the block, putting little packets through letter-boxes. They were little parcels of money and foods to help poorer families celebrate the coming Sabbath. They were given at night so that giver and receiver would never meet, and neither would feel obligation or shame. Occasionally we would meet other *bubbes* wrapped in shawls and shadows waddling from house to house. I was surprised when I first saw a picture of angels after I was evacuated. Who could believe in their too sweet smiles, the peroxide blond hair, and the fairy wings. My angels were solid from the neck down. They were Semitic, rheumatic and waist-less. When the messiah comes they might levitate. In this reality their poor bodies were stuck only too closely to the earth.

Source: Lionel Blue and June Rose, *A Taste of Heaven*, p. 47.

# 7

# CHRISTIANITY

Judaism's relationship with Christianity has been quintessentially different to its relationship with any other faith, and for a variety of reasons: Christianity developed out of Judaism; Jesus and his initial followers were Jewish; both faiths share the same sacred scriptures in the form of the Hebrew Bible; Christianity regards itself as the true heir to Judaism (the 'New Israel'); the Christian story has Jews playing a central (and villainous) role in it; Christianity has constantly sought the conversion of Jews; the blood-splattered conflict between the two faiths for most of the last 2000 years in Europe. It means that the two religions have an enormous amount in common and yet also have a history of unparalleled animosity. The moves towards reconciliation in the last fifty years have had to contend with this dual legacy.

## 7.1 Morris Joseph on the Lure of Christianity (1893)

*In the more tolerant climate of the late nineteenth century, it seemed that Christian welcome could be as dangerous as Christian hostility. Some Jews found Christianity very attractive because its emphasis on spirituality and the aesthetic appeared to contrast favourably with the obsession over ritual minutiae which they felt characterized much of Jewish life. There were also those who, more cynically, saw it as offering a gateway into social acceptance and political opportunity. Reverend Joseph was sufficiently concerned to issue a public warning to those considering conversion.*

Now and then Jews of an impressionable age are caught by the glitter of the Church, and think, with a sigh, how beautiful it would be if the rites of the Synagogue were not characterised by so severe a simplicity. They are attracted by the Christian service with its impressive ritual, its stirring and tuneful hymns, or they are captivated by the winning hero of the Gospels. Occasionally, regret manifests itself in action of a pronounced kind, and the homely religion is abjured for the more romantic one. It is well that young people of our race, who exclaim 'how superior!' when they think of the religion of their Christian companions, should be at pains to examine it in its entirety before pronouncing judgement. A religion whose surface looks so beautiful may prove to be far less satisfactory when examination is extended to the core. Music and incense, even religious stories, however inspiring, do not make a religion. It is made by cardinal truths – truths to live by, and which, if one is to live by them, must be felt to be truths. If there are people who can honestly believe in the dogma of Original Sin, of the Atonement, of the Justification by Faith and similar essentials of Christian teaching, and lead better lives for their belief, let no man disturb their minds. Their faith is justified by their righteousness. But it is another matter altogether when we are attempting to reconstruct the religious edifices for ourselves. Then we must be careful, as befits the solemnity, the momentousness of the task we have in hand, that all our materials are sound, that the superstructure shall not only be beautiful, but stable; above all, that the foundation shall be strong. It is easy enough to join in a melodious hymn, or to admire the nobility of the central figure in a religious story. But Christianity is far from being so simple an affair. It requires its adherents to accept every word of the Gospel narrative as absolutely true, as Divinely inspired – nay, to subscribe to doctrines saturated by mysticism – doctrines which are almost in perpetual conflict with reason, and which strain belief to breaking point. Surely, all of us who wish to preserve a character for sobriety of thought, must hesitate long before complying with so exacting a demand.

Why do I say all this? Only to bring out more clearly the reasons we have for being eminently satisfied with our own religion, eminently indisposed to recognise any other as its superior. As regards the inspiration which the Christian undoubtedly does draw from the contemplation of the virtues of his Master, the Jew is furnished with a similar incentive to nobility of life if he will only think of it. It is to be found in the heroism of Israel, in his fortitude under unique suffering, in his living for an idea, which, considering what life has meant for him, has been even more glorious than his dying for it.

Source: Morris Joseph, *The Ideal in Judaism*, pp. 32–5.

COMMENT: *Joseph manages to be very honest about the attractions of Christianity – particularly the style of its services – without ceding any ground to it. Instead he emphasizes that these attractions have to be weighed against more important considerations, notably the actual beliefs to which Christians are expected wholeheartedly to subscribe and which he considers totally unacceptable. He avoids the trap of just criticizing Christianity, and also offers positive reasons for remaining faithful to Judaism. However, it could be claimed that he merely appeals to a sense of history rather than deriving inspiration from what Judaism offers currently. It is also evident that Joseph is walking a tightrope between a wish to dismiss Christian beliefs and a desire not to offend existing members of the faith. Although he states that Christian doctrines can lead to righteousness, his description of them as being in 'almost perpetual conflict with reason' reveals his true feelings and is his main argument against Jews joining the Church.*

## 7.2 Ignaz Maybaum on the Differences between Judaism and Christianity (1944)

*Rabbi Maybaum's concern was not so much the attraction of Christianity to some Jews, but the ignorance of both Jews and Christians alike as to where the faiths differed, apart from the obvious areas of the person of Jesus and certain doctrinal distinctions. He was keen to combat the assumption common in the popular mind that the two faiths were 'all the same underneath' and to point out the very different approaches that shaped the thinking and practice of the two religions. His object was not to erect a barrier between Jews and Christians, but to promote a clarity of thought which in itself would lead to better mutual understanding.*

The Jew prays to God, justifies his deeds before God, and regards the world as God's creation. But he knows no sudden transformation, no conversion. He knows nothing of such an experience of faith. Yet he is no heathen. Yet as a Jew he follows God, who is also the true God of the Christian. The Jew is true to the God of Abraham, Isaac and Jacob. Where the Christian speaks of his conversion, of his changed life because of his baptism, of his faith, the Jew speaks of the God of his fathers. The Jew is a Jew because he is part of the chain of tradition. The Prophet's call to repentance does not mean a call to conversion, but a return to what the fathers taught and did . . . We know of God. That is why nothing can be found in our Bible which may in any way be interpreted as a parallel to Paul's Damascus experience in the New Testament. That is why as a Jew we speak of a contrast between Christian faith and Jewish tradition . . . Fear of God, hope, trust, thankfulness, humility, obedience – these are all words with which the Jew can explain his relationship to God. But the word 'belief' – as Paul understood it has no meaning for the Jew. There is no 'Jewish belief' to correspond to 'Christian belief'. The Jew is true to an event in history to which we are heirs. This historic event must be understood on the ethical and political plane as a bond, and on its rational side as a revelation – that is to say, as the reception of the *Torah*.

. . . This was the difference between Judaism and Christianity at the time Christianity left Judaism in the days of Paul: Christianity baptised the *Am Ha'aretz* (uneducated person). Judaism throughout its entire education system tried to stop the *Am Ha'aretz* being an *Am Ha'aretz*, to make him a man who learns from the Jewish books. The difference between Paul and the Pharisees is this – the Pharisees tried to reach the *Am Ha'aretz*, the man who had no ties with Jewish history and was ignorant of it, and to bring him into it. The Pharisees saw in the *Am Ha'aretz* an educational task. Paul's approach was different. He too wanted to bring the pagan world to the God of Israel, true God of Abraham, Isaac and Jacob. But he did it in a new way. Not through Pharisaic adult education. Paul tried to win the heathen by the faith which can transform a man . . . The absoluteness of the *Torah* is expressed in our customary formula, 'the *Torah* from Sinai'. But its holiness and absoluteness do not make of it a sacrament, an object which like a body has a place in space. We do not believe in the *Torah* in the Christian sense of the word. We study it, trusting in the teachings and prescriptions by which our fathers walked with God, we too will in our own time find the road by which we may also walk with God. The word 'studying' Holy Script is an expression found only in Judaism. Christianity does not know this religious activity of study to the extent where it applies to every individual, as it does in Judaism. Where the Christian believes, the Jew studies.

... When we Jews use the word 'layman' we must realise that the word has been borrowed from Christian terminology, and cannot therefore just be taken over with nothing more to it. The word is borrowed from a world in which there is a Church. Judaism has no Church. As far as the layman is in Christianity the man who is not a member of the clergy, who is not an ordained priest nor a recognised theologian, we may accept the word 'layman' and say that Judaism is a religion in which the layman plays a leading part. As far as the layman is in religious affairs not an independent man, but is directed by the officers of the Church, by his ordained priests and recognised theologians, we cannot accept the word 'layman'. No Jew may in this sense be a layman. The Jew must never recognise an ecclesiastical tutelage. 'You shall be a kingdom of priests unto me' ( Exodus 19.6). Judaism is a lay priesthood. All great creative Jewish movements were always lay movements. The prophetic movement in Biblical times and Pharisaism in post-Biblical times were lay movements. In modern times Liberal Religious Judaism and Zionism are lay movements.

... The Synagogue cannot utilise music in its services to the same extent as the Christian Church. The Synagogue is a place of religious popular assembly. Jewish people assemble in the Synagogue to pray, also to study and teach, as citizens assemble in the town hall. Time does not stand still as in the concert hall, nor is it in the Church, where a single point in time submerges all past and subsequent points. The assembly in the Synagogue is concerned with time past, present and future. The praying Jew deals with time, for in it the Jewish people lives, wanders, suffers and renews itself, [be it] Jerusalem, Rome, Paris, Wittenberg, Whitehall, Moscow ... When the church door closes behind the worshipper, the world remains outside. The Jew praying in the Synagogue remains in the world ... Christianity has for nearly two thousand years been celebrating in its divine service the end of time. We Jews, though we look to the end of time, and which indeed every individual experiences at the end of his personal life, and we live and act accordingly, cannot in the Synagogue celebrate the end of time in the Christian fashion. The Christian says, the time is fulfilled. The Jew says, the time is not yet fulfilled. The Jew prays for the coming of the kingdom of God, with his eyes turned from the present to the future of the world. Both Jew and Christian pray for the Coming of the Kingdom. But the Jew prays for it with an intensity which the Christian does not know, which makes the Jew always stand out as a pattern for the Christian. The idea of the second coming of Christ may have its place in the theological dogma of Christianity. But there is no place for it in the heart of the Christian. Not only the resurrected Christ, but the infant Christ is already called Saviour and Redeemer. This is the difference between Jew and Christian. And this difference makes Jewish prayer different from Christian prayer.

... Those assembled in the Synagogue are a community of lay-priests, without the aristocracy that raises the priest above the laity, an absolute religious democracy. We are all priests, lay-priests. Lay-priesthood differs from that priesthood which constitutes a class, because it is not open to the danger of clericalism. The Jewish lay-priesthood is protected from that by its position in relation to the Prophets. Between priest and prophet, the higher rank belongs to the prophet. Any Jewish child knows that Moses the prophet stands higher than Aaron the Priest.

Source: Ignaz Maybaum, *Synagogue and Society*, pp. 68–70, 75, 80, 83, 118 ff., 132.

COMMENT: *There is nothing cautious about Maybaum. He has no hesitation in painting in broad brush strokes and with vivid colours. He confidently asserts the fact that Christianity involves conversion, whereas Judaism means following tradition; that Christianity is a matter of belief, whereas Judaism is concerned with education; that the Church has a hierarchical divide between priests and laity, whereas the Synagogue is a lay democracy; that Christianity revolves around a single point in the past, whereas Judaism is at home in living time. In some respects these generalizations are enormously helpful in providing evidence of the major delineations between the two faiths at a very deep level beyond the surface differences. In other ways, their over-generalized nature makes them risk being open to question: Judaism, for instance, could also be said to be fixated on one moment in time, the revelation at Mount Sinai, while many would argue that rabbinic obfuscation meant that Judaism too suffered from clericalism. Presenting Judaism as if belief plays no part whatsoever is equally controversial. For their part, Christians may question the accuracy of his analysis of their faith. Nevertheless, Maybaum's swashbuckling ap-*

*proach is refreshing and challenging, even if it glosses over some important qualifications.*

## 7.3  Leo Baeck on Reclaiming Christianity (1958)

*Rabbi Dr Baeck was well aware of the differences between the two faiths and had written on them extensively. However, he also desired to show the Jewish roots of Christianity – not as a polemic against the Church but as a lesson to fellow Jews, whose vision of Christianity was often coloured by centuries of persecution and for whom the Jewishness of Jesus tended to go unnoticed. Baeck analyses the Gospels and tries to extract what, according to him, is the 'old Gospel'. He regards this as the original Jewish record of Jesus without the later Christological overlays that were added to the accounts.*

In the old Gospel which is thus opened up before us, we encounter a man with noble features who lived in the land of the Jews in tense and excited times and helped and laboured and suffered and died: a man out of the Jewish people who walked on Jewish paths with Jewish faith and Jewish hopes. His spirit was at home in the Holy Scriptures, and his imagination and thought were anchored there; and he proclaimed and taught the word of God because God had given it to him to hear and to preach. We are confronted by a man who won his disciples among his people and they believed in him even after his death, until there was nothing of which they felt more certain than that he had been 'on the third day raised from the dead'. In this old tradition we behold a man who is Jewish in every feature and trait of his character, manifesting in every particular what is pure and good in Judaism. This man could have developed, as he came to be, only on the soil of Judaism; and only on this soil, too, could he find disciples and followers as they were. Here alone in this Jewish sphere, in this Jewish atmosphere of trust and longing, could this man live and meet his death – a Jew among Jews. Jewish history and Jewish reflection may not pass him by nor ignore him.

When this old tradition confronts us in this manner, then the Gospel, which was originally something Jewish, becomes a book – and certainly not a minor work – within Jewish literature. This is not because, or not only because, it contains sentences which also appear in the same or similar form in the Jewish works of that time. Nor is it such because the Hebrew or Aramaic breaks again and again through the word forms and sentence formations of the Greek translation. Rather it is a Jewish book because the pure air of which it is full and which it breathes is that of the Holy Scriptures; because a Jewish spirit, and none other, lives in it; because Jewish faith and Jewish hope, Jewish suffering and Jewish distress, Jewish knowledge and Jewish expectations, and these alone – resound through it – a Jewish book in the midst of Jewish books. Judaism may not pass it by, nor mistake it, nor wish to give up all claims here. Here, too, Judaism should comprehend and take note of what is its own.

Source: Leo Baeck, *Judaism and Christianity*, pp. 100–2.

COMMENT: *Baeck is passionate in his assertion of the Jewishness of Jesus and the totally Jewish context in which he and his followers existed. He is by no means the first to make the claim, although others have largely been Christians or academics rather than rabbis. However, he is strikingly original in his attempt to persuade fellow Jews to reclaim the Gospel as part of Jewish literature and to appreciate its teachings, rather than dismiss them as inconsequential or condemn them as heretical. Of course, much of his thesis depends on whether his ability to extract the 'old Gospel' from within the received text is regarded as credible. It is also not easy to ignore how a text has been used by others for two thousand years. Nevertheless, Baeck attempts to roll back Christian claims and Jewish assumptions and he presents a powerful call for a re-evaluation of how Jews relate to the Gospel.*

### 7.4  Percy Selvin Goldberg on Christmas (1957)

*Rabbi Goldberg had a very different concern, far removed from academic or theological matters. As a congregational rabbi whose members were highly integrated into society at large, he faced the annual practical problem of trying to prevent adults and children alike from being sucked into the all-pervasive Christmas celebrations surrounding them.*

Undoubtedly at Christmas time with its ideal of 'peace on earth and goodwill to all men', with its giving and receiving of gifts, with its lights and its laughter, there is festivity in the atmosphere and festivity is contagious: any excuse is good enough for a party. The real problem is: shall we as Jews become poor and passive imitators of what the majority are doing (because obviously insofar as Christmas celebrates the birthday of the central figure of the Christian faith, the 'soul' is lacking) or shall we rather take a positive and determined stand to prevent the schizophrenic effects of the strong appeal which this season has upon our children by giving them a well-rounded Jewish education in religion school and home? I can see no other alternative. Christmas can never be a festival which Jews can celebrate – it is one of the theological differences between Judaism and Christianity. Not only do parents have to accept this situation, however, but they must make it clear to children in their most tender years. Most of the celebrations of Christmas in Jewish homes arise out of the fact that we over-pasteurise our children, and because the child next door enjoys a tree and gifts, we feel that our children are entitled to nothing less, that they should not be made to feel 'out of it'.

Then how about saying something like this, when our child asks us about having a Christmas tree. 'Most Jews don't have Christmas trees because they are used by Christians in celebrating Christmas which is a Christian holiday. Yes, there are some Jews who have them. They say the tree is pretty and decorates the house and that they don't want to be 'different'. But what's wrong with being different? I am different from Mummy and you are different from both of us. No two people – except twins – look alike. God must have meant us to be different. Jews are different from Christians because we have *Simchat Torah, Purim, Bar Mitzvah*, and they have Christmas. Let's ask Willie Smith about their Christmas customs. Perhaps they'll let us see their tree too. Then we can invite them over and tell them about *Hanukkah* and show them our *Menorah*.

What then should we do about Christmas? Just this. We should celebrate *Hanukkah* as fervently as our neighbours do Christmas. We should tell our children the story of *Hanukkah* in the weeks that precede the festival. We should discuss together the house decorations, the gifts we are going to give each other, how we are going to make the Synagogue party the 'best ever'. As grown-ups we should have our house-parties during *Hanukkah* week, and by all means let us invite our Christian neighbours. Then if we are invited back to their Christmas parties it takes on an altogether different aspect. These are some of the ways in which we can maintain our self-respect as Jews and not have leveled against us the accusation of 'phonies' because we enjoy all the trimmings and trappings of a festival in which we do not and cannot believe.

Source: P. Selvin Goldberg, 'What should We do about Christmas?', *The Synagogue Review*, 32, pp. 91–3.

COMMENT: *In some respects Goldberg's attempt to solve the Christmas dilemma may seem banal. He ignores the fact that the main theme of Hanukkah is pride in one's faith and resistance to assimilation, and he does not utilize its value as a clarion call to Jewish identity. Instead he seems to mould Hanukkah into being a Jewish equivalent of Christmas, when in fact it is Purim which is the traditional time for parties and gifts. However, it is clearly a real attempt to be practical in an effective way and one that prefers compensating Jews for missing out on Christmas to merely castigating them for being drawn to it. While much of his advice is directed at children, there is an equally clear message for adults too. He also makes the distinction between attending a neighbour's Christmas party solely as an act of personal socializing and attending it by way of reciprocating hospitality from one's own festival. For Goldberg, it is the difference between 'selling out' and still being rooted in one's own faith.*

### 7.5  Michael Hilton on a New Model for Joint Study (1988)

*Rabbi Dr Hilton was part of a new generation of rabbis for whom Jewish–Christians relations was no longer an optional extra for a few outward-looking rabbis but a compulsory part of the training of all rabbinic students. Moreover, this was conducted not just by Jewish teachers but also by Christian teachers, and involved understanding the faiths and their relationship from a Christian perspective too. Hilton was keen to share the insights arising from this new approach with a wider Jewish circle.*

It is often stated that Jews worship with their heads covered because Christians pray bareheaded. Whether that is the real origin of Jewish headcoverings is lost in the midst of medieval history: what is important is that people believe this to be the origin, and still feel it is a distinction worth keeping. It is thus a commonplace idea that Judaism and Christianity have developed many practices in contradistinction to each other, practices born out of centuries of enmity and misunderstanding. Today, the hatred of the past has been replaced by rivalry. It is all too easy for those involved in Jewish-Christian dialogue to adopt a competitive spirit, of holding discussions in which their motive is simply to prove their own faith superior to the other. Such debates do nothing to help us realize how an understanding of the other tradition can help enhance an understanding of our own faith.

. . . In the past much of the debate between Jews and Christians has centred on each trying to prove to the other that their side came up with the better ideas first: that their side embraces wider ethical principles. This then is a starting point: we cannot advance the dialogue if we try to prove each other wrong. We are required to wipe away the pain of centuries and the assumptions of a past when one of the main reasons for reading each others' texts was to prove them wrong . . . Often, when Christians come to Jews to discover their 'authentic roots', they assume the existence of a Hebrew tradition, which has had a linear development right through to contemporary Judaism: somewhere along the route was an offshoot which we know as Christianity. The traditional Christian outlook is very different from this. The Church Fathers, like many theologians right up to the present day, regarded the Hebrew tradition as showing a linear development right to Christianity, from which, at a particular period of time, the Jewish people somehow became diverted.

Obviously the model we adopt for dialogue will make a tremendous difference on such issues as how we view the possession of the Hebrew scriptures. These two models are mirror images of each other. The reader is invited to ponder whether it is not now possible to create a new model for dialogue. In this model as in the others, the Hebrew tradition developed up to a particular time of division. It suggests, however that Judaism (as it develops through the rabbis and continues) and Christianity (as interpreted through the Gospels) can both be seen as equally authentic interpretations and developments of that one common Hebrew tradition and scripture. In other words, the parent-child image of dialogue is not necessarily the best image, but another model is possible, in which we see ourselves as twins from the same parent.

... Many of the issues cannot be explored without pain. There is the question of polemic, of the reading and study as 'Gospel truth' of texts hostile or insulting to 'The Jews'. It is the later Gospels which contain more anti-Jewish remarks, as the two faiths became separated and bitterness grew between them. Some Christians are beginning to recognize a need to work on an understanding of Jesus, which says that the presence of Christians in the world can be a blessing for the whole world without the whole world being Christian. There is also a need for Jews to be more prepared to study the Gospels, and to speak openly about their shock and concern. Why should we endure that pain? We must, if we are to take that dialogue forward.

Source: Michael Hilton and Gordian Marshall, *The Gospels and Rabbinic Judaism*, pp. 1, 36, 114–16, 154.

COMMENT: *Hilton is honest about the problems of dialogue. If it is to be meaningful, it entails giving up attempts at religious one-up-manship and the comfort of familiar assumptions about the other. Instead it is a matter of engaging in a genuine search together. It also involves confronting the prejudices of the other faith and not allowing them to hijack the debate or stymie the search, as well as admitting one's own faith's prejudices and not downplaying them or condoning them. Hilton's proposal of a new model for dialogue – as twins rather than as parent and child – is not only more accurate historically, but is a useful tool with which Jews and Christians can explore their common religious heritage side by side. Twins are still liable to play games of 'me first' and 'I'm better than you', but whereas a parent can pull rank and insist on being the one to whom the child owes its existence, twins have to accept a shared source and mutual co-existence.*

### 7.6 Jonathan Romain on Jews for Jesus (1991)

*The fear of Jews converting to Christianity, which had so concerned Reverend Joseph earlier, waned markedly in the twentieth century. This was partly because conversion was no longer seen as a passport into society or useful for career advancement as secularism grew and prejudice against Jews declined. Horror at the Holocaust by non-Jews and pride in the new State of Israel among Jews also played a part. In addition, the growth of interfaith dialogue led many within the Church to regard efforts at conversion with increasing disfavour. However, in the 1970s a new missionary movement arose – Jews for Jesus – which caused considerable anxiety in the Jewish community. It also begged the question of whether Jews who now accepted Jesus could still be considered Jewish.*

The 'Jews for Jesus' movement is a recent phenomenon, although in character it is merely a modern version of a centuries-old attempt to convert Jews to Christianity. The only difference with 'Jews for Jesus' is that they claim to believe in Jesus while still retaining their Jewish identity. Thus they observe many Jewish practices such as lighting candles to welcome the Sabbath on Friday evening, reciting the *Shema*, wearing a Star of David and supporting the State of Israel. Despite these outer Jewish symbols, their beliefs are totally in conformity with Christian theology and they accept Jesus as their Messiah and Saviour, as well as doctrines concerning the Resurrection of Jesus and Atonement. They harmonise this inconsistency between practice and belief by describing themselves as 'fulfilled Jews', 'completed Jews' or 'Messianic Jews'. It would seem that this terminology, along with the maintenance of Jewish customs, is a way of assuaging their guilt at adopting Christianity, and is designed to reassure themselves that they have not betrayed their Jewish roots and family. By all objective Jewish standards, however, they have adopted beliefs so alien to Judaism that they must be considered to have left the Jewish faith, even if they genuinely believe otherwise. 'Jews for Jesus', therefore, are viewed as Christians.

A difficulty associated with 'Jews for Jesus' is that they place great emphasis on missionary work and, in particular, persuading other Jews to accept Jesus. Naturally, everyone is free to follow whatever faith in which they believe, and indeed to change their faith, but this should be the result of their own free-will and not from any religious coercion. This means that, although 'Jews for Jesus' are as welcome to attend a synagogue service as any other non-Jews, extreme care has to be taken that they do not take advantage of their welcome to distribute leaflets or influence others. This applies especially to young adults and the lonely. The emphasis on mission is also regrettable because of the harm it could do to the enormous progress in religious dialogue between Jews and Christians that has occurred in recent decades. Such dialogue is founded on a willingness to accept the validity of the other's faith, and is under-mined by any attempts at conversion. It is important that Christian authorities stem as much as possible the missionary activities of organisa-tions such as 'Jews for Jesus' ; for its part, the Jewish community should recognise that 'Jews for Jesus' are a small minority within the Church and it should maintain its inter-faith contact with the mainstream bodies.

Source: Jonathan Romain, *Faith and Practice: A Guide to Reform Judaism Today*, pp. 170–1.

COMMENT: *The adamant assertion that members of 'Jews for Jesus' are not to be classified as Jews reflects a desire to counter what was con-sidered to be the most insidious aspect of the movement: that whereas in the past conversion to Christianity has meant abandoning Judaism for the new faith, now one could remain within the Jewish fold. Indeed, it was claimed that one would thereby be fulfilling one's Judaism and could happily marry together the practices of Judaism with the beliefs of Christianity. This made conversion appear to be a much less drastic step and removed a barrier that may have prevented some Jews from converting in the past. The response also addresses the tactic of 'Jews for Jesus' of targeting groups that were con-sidered most receptive (or 'vulnerable'), especially young people at univer-sity or those living alone without any support group. Another concern was that interfaith dialogue was only just emerging from its infancy, promoted by some within the Jewish community, but with many having reservations as to its desirability. The high profile campaigning of 'Jews for Jesus' threat-ened to halt the gradual thaw in Jewish attitudes even though it had very little success in the number of people it actually attracted.*

## 7.7  Tony Bayfield on Making Theological Space (1992ff.)

*With the passage of time, Jewish–Christian relations gradually developed from being a truce from previous rivalries to a mutual acceptance of the other's validity. The question then arose as to how far this rapprochement could progress. Was friendly co-existence the final stage or could there be a deeper level of connection? As someone who was immersed both in Jewish tradition and English heritage, Rabbi Bayfield found himself deeply engaged in that debate. An experience while visiting an old church during a summer holiday in Northumberland helped clarify the issue for him, while a second passage, written later, extends the significance of that realization.*

I look up to the roof soaring above me heavenwards. And around at the empty pews. The prayers prayed in this place for centuries are almost tangible. Real prayers, honest prayers, true prayers, prayers which are heard. People reach out to God here, just as I strive to reach out to God in synagogue. And if they reach out to God, God comes to meet them here. The smell, the flavour, the accoutrements may not be of my home, but God is at home here as God is at my house.

In the course of my career and life I have encountered a number of Christians whose life and faith have so impressed me that a conviction has been brought home to me with ever-growing strength. That conviction has to do with the integrity of their place of worship, with the validity of their prayers, with the acceptability to God of their faith. If that intuitive understanding has any importance (and I believe it has), then it is necessary for me to formulate my own self understanding and theology as a Jew in a way that leaves space – uncondescending, unequivocal space – for my Christian friends. This is a space which (I should add lest there by any confusion) does not compromise in any way the integrity of my own Jewish faith and commitment . . . In dialogue, I journey to the land of my Christian partners and admire, puzzle, study, challenge, value and learn. I go home wiser and inevitably changed. Which many see as a risk, but others, myself included, as enrichment. Though I will never cease from pointing out its failings towards my faith and the consequences of teachings I regard as misguided, I have no need to denigrate or condescend. The land is real and true, though, like mine, imperfect. It is no betrayal of my own country to offer respect and honour and recognition of our common source and goal. In the mutual granting of space, ungrudgingly and unreservedly, lies the hope for new growth and insight into the Oneness out of which our purposeful diversity flows.

Source: Tony Bayfield, 'Making Theological Space', in Tony Bayfield and Marcus Braybrooke (eds), *Dialogue with a Difference*, pp. 4–5, 28.

I believe that many Christians find in the life, death and resurrection of

Jesus as described in the New Testament and in the tradition that flows from those events the fullest disclosure of the nature of God and God's will for them. Such faith involves no necessary error or illusion. Just as Sinai was the central episode of revelation, the covenantal moment for the Jewish people, so too, from my Jewish perspective, is Calvary for Christians and Christianity . . . [although] I remember vividly the very first time that I acknowledged the New Testament as a book of revelation for Christians. A Jewish friend, a gentle, scholarly man, a member of the group within which I was in dialogue, reacted with uncharacteristic anger and hostility. 'You are giving much too much away,' he protested. After two thousand years of untold suffering, after all the vicious stereotyping, demonization and persecution, there is much more restitution and repentance to be made before so much can be conceded.' I understand that objection and even experience a certain amount of guilt at 'letting the side down'. But, in the last analysis, theology is not improved by being tempered with political expediency.

A second colleague later chided me more gently, acknowledging revelation in the lives of individual Christians, but denying to the text and the events they portray the same quality. That too I understand. I still feel shocked at myself for giving such acknowledgment to a book which contains so much anti-Judaism, which has served as a proof text for expulsion, forcible conversion and murder. I am not sure that I gain much other than inviting criticism from every side by saying that there are also texts in the Hebrew Bible that I find repugnant. But texts that speak of revelation, whilst bearing the fingerprint of God, are written by human hands as well and are limited flawed, partial, historically constrained, as are all human beings. . . . I am arguing that the best metaphor for the relationship between Judaism and Christianity is that of siblings. Each sibling owes its existence and identity to a founding revelatory experience, depicted in its scriptures. Each revelation establishes a covenant for those who understand themselves to be part of the story, part of the people whose story the scriptures tell. Each revelation, each covenant, each sibling warrants the acceptance, respect and independent space that is every sibling's birthright.

Source: Tony Bayfield, 'A Partnership in Covenant', in Tony Bayfield, Sidney Brichto and Eugene Fisher (eds), *He Kissed Him and They Wept*, pp. 31–3.

COMMENT: *Bayfield goes further than previous writers in accepting that Christianity is not only a valid faith for those who practise it, but is as valid as Judaism in the eyes of God. In many ways this is nothing but the logical culmination of decades of dialogue between Jews and Christians – granting religious equality to a members of another faith inevitably leads to granting religious equality to the faith itself unless it is deemed to be harmful in some way. However, this is still a radical development compared to the centuries of religious competition that preceded it. This is especially so in the case of Judaism and Christianity, whose relationship was characterized by so much hostility and bloodshed. Hence Bayfield is understandably nervous about breaking such new ground and has to defend himself both against accusations of betrayal by others and against his own sense of disquiet. He also acknowledges that there are risks inherent in this approach. He is therefore quick to point out that he feels no less committed to his faith, but this still leaves open the possibility that others who are not so deeply rooted in Judaism might take his words as implying that it does not matter switching to Christianity, or another religion, as God welcomes prayers from all sources. Either way, though, there is a genuine sense of break-through in his writing: a religious milestone has been passed, and all subsequent discussion must take account of it.*

## 7.8 Albert Friedlander on Relating to the New Testament (1992)

*If Jews could now accept that Christianity had religious validity, how did they themselves relate to it? Was the New Testament a source of inspiration just for Christians or could it also have significance for Jews? This radical extension of the debate exercised Rabbi Dr Friedlander whose searing childhood experiences in Nazi Germany had propelled him in adulthood to a life dedicated to the pursuit of reconciliation between the two faiths.*

Judaism has recognized Christianity as a true faith, as proper worship based upon divine revelation, throughout the centuries. We recognize many roads towards salvation, and respect the inner mystery of those ways, looking more towards an outward manifestation of ethical action where those paths parallel ours. It often occurs to me that the Christians with whom I have engaged in dialogue are closer to God than I am. I cannot judge the New Testament and declare it to be a revelation. I can and do judge the Christian I meet and can accept that he or she has been addressed by God in a special way, that their life is filled with revelation. I felt this when I met Albert Schweitzer: I feel this simply knowing about Mother Theresa; and there are members in our dialogue group who convince me that when I am near to them I am closer to God.

How, then, do I deal with the New Testament when I recognize that my Christian colleagues are filled with its spirit and cannot be divorced from the text? In a strange way, an inversion of authority takes place: they make it authentic because of God's movement through their own lives. A personal revelation exists here, and I honour it even when it remains a mystery. And I am also able to pray alongside of them – in St George's Chapel at Windsor, with the Carmelite nuns in Berlin – even though I cannot pray with them: the Christian doctrine of the words pushes me away even as I come closer to their anguished faith. I do have a special relationship with the Gospels as well; but it differs from the way in which it serves as their bread of heaven.

Source: Albert Friedlander, 'The Geography of Theology', in Tony Bayfield and Marcus Braybrooke (eds), *Dialogue with a Difference*, p. 35.

COMMENT: *Whereas Baeck had sought to approach the New Testament as a Jewish book and reclaim it for Judaism, Friedlander accepts it in its own integrity as a profoundly Christian faith-text. Like Bayfield, Friedlander finds that the religious aura of Christian individuals leads him to acknowledge the religious power of the Scripture from which they derive their faith. This in turn persuades him that he too can have a relationship with that text and that he can even be present with Christians in their worship. Friedlander is careful to distinguish between praying alongside them and praying with them, and thereby seeks to assert that he is praying from a Jewish perspective even if the liturgy he is holding at the time is Christian. Nevertheless, this is a step much further than merely engaging in mutual understanding. It indicates that those who expressed doubts as to the wisdom of such dialogue because of the consequences to which it would lead were certainly right that it has taken those involved far beyond their original starting point, even though the value judgement attached to this development is open to debate.*

## 7.9 Michael Hilton on Recognizing the Symbiotic Relationship Between Judaism and Christianity (1994)

*In his earlier book on the Gospels and Rabbinic Judaism, Rabbi Dr Hilton had argued for the need to abandon pre-conceptions about the relationship between the two faiths and had suggested that instead of a parent-child model, that of siblings was more appropriate. His subsequent book used this approach to re-examine many of the rituals and beliefs in Jewish and Christian life. It found evidence that there was a much greater level of reciprocity between the two faiths than had been admitted previously.*

While Christians like to regard Judaism as older and therefore outdated, Jews like to think of Judaism as older and therefore purer, untainted by change. But there are very many Jewish practices which are not necessarily older than Christian ones, and many Jewish beliefs which do not necessarily pre-date Christianity. Judaism as we know it is the religion of the rabbis – men who lived in a world in which Christianity had already been born, a fast-changing world with many different religions and sects. Both Judaism and Christianity had to come to terms with the destruction of Jerusalem by the Romans, the loss of Jerusalem, of the Temple, of the sacrificial system – the loss of a whole way of life. Christians and Jews developed different responses, theologies and practices in responses to these events. A detailed examination shows that the rabbinic theologies and practices are not necessarily older than Christian ones – on the contrary, Judaism often developed and changed in response to Christianity.

. . .*Instead of reading about the rabbinic Passover *seder* to learn about the last supper, we can read the last supper to tell us a little of the origins of a Jewish festive meal. Instead of looking for examples of Jewish ritual and law in Paul to tell us whether he was really a Pharisee, we can use Paul's knowledge of Judaism as evidence for the development of various Jewish laws. Instead of reading the Mishnah to find out what kind of synagogue service Jesus might have attended, we can use Luke's account as evidence of the origin of prophetic readings. Books written to be contributions to the history of Christianity are equally contributions to the history of Judaism.

. . . There are obvious reasons why the church should have sought to borrow from the synagogue – by its use of the 'Old Testament' it sought to proclaim itself as the heir of both Temple and synagogue of Israel. But what motivation might there be for the reverse? The conventional history of Jewish–Christian relations is mainly a history of anti-semitism: many libraries to this day classify all books on the relationship between the faiths under that heading. This provides no understanding of the extent to which Jews borrowed ideas and customs from their Christian neighbours. A more accurate understanding of the story of the relationship between the two faiths is vital to Jewish–Christian dialogue today. We cannot accord the two faiths an equal and distinct right to exist while we continue to regard Judaism as the unchanged word of the Bible from which Christianity deviated, or Christianity as the true fulfilment of the prophets, which the Jews rejected.

. . . I am fully aware that this is a highly controversial area. It is indeed painful to discover that someone you have always thought of as your parent is in fact not parent but brother or sister. Both Jews and Christians have long supposed not simply that Judaism is an older religion than Christianity, but that everything Jewish therefore has to be older than every Christian custom. There are still many, I am sure, who will wish to reject the idea that Judaism is or can be anything other than the 'parent faith' of Christianity. To recognize that there has been for two thousand years a symbiotic relationship between twin faiths has profound implications for Jewish–Christian relations today.

Source: Michael Hilton, *The Christian Effect on Jewish Life*, pp. 2, 4, 209.

*This paragraph occurs later in the book but is inserted here as an illustration of the previous paragraph.

COMMENT: *Hilton is right to suggest that centuries' worth of conditioning regarding the relationship between Judaism and Christianity needs to be radically revised. Abandoning the parent-child model in favour of a sibling one – hinted at in an earlier passage (7.5) – could lead to practical benefits. It might help remove the sense of superiority that many Jews have felt and which has led to them dismissing Christianity as irrelevant and with nothing to offer, while it may remove the sense of inferiority that many Christians have felt and which has led to them developing a replacement theology by way of compensation. This profoundly changes the nature of dialogue. Moreover, if his academic research is correct and many Jewish customs have been shaped by Christianity just as Christian ones have been by Judaism, this dramatically alters previous assumptions about a one-way influence. Henceforth Jews and Christians should learn from each other as equals, not just, as hitherto, out of politeness, but because that is their true status.*

## A Final Thought . . .

Many years ago when I was very inexperienced, I was let loose on a congregation to practise my ministry. Unfortunately I decided to practise it on Christmas eve. The house was lit up and so were some of my congregants. I heard sounds through the door. I rang the bell. A voice shouted out 'My God, it's the rabbi'. I heard a large object being hurled in the cupboard (the Christmas tree?), and bottles being slammed into a cocktail cabinet. I peered through the curtain and saw little twinkling lights going out. In ancient Egypt they used to bring a coffin round at parties to sober the revelers. I was the kosher coffin, the death's head at the party. After some stilted conversation I left quickly. As I turned the corner, the music resumed, reassuring me somewhat unnecessarily that 'Baby It was Cold Outside'. It is difficult being a Jew at Christmas.

Source: Lionel Blue, 'God and the Jewish Problem', in Dow Marmur (ed.), *A Genuine Search*, pp. 61–2.

# 8

# COMMANDMENT AND
# JEWISH LAW

Ever since God instructed Abraham to circumcise his son Isaac as a sign of the covenant between them (Genesis 17.10) Judaism has been associated with commandments, both ritual and ethical. According to rabbinic calculation there are a total of 613 commands in the Five Books of Moses, and they in turn have led to a host of additional commands as extensions of them, all of which form Jewish law, the *halacha*. The collection of laws referred to as 'The Ten Commandments' may be particularly well-known, but is neither a summary of the 613, nor a minimum list for Jewish observance. Judaism would not be Judaism with the Decalogue alone. The Orthodox regard all 613 commands as divinely-given, uttered directly by God, and therefore immutable. Reform considers them to be of human origin, albeit under divine inspiration, and therefore open to change should they need to be adapted or even abolished as new circumstances develop. The founders of Reform Judaism were not afraid to institute any changes they considered necessary, but did not exercise themselves over creating a new theoretical framework in which to house them. However, in more modern times the nature of the commandments and their role in Jewish life has been a key issue in Reform thinking. They have become a litmus test of Reform's ability to marry tradition and modernity without either abandoning core practices or ignoring current realities.

## 8.1 Leo Baeck on the Meaning of Commandment (1947ff.)

*Rabbi Dr Baeck was a scholar equally well versed in both Jewish philosophy and Jewish law. For him, the main challenge posed by Judaism was theological rather than legal. The key question concerning commandment was how it expressed our relationship with God rather than which particular set of laws we should or should not observe. It was this aspect that engaged him most and which he sought to clarify in two of his works.*

In every act that is demanded of him, man experiences the commandment, and this, too, is the experience of infinity. The commandment for man is God's commandment, born of the infinite and eternal depth, full of divine restlessness and sacred movement. Every duty to which he is summoned begets a new duty; whatever he accomplishes is only a step on his way, a step that must be followed by other steps, a step that always has its goal, but never attains its end. He is never finished, his peace is the peace of final fulfillment. In every commandment that he carries out, he is possessed by God's absoluteness and eternity, by the tension between the finite here below and the infinite beyond. However determined and limited his life, the imperative is unlimited, ultimately it lives in the absolute, in the constantly unfulfilled, it is never past, but always future, it is always renewed. Here, too, there is nothing final, nothing completed, nothing perfect in the life of man; in his action, too, he is surrounded by infinity, it irrupts into him, and his path leads to it. Every commandment is a force that tends to become force. Just as God creates to continue creating, so he commands to continue commanding. The pious man, as the Talmud says, is a man 'without rest here or in the beyond'.

Source: Leo Baeck, *The Pharisees and Other Essays*, pp. 139–40.

The experience of the One revealed to Israel that a commandment confronts man. It is always the same commandment, because it is the commandment of God. Yet it is also new, because it is the commandment of each and every hour. Man is to fulfill it; a purpose is set before him. As long as he lives, he is on the way; as long as he lives, the way lies before him. Fulfillment itself can only be found at the end of the way. Man can only direct his vision towards it, for man is finite. But that is the great design, man's answer to the limitations of human existence. Wherever a man travels on the right way, achievement is already his, for he fulfills there and then the commandment of God.

God demands from man, and with this the greatest has already been given to him. God has awaited him, and with this the greatest has already been assured. It is a paradox that God's will can be realized through man. The Eternal's everlasting will can be, and is to be, the will of mortal man.

What is demanded is the pledge; the commandment is the promised possession. Through the fulfillment of the commandment man becomes an I out of God's I: I by the grace of God. The individual becomes a personality, the chosen one . . . The law becomes a reality by the fact that man realizes it. He now shares the law, shares God's covenant. This vision of decision, this certitude went forth from them and becomes the experience of their people, and afterwards an experience for the peoples of the world.

Source: Leo Baeck, *This People Israel*, pp. 15–16.

COMMENT: *Baeck typifies the massive shift in emphasis in Reform thinking compared to that of Orthodoxy: for the latter, Judaism is a matter of obeying the divine will through observing the commandments; for the former, it is a matter of seeking communion with God via the commandments. For Orthodoxy, the commandments have an absolute value in themselves and are to be adhered to rigorously; for Reform, the commandments are utilitarian and their validity depends on whether or not they fulfil their purpose. Baeck is not at all interested in the minutiae surrounding the commandments, but the concept that they represent and the way in which they are a means of experiencing finite appreciation of the infinite.*

## 8.2 Rabbinic Debates on a Reform Code (1964–66)

*After several decades of little growth in Britain, Reform began to attract new members who had belonged previously to Orthodox synagogues. They were used to a much more rigorous presentation of the obligations of Jewish law than the ill-defined and largely ad hoc approach that had character-*

*ized Reform Judaism until then. Pressure grew to explain both to them and to the Jewish community at large which commandments still applied and what principles were used to make decisions. It led to a rabbinic debate that contained greatly contrasting views.*

In the past years there has been an increasing desire on the part of many for a reasonably authoritative set of rules for Jewish observance. No matter how reasonable it is, the move is undoubtedly towards a Reform *Shulchan Aruch*, and though I consider a guide may well be necessary, anything more final would to my mind be fraught with dangers. These dangers would be the greater because they are not obvious, and I set them down so that you may consider them. The very people who cry out 'Tell us what to do!' may not keep the rules if they were told them. A set of printed orders, to my mind, will make little difference to the actual situation. The same number will pray, the same number will make *Havdalah*, and the same people keep the same degree of *Kashrut* as they have always done. This is not the time to order, but to educate. Rules cannot help being pietistic, and there is a great danger that Judaism in the home will be identified with a list of ritualistic dos and don'ts. In other words, interest will be focused on the outer husk of religion and the technical, as opposed to the spiritual, side of religion.

We all know the things that are wrong in Jewish suburban society – low cultural life, primitive religious attitudes, concentration on outer show and status seeking. These attitudes can exist, for example, with *Kashrut* or without it. In other words, the ritualistic requirements, though having a validity of their own, do not deal with the main points, and ritualism will evade and not solve the problems. Religion is always in danger of being identified with ritualism, especially in an irreligious age. If this identification is made, then it is logical to say that the man who is most religious keeps the most details. This attitude has been all too common in Anglo-Jewry and its result has been to make Judaism a mass of pettiness and trivialities. This has also been responsible for making the minister a man who is paid to keep the technical details his Congregation don't – a degrading situation. At the moment the social situation is still chang-ing, and any attempt to finalise Jewish Law in our time is doomed to failure. The foundations of the Jewish society of the future have not yet settled, and until they have one cannot build firmly on them. A last point

– but for me the most important. I regard religion as a questing of the spirit. It is the greatness of Progressive Judaism to have kept our sense of identity yet given us freedom of spiritual expression – guidance but not authoritarianism. This spiritual freedom should not be sacrificed to the conformism of the sheep-like tendencies of our age.

Source: Lionel Blue, 'Guidance or Order', *The Synagogue Review*, 39, pp. 54–5.

Our historic guides or codes described and systematised a vast body of existent practice, gave classic expression to long established standards of behaviour. They did not arrive out of thin air to initiate ritual or tradition. They possessed theological backing in that the authority of the Pentateuch was accepted and the chain of *halachah* which flowed from it was not questioned. In our Reform Jewish life neither of these conditions exists. The medieval world is quite dead. Both in practice and in theory we lack any basis for a guide or code ('guide' is intended as a weak or neutral term to mask the code-like intentions which it will inevitably display). We lack those responses and that dynamic ritual life which codes can summarise or describe. We can certainly use the words 'code' or 'guide', but their substance, function or authority are different from their classical predecessors. We should make it clear both how and why our usage differs. We do not, for example, believe in that unitary and infallible verbal and written revelation on Sinai, without which ab-solute authority and metaphysical backing to any past code would have been impossible. Worse, a code or guide which has nothing of note to describe might cut at the roots of that hope for spiritual regeneration which Reform Judaism embodies. By holding up certain standards and norms it hopes to give a mechanical solution to our problems, to make a spiritual vacuum disappear by prescriptive magic. Can we call a robot alive because it moves its limbs? Weak at heart, we call upon an arbitrary anthology of past Jewish practice to revive us.

Any code or guide which proposes certain minimal standards can outwardly appear to have satisfied the desire for religious service, but in fact it has elicited no real thought, action or devotion on the part of the individual. When the natural drive towards some sort of piety or service of the heart has been guided towards a prescribed ritual, any individual religious contribution or need for personal decision has been thwarted.

Our Reform search for new meanings, deeper spiritual insights and quest for religious truth in the prophetic tradition would be called off. What started out as minimal standards would soon become the only standards. There is then no longer a pressing need to question, to experiment, to study, to take existential risks. When piety is both measured and circumscribed by ritual prescription, some of the risk and adventure involved in Reform Jewish life has departed.

The call for a guide represents a spiritual longing which cannot be spurned, but before any guide arrives the ground must be prepared at theoretical and practical levels. Today, if a Reform guide said 'no pill' or 'no work on Sabbath', who would follow it? First we must evolve a coherent Reform attitude to our tradition. Only a clear theology and philosophy of Reform can effectively review the whole sweep of the tradition and prevent an abortive, piecemeal approach. Parallel with these theoretical considerations, practical work is possible at the congregational level. A Congregation in consort with their Minister could make some initial decisions. For example, the existence, length and format of the *Shiva* could be reached only after prolonged study, discussion, heartsearching and choice. The decision which is democratically arrived at is then morally binding only upon the group that made it, those who 'bound the *Mitsvah* upon themselves'. Its future life is connected only to that group. There is no unilateral manifesto or guide . . . This endeavour is only the beginning of the journey, and even should all the personal and lived decisions be combined, they could only then form a guide of relative authority. In our subjective choices we will say merely that, flanked by our Jewish tradition, we 'commanded ourselves'. Only the future can say whether it was also *Mitsvah*, the command of heaven.

Source: Michael Goulston, 'Perplexity Over Guides', *The Synagogue Review*, 39, pp. 56–7.

A Reform Movement relevant to the mid-twentieth century which states its position clearly is now required, and I believe that a clarification in terms of 'ritual', amongst other things, is a good beginning and is clearly demanded. No one is suggesting that there should be a Code because it obviously cannot be enforced, and anyway our non-fundamentalist position precludes this. We must depend on persuasion, but congregants

must know what they are being persuaded about . . . Both Rabbi
Blue and Rabbi Goulston speak continually of the 'spiritual' side of
Judaism and the Reform 'hope for spiritual regeneration', making an
un-Jewish distinction between the spiritual and the earthly. The genius
of Judaism is that it has evolved customs and ceremonies which have
concretised spiritual ideas: the *matza* is the 'bread of freedom', the
sabbath candles represent sabbatical peace. The great achievement of the
Talmudic rabbis was to put the ideals of the Prophets to work, to give
them a concrete expression. True, there is the danger that rituals may
become mechanical, an outer husk, but a still greater danger exists in
relying on high-flowing ideals in vacuo. Furthermore, our ceremonial
life emphasises our distinctiveness – a counterblast to assimilation.
Rabbi Goulston is troubled by the theoretical basis for any rituals in a
Guide. The fact that I have a non-fundamentalist attitude to the authorship of the Pentateuch does not nullify my belief in a Sinaitic Revelation
and, hence, the Finger of God on subsequent Jewish law and life, a process in which I wish to participate. Rabbi Goulston wants first to 'prepare
the ground at theoretical and practical levels' before committing himself
to any ritual way of life. Jewish thinkers have been preparing the ground
since the early 19th-century, with no great success. Meanwhile, Jewish
life and practice are slipping away. People want guidance and advice
through the maze of inherited ritualistic attitudes – a source of great
Jewish loyalties which should not be dissipated – in order to help deepen
their home and personal Jewish lives. They are quite entitled to look for
rabbinic guidance and advice and would resent Rabbi Goulston's naive
suggestion to make democratic decisions amongst themselves at congregational level. Members would admit their ignorance in such 'halachic'
discussions, and anyway they may feel that they were contributing towards an anarchic situation on a national, let alone international, level.

Source: Michael Leigh, 'Guides', *The Synagogue Review*, 39, p. 93.

There is no authority for a Reform code as a theological document.
Orthodox Judaism, because it can attach all the details of ritual observance to an infallible revelation at Sinai, can say of any *Mitsvah*, any ritual
deed, 'this is what the Lord requires of you'. Reform Judaism is not sure
that God revealed the laws of *shatnez*, mixed fabrics, to Moses. Once the

written law or the chain of oral tradition is called into question, we can never again be sure of anything, at least in an objective sense. A Reform code is a contradiction in terms. A Reform code encourages Judaism by proxy. We do have absolute demands in Reform Jewish life, but they cannot be learnt from a book. They are appropriated, personally experienced, individually understood, by involving ourselves in the experiment to evolve religious expression at the communal level. Our Reform movement is too young to allow codal sclerosis to harden the arteries of our spiritual endeavours. Just as all previous codes have merely crystallised hundreds of years of communal experience and adaptive experiment, so too we need time for our own unique zest to produce its own definable path. A Reform code is premature. I am not impressed by the argument that our members want a code. At the Exodus, the Israelites also wanted a visible God, and out came the calf of gold. Those who want the type of tangible authority that a code offers, those who repine for a sense of guilt codally induced, those who seek a sense of salvation by ritual efficiency will, I fear, be disappointed. Perhaps they have yet to come to terms with Reform Judaism, with religious existence without the Law.

Source: Michael Goulston, 'In My Opinion', *The Synagogue Review*, 40, pp. 34–5.

One of the problems which we face as a non-Orthodox religious movement is a clear definition of what Judaism requires of the individual Jew. This problem has recently been brought to the surface by the desire of some of our friends to be told exactly in detail what they have to do in order to comply with the commandments of Judaism, as we interpret it. At least in this respect, Orthodoxy is the easier religion. It states categorically that every Jew has to comply with the laws of the *Torah* as interpreted in the traditional codes and especially in the *Shulchan Aruch* which was compiled in the sixteenth century. Its more enlightened leaders must know, however, that this aim is quite impossible, and even in some respects undesirable, in the context of modern life. In practice, this often leads to insincerity and a wide cleavage between religious demands and the actual practice of the vast majority of Jews. The Reform Movement must be intellectually honest and must not demand anything which is obviously impossible or undesirable to fulfil in the second-half of the twentieth century. We must try to define the words of the prophet Micah:

'what does the Lord require' of us today. Reform leaders of the past century rejected fundamentalism (as we do today) and made a distinction between the two kinds of commandments. The moral commandments were considered of divine origin and therefore an end in themselves, whilst ritual and ceremonial was a means to an end. Its aim was to bring man nearer to God through the creation of an atmosphere of sanctity and holiness. Moral laws therefore were considered absolutely binding whilst ritual could be modified, and reinterpreted to guarantee its beneficial influence or even abandoned if it failed to have such an effect. As a general rule this distinction should still be valid for us today. Sometimes, laws which were considered as moral by our ancestors, may be looked upon in a different way in our time. Laws like the exclusion of the so-called *Mamzer* from the congregation of Israel and the prohibition of a *Cohen* to marry a divorcee, fall under this category. We cannot always accept the letter of the law but must be prepared to follow the advice of our own conscience. It tells us clearly what is moral and what is immoral. Reform Judaism has always based itself largely upon the teachings of our great Prophets and these men often overlooked the letter, following their own conscience in expressing God's will and told their contemporaries what was good and what was evil. Although we are unable to reproduce their moral fervour and enthusiasm, we must try to emulate their example according to our own lights, taking into consideration the circumstances and conditions under which we live. Therefore we must of necessity be selective when it comes to Ritual laws. The test must always be whether compliance helps us to strengthen our Jewishness. What then, is a *Mitsvah*, a Divine commandment, in our eyes? It is to comply strictly with the moral commandments of scripture if they are still such commandments in the context of modern life; to follow the dictates of our conscience, which tells us what is right and what is wrong; to be charitable in thought and in deed; to uphold and cherish the messianic aims for the future of mankind; to join with our fellow Jews in carrying out meaningful ceremonial in the Synagogue and in our homes.

Source: Charles Berg, 'What is a Mitsvah?', *The Synagogue Review*, 40, pp. 125–7.

COMMENT: *The heated nature of the debate among Reform rabbis reflected the intense passions released by the issue, which was not just about whether or not to produce a written document called 'guide' or 'code' or some other title, but was a struggle for the future direction of Reform Judaism in Britain: was it to follow the model of 'Classical Reform' associated with the early American Reform movement, which valued spirituality and ethics above ritual and practices, or the American Conservative movement which sought to identify a core set of Jewish observances, linked to a chain of tradition, albeit open to interpretation. Blue's opposition to such a code was two-fold: partly based on pragmatism – that in reality it would have no effect on the everyday lives of ordinary Reform Jews who would ignore its guidance – and partly based on the fear that it would distract attention from the more important task of deepening Jewish spirituality. In his eyes, it would be all too easy to measure one's religiosity by what one had or had not done, rather than by the quality of one's relationship with God. He also feared that any code would inevitably mean the reintroduction of a level of authoritarianism that Reform had spent much of its previous energies shaking off.*

*These objections were given more systematic expression by Goulston, who posited that the religious perspective of Reform meant that codes were no longer feasible, lacking both the content and authority that they had enjoyed in previous generations. Dismissing any attempt at imposing religious rules as 'prescriptive magic', he insisted that Reform instead focus on the Prophetic tradition. Nevertheless Goulston did suggest that some locally-based decision-making process could be encouraged so as to satisfy those seeking some guidelines. However this proposal could have led to huge variations in practice, leading to major variations between one Reform community and another, and be a recipe for religious anarchy. It is a defect that Leigh identifies in his forthright riposte to both Blue and Goulston. He also lambastes them for over-emphasizing spirituality at the expense of practical Jewish life, and is adamant that it is precisely because of the crisis that guidance is needed. Goulston's response was equally uncompromising, challenging those who demanded a code as to whether they even understood what it meant to be a Reform Jew. For his part, Berg was more concerned with cooling the debate rather than resolving it, and he was content to re-state the somewhat hazy conscience-based position that had sufficed earlier generations. This may have avoided further controversy but left Reform open to the charge that it relied too much on individual whims and lacked a definitive standpoint. Moreover, his suggestion that commandments*

*be judged according to whether they strengthened Jewishness reflected a
third position, that of the American Reconstructionist Movement, which
emphasized peoplehood over observance and preferred to concentrate on
the commanded rather than the Commander. All three groupings in the
United States held a certain appeal, but none persuaded all of the British
Reform rabbinate. There was no bridging such a divide, and another thirty
years were to lapse before a uniquely British solution was reached, with the
publication of a non-binding guide* (Faith and Practice).

## 8.3  Ignaz Maybaum on Morality in Jewish Law (1975)

*Rabbi Dr Maybaum frequently railed against what he considered to be the
medievalism of blind adherence to the law without any reference to conscience or context. His last book,* Happiness Outside the State, *was completed in 1975, but Maybaum died the following year and the book did not
appear until 1980.*

Today *halachah* can be very well defined as legality. There is a law of
some kind. Obedience to this law produces an action. The motive for
this action does not play a part in its performance. The main thing on
this level of activity is the result. I may give alms to a needy person in
order to get rid of the annoying picture of distress. On the other hand
I may act differently: I give my bit to the needy out of charity. The
result in both cases seems to be identical. But something very important
makes the actions very different: the motive. Whether an action is in
truth a moral action depends on its motive. An action performed out of
unreflecting obedience to a law, military obedience for instance, is without the splendour of morality. As an action on the level of mere legality
something has been done because it had to be done. The heart and soul
of a moral motive is missing.

   All this amounts to a weakness inherent in a Judaism reduced to one-
sided halachic order. *Halachah* demands obedience only in the fields of
legal activity. The motive alone can make an action performed according
to the *halachah* a moral action. In a Judaism which consists entirely of
*halachic* precepts the absence of consideration of motive can lead to an
atrophy of morality, of moral thinking and of moral practice. Atrophy

is the dangerous disease in which, say, a limb of the human body wastes away because it has not been used for a length of time. The same can happen to men's character. If action with negligence of its motive has lasted for a long time, in the end the sense of moral motive dies. If you teach a generation that mere morality suffices, moral cripples will grow up who will become convinced that the highest principle is not to be caught. Numerous examples exist where rituals can be carried out mechanically. What kind of man will a child grow up to be who is told he is permitted to listen to the wireless on *shabbat*, provided somebody else, but not he himself, has switched it on? When Reform Judaism teaches that 'The *halachah* must not be dictated, it must be taught', the door to the end of *halachic* legality has been opened. The urgency of this emancipation from *halachic* Judaism in Israel and in the diaspora cannot be stressed enough.

Source: Ignaz Maybaum, *Happiness Outside the State*, pp. 21–3.

COMMENT: *Maybaum's comments on Jewish Law were usually directed against Orthodox interpretation of it, for during much of the time of his earlier writings there was no definitive Reform position. In this book, however – aware of the diverse and heated views among the Reform rabbinate – he considers the contribution which Reform needs to make.*

*Maybaum sought to turn the discussion about Jewish Law away from how directive should be any Reform guidelines on the subject. He was keen to stress instead the moral purpose of the commandments – an aspect that once featured high in such debates but which had been absent from more recent ones, as evident above. The momentum for a Reform perspective on halacha among other rabbis was already too far advanced to be affected by Maybaum, as will be seen below, but his words act as a powerful echo of one of the hallmarks of Reform – the emphasis on the ethical in Judaism – and serve as a useful reminder of religious priorities.*

## 8.4 Dow Marmur on a Search for New Ways (1979)

*Rabbi Marmur edited a collection of essays in 1973 entitled* Reform Judaism *but was keen to state in his introduction that 'This book makes no claim to be a definitive work on Reform Judaism in Britain today. Many of us hope that such a work will never be written, that British Reform will always retain its dynamic character and thus remain truly progressive' (p. viii). In his introduction to a second collection of essays, he repeats that sentiment yet also seeks to develop a new procedure for establishing standards of Jewish practice.*

The old ways do not solve the new dilemma. They offer either personal freedom without Judaism, or a kind of Judaism without freedom. But we need both. Our search for new ways may, therefore, bring us to an attitude normally associated with community decisions, of letting the group, the extended family, the individual congregation, shape its *Halacha* in the light of its search for the meaning of revelation, under the guidance of the rabbi who, by virtue of his training, is the expert, though never the sole authority. We must seek a system of Jewish practice that each community takes upon itself and which is binding on its members as long as they remain in that community. What they do outside it must be a matter of their discretion, although it is reasonable to assume that they are likely to live by the same standards. Inevitably, standards would vary from congregation to congregation, but it is not a tidy and uniform platform that we should be striving for. Our concern is to make Judaism active in the lives of our members. Our quest for authenticity must lead us along these paths. For Judaism without a *Halacha* is impossible, but Judaism on the basis of the *Halacha* of Orthodoxy is unsatisfactory. Hence the search for new ways.

Source: Dow Marmur (ed.), *A Genuine Search*, pp. 34–5.

COMMENT: *Marmur articulates the perennial problem for Reform of how to combine a definite sense of authoritative Jewish law with the freedom to interpret and adapt according to conscience and circumstance. He shies away from what might have been the most honest course – to admit that it is an impossible dilemma to reconcile – and instead opts for a localized solution, similar to that advocated by Goulston fifteen years earlier. Marmur recognizes that this will fail to provide a coherent position for the Reform Movement as a whole. He solves this in his own mind by declaring that such uniformity is unnecessary, although he ignores the fact that the debate over the commandments was prompted largely by a perceived need to state clearly and publicly what Reform did and did not accept.*

## 8.5 Henry Goldstein on the Problems of Reform (1979)

*Rabbi Goldstein's essay on observance in Reform Judaism was not written from the perspective of a theologian but as a congregational rabbi noted for his honesty and plain-speaking. He had no time for erudite expositions that bore little relation to reality and instead preferred to focus on what Reform Judaism represented for those who actually practised it.*

If dedication to deeds is a criterion for judging Jewish religious behaviour then Reform Judaism has passed the test; yet dedication is more often composed of affirmation than fulfillment. Reform Jews certainly affirm, but to a great extent their commitment to deeds, in the classical Jewish sense, never reaches actual practice. That Reform Jews in this country often indulge in slogan-making is possibly an indication of this. Diversity of practice is distinctive of Jews in general, but diversity is allowable only when it flourishes on top of a basic system to which Jews have given common agreement. Reform Judaism is an umbrella title for what common system exists in diversity, and for the doubts and weaknesses. Understandably many people find the current situation in Reform perplexing. If *kashrut* is regarded as fundamental by most of Jewry, the emphasis on personal choice might not be just a sign of development but an inability to know which way to develop. Reform Judaism does have something of a teen-age mentality. It has strength, it is conscious of growth and future; yet it displays weakness, uncertainty, and inconsistency. That one person feels justified in behaving in one way on Sabbath and another in the same synagogue has a different attitude, is rather like the limbs and mind of the adolescent not quite knowing the meaning of harmony or experiencing its benefits. Reform Judaism is very much an approach to a problem, but that is hardly enough. Reform Jews have to resolve that problem and develop a basic system. A method of achieving this is to discover criteria based on the values of Judaism. Part of the strength of Reform Judaism is that it recognises the values of Judaism; part of its weakness is that it has difficulty putting them into practice.

Source: Henry Goldstein, 'Criteria for Observance in Reform Judaism', in Dow Marmur (ed.), *A Genuine Search*, pp. 153-5.

COMMENT: *Goldstein does not mince his words. Rather than try to construct a theoretical framework to place in respectable terms the inconsistencies of Reform Judaism, he bluntly describes its theological weaknesses. In one sense the image of a teenager is very appropriate: at the time of writing, Reform was only 139 years old, and so it was comparatively young as a religious movement. However, Goldstein was using that image more as a reflection of its immaturity than its chronology, and although some may object to envisaging Reform as a gawky adolescent unsure of his future, others will find it a highly accurate portrayal, along with more positive connotations of hope and potential.*

## 8.6  Tony Bayfield on Guidelines for Reform *Halachah* (1981)

*Whereas many rabbis had approached the question of Reform's relationship with Jewish Law from a theological point of view, Rabbi Bayfield was influenced by his background in English law to attempt a more legalistic solution. As Reform did not adhere to the system of legal interpretation developed by Orthodoxy, it had to establish its own methodology, which combined consistency with flexibility. He therefore offered ten guiding principles as a way of achieving that.*

Guideline One: Tradition is innocent unless proven guilty.
Guideline Two: A hierarchical approach to *halachah* may be helpful.
Guideline Three: Pluralism will be a feature of Reform *halachah*.
Guideline Four: Careful consideration must be given to the role of the 'official community'.
Guideline Five: The origins of a custom are no sure guide to its present value but its underlying meaning may be.
Guideline Six: We must work in everyday, practical detail.
Guideline Seven: Discretion must have a place in modern *halachah*.
Guideline Eight: The past was not necessarily better; maybe just different.

Guideline Nine: We must restore common sense to the *halachic* debate.
Guideline Ten: This is work for both rabbis and congregants.

Source: Tony Bayfield, *God's Demands and Israel's Needs*, pp. 7-11.

COMMENT: *The ten guidelines offered a coherent and systematic frame-work to a decision-making process that had previously been guided largely by instinct. They did not set Reform thinking on a distinctive new path, but articulated the unspoken or ill-defined criteria already in existence. Moreover, they provided a basis for answering the increasingly urgent calls to explain Reform's relationship with the commandments and detail what that meant in terms of practical observance. However, although Bayfield's guidelines received a broad welcome at the time, they were left in abeyance and no attempt was made by him or others to apply them to the broad corpus of Jewish law.*

## 8.7 Collective Theological Essay on Jewish Law (1990)

*The collective essay attempted to formulate a broad consensus on a range of key issues. Despite the widely varying views that had existed previously on Reform's relationship with Jewish Law, the essay was able to present a view that was broadly representative of current Reform thinking.*

Rabbinic Judaism developed a code of law or practice, *halakhah*, which sought to express revelation in the details of everyday behaviour. Whilst respecting the *halakhic* system as a dominating aspect of our inheritance, we do not believe that a system of law is adequate to enable all contemporary Jews to express their relationship with God and other human beings. This is, first, a reflection of the shift from a society which addressed groups and classes to a society which addresses individuals. Secondly, it stems from a process whereby the Jewish community has handed over responsibility for such areas as criminal and civil law to the state, leaving only the deeply personal area of ritual and subtle issues of ethics to the domain of *halakhah* .

There should always be a presumption in favour of *halakhic* tradition, a respect for traditional methods of analysis and a recognition that *halakhic* literature contains the distilled wisdom of many generations. Nevertheless, Progressive Judaism believes that individuals must formulate their own patterns of Jewish practice. This is to be achieved through a process of study and exploration, an understanding both of the needs of the individual and the community, and an awareness of the norms and values taught by the synagogue. We accept the plurality of responses that emerge. We recognise the primacy of individual judgement and conscience, but individuals have to recognise that they exist also as part of a community and a tradition. The preservation and transmission of the Jewish heritage are the unique responsibility of each Jew.

Jewish practice and observance evolved over the centuries in response to changing circumstances and needs. Progressive Judaism embraces that process of creative change and development, which brings with it new patterns of Jewish practice. There is much merit in the injunction to renew the old and sanctify the new.

Source: Tony Bayfield, 'Progressive Judaism, a Collective Theological Essay and Discussion Paper', *Manna*, 27, Theology Supplement C. 2.

COMMENT: *The essay throws it weight unashamedly behind those who had argued that, by definition, Reform Judaism is no longer part of the halakhic system, nor can it ever be even a modern variation of it (as the American Conservative movement attempts to be). Despite mention of the value of tradition and the importance of community, the emphasis is primarily on individual responsibility. The problem of grossly varying standards to which this inevitably leads is dealt with by being legitimized as 'the plurality of responses that emerge'. There is still no unifying method for determining Reform Jewish observance, but the essay does at least provide a theological framework for major divergences. Notable, too, is the absence of any calls for a Reform code – a concept that had so exercised previous rabbis.*

## 8.8  Tony Bayfield on Responsible Autonomy (1993)

*The puzzle as to why Rabbi Bayfield never pursued his ten guidelines to develop a major work on Jewish Law is partly answered by the extract below a decade later, which – as hinted in the collective essay above – indicated the shift in his thinking away from communal standards to individual perspectives.*

The idea of an autonomous or self-determining individual is addressed from time to time in classical Jewish sources. But it is clearly a dominant theme of the modern western world. Whatever force it may have had in pre-Enlightenment society, it is the strongest 'spiritual' force of our times, expressing itself in our political structures, through democracy, our economic structures, through the free market and in every aspect of life. Modern western human beings, Jews included, experience themselves as being choosing, self-determining, autonomous individuals. Relatively few are either able or willing to surrender that right/duty of choice in matters as personal as those dealt with by the *halakhah*. The blueprint model, *halakhah*, is significantly out of tune with contemporary self-perceptions. Of course, that does not, as its proponents point out, ipso facto invalidate it. But it does effectively mean that it does not work for very many Jews . . . If Judaism is to move, as for many Jews it has already done, into a post-*halakhic*, post-legal mode, what is to happen to the *halakhic* tradition? And, perhaps, more urgently still, what is to stop mere anarchy being loosed upon the Jewish world? How can Judaism survive the whims of the autonomous individual? Moreover, is not the elevation of autonomy, the ultimate arrogance and dethronement of God? Does this not represent the triumph of modern, western, secular thinking over religion? The answer to the last two questions, I believe, is emphatically 'no' because the Jew is not a mere autonomous self, but a Jewish self. We are our individual selves but we are also contractually part of a story and a people. Our autonomy has to be exercised in tension with and in dialogue with God, history and peoplehood. The Reform Jew opts in and accepts the self-discipline and responsibility that comes from standing in active dialogue with the community, tradition and God. Thus, in the age of the voluntary covenant, is the autonomous self voluntarily limited.

In the sphere of religious practice, the question 'how does this behaviour deepen my faith and spiritual life?' should never be far from consideration. And in both ethical and ritual matters the question of how best to fulfil God's purpose for us and how best to deepen our understanding of what it is we must give to life are of the utmost importance. The autonomous Jewish self [also] turns to tradition and asks: what voices can I hear? What does tradition say? What truths is tradition seeking to teach me? How can I understand, respond, enrich, purify and refine? There are [other] probing questions. What are the needs of my people, my community and my family and what are my obligations to them? How do I respect and balance those needs with my own? What bounds and limits does the community set and why? . . . It is far easier to waive the old rulebook or to call for its revision than to face up to the paradigm shift from a *halakhic* to a post-*halakhic* way of life. Responsible autonomy is both the challenge and the reality of the new paradigm and can alone ensure the continuing flow of *Torah l'Moshe miSinai* [Mosaic law from Sinai], enriching and informing the lives of each and every responsibly autonomous Jew.

Source: Tony Bayfield, *Sinai, Law and Responsible Autonomy*, p. 14–16, 18–20, 30.

COMMENT: *Bayfield offers a way of harmonizing the need for objective standards of Jewish behaviour and the all-powerful desire for individual freedom: he declares that although individuals are no longer obliged to keep traditional observances, they can still choose to do so – and ought to choose to do so – and should exercise a degree of self-regulation for the sake of the Jewish past, present and future. This is a radical solution, and also a significant departure, with Jews no longer being commanded, but electing to command themselves. Bayfield cannot escape the need for compulsion if any semblance of community is to be maintained, but insists that it is now self-imposed rather than externally commanded. It is a viable solution in theory, but whether in practice it can provide sufficiently strong guidance for family life or communal cohesion is open to debate.*

## 8.9 David Kunin on the Halachic Self (1994)

*Rabbi Kunin was concerned that if, as Rabbi Bayfield suggests, many Jews consider halacha to be locked in the past and of little use, then the modern autonomous halachic Judaism that he proposes will be an impossibility. Kunin himself was not prepared to abandon the halachic system and, in a critique of Bayfield and others, sought to show that it could still be appropriate.*

There is another modern approach embracing both the *halachic* tradition and individual autonomy. This approach would create a new paradigm of religious authority, the paradigm of the individual autonomous self making Jewish decisions using the tools and parameters of the *halachic* system.

. . . Within autonomous *halachic* Judaism there should be a differentiation between the role of the rabbi, as *halachic* authority, and the individual's halachic authority. Rabbis are needed to fulfill the obligation to teach, in all its meanings. In order for any model of autonomous Judaism to function, whether *halachic* or not, knowledge is essential. Source material must be collected, translated and communicated. The parameters of the halachic system must also be explained. The rabbi must protect the boundaries, ensuring that decisions which are reached are consonant with the *halacha*. The rabbi is the one, licensed through ordination, to guide and enable the community and the individuals to reach their own decisions. As argued elsewhere, *Halacha* is not a unitary list of laws, rather it is a system which allows for a multiplicity of answers. In many cases, the rabbi's most important role should be to present the choices and the sources behind them, thereby allowing the community and the individuals to choose from the different options.

The rabbis would also help to ensure the basic standards of the community. Autonomous *halachic* Judaism, by its very nature, does not permit free choice by its adherents on all issues. Choices must be made within the framework that is acceptable to the Jewish tradition. Changes and choices can be made only within the *halachic* system. Whilst this may appear stifling, and stultifying, the scope for change within the *Halacha* is tremendous. Indeed, most of the important changes made by Reform Judaism could have been made using *Halacha*, and are consonant with autonomous *halachic* Judaism. Rabbis would also be there to fulfill their traditional function of answering questions or guiding people to find their own answers. Indeed, it is interesting to note, the biblical verse cited as the source of rabbinic authority [Deuteronomy 17.8] does not state that the Judge will make all the decisions on small matters as well as great. Rather, it states that one should go to a judge if the matter is too difficult for the individual to come to a decision.

Source: David Kunin, 'The *Halachic* Self', *The Journal of Progressive Judaism*, 3, pp. 85, 90–1.

COMMENT: *Kunin's approach is very similar to that of the American Conservative movement, which claims it is able to maintain the halachic system yet use the flexibility within it to introduce a variety of far-reaching reforms through traditional methods of interpretation. Kunin's paradigm is particularly attractive to Jews who are both free-thinking yet concerned about tradition, because it appears to offer much greater decision-making authority to informed individuals. However, this freedom might be negated by the rabbinically-determined framework within which he insists that all such decisions should be made. Moreover, the very criticism he levels against Bayfield's approach – that Bayfield's claim that the halacha no longer has any relevance for most modern Jews removes any credibility for Bayfield's solution – also undermines his own suggestion, which can only succeed given an acceptance of the halacha. The problem of imposing communal uniformity on autonomous individuals remains elusive, whatever the merits of theoretical systems.*

## A Final Thought . . .

The most special moment is when I put my tallit on. I need space to do it. Not just because it's so big – but because I need to feel 'separate' from other people. As I stretch it out in front of me, I feel small, a little hesitant and excited too. Then, when I hold it for a few moments over and around my head, I feel totally sheltered – as if from a storm, raging just a few feet away.

That feeling is broken as I take my tallit from my head and let it fall on my shoulders: I'm connected to things again; to the people around me – and yet not in the same way I was a few moments earlier. In some way, the whole process of putting on and wearing my tallit is a differentiating, a secluding experience, ensuring that my task as an individual standing before God remains distinct and necessary even as it is an integral part of the whole. The community's relationship with God can never be a substitute for my relationship with God – even as we are all sureties for one another.

But there is another issue entangled here: whatever personal meaning wearing a tallit may have for me in establishing and maintaining my relationship with God, my tallit is infused with eternal, very specific Jewish meanings, which force me to ask: what am I doing when I wear a tallit . . . when I undertake this, or indeed any other *mitzvah*? . . . What does 'personal choice' mean? Why do individuals 'choose' one practice or another? . . . Am I simply gratifying personal needs when I choose to light Sabbath candles or wear a tallit?

. . . [it] is complicated by the implications of being a Progressive Jewish woman. As a woman I am aware of the extent to which the *mitzvot* defined by God's Commandments have been mediated and interpreted by men . . . It is a structure which I, as a Jewish woman am struggling to make more fully Jewish by participating in it and by bringing my own experiences with me. This is, after all, a very Jewish process: the transformation of elements drawn from the past in the context of the needs of the present.

Source: Elizabeth Sarah, 'Wearing my Tallit: Some Thoughts on the Hidden Agenda', in Barbara Borts, Dee Eimer and others, *Women and Tallit*, pp. 32–3.

# 9

# CONVERSION

Ever since Abraham first discovered the One God, converts were attracted to the new faith. Reference to the 'souls gotten in Haran' by Abraham (Genesis 12.5) implied that he encouraged adherents. In later times, Joshua forcibly converted many of the Canaanite tribes he conquered, while the ringing declaration of Ruth – 'Your people shall be my people, your God my God' (Ruth 1.16) – indicated that others joined of their own accord. Judaism was undoubtedly a missionary faith until banned from making converts by the Christian powers in the fourth century. This, along with the social hostility that arose between Jews and their neighbours, developed into an almost pathological unwillingness by rabbinic authorities to admit any newcomers. This reluctance was especially strong in Britain, even in the nineteenth century when the ban had long ceased to exist and the social divide between Jews and others lessened. It was only in more recent times that the question of permitting, or even encouraging, proselytes re-emerged.

## 9.1 Leo Baeck on Active Mission (1949)

*Rabbi Dr Baeck had been a leading member of a German Jewry that was deeply attached to the notion of universalism and the onward progress of civilization, with Jews being part of German society and immersed in German culture. He had also witnessed the death of all such hopes in the Nazi extermination camps, when it appeared that much of the world still did not accept Jews as fellow human-beings. After the Second World War, at a time when many Jews were re-assessing their relationship with wider society, Baeck spoke about the direction he felt it should take.*

108

Mankind is hungry and thirsts for that which Judaism can say, what Jews full of Judaism can say. Throughout our history, many gentiles became attracted to Judaism and became proselytes, educated people, high-minded people. Should we not begin anew? Should we not send our missionaries to Asia, to East Asia and to other places to the people there waiting for us? We are in need of expansion for our own sake . . . We must free ourselves from the narrow mind, from the little thought. Only a people, only a community with great ideas, with the great way of thinking, is able to have a mission, to send out missionaries. All depends on us. Our God waits for us.

Source: Leo Baeck, 'The Mission of Judaism', in *World Union for Progressive Judaism Report* (Sixth International Conference), p. 74.

COMMENT: *Baeck brushes aside those who, after the Holocaust, wished to withdraw from the outside world and concentrate on rebuilding internal Jewish life. Instead, he not only re-asserts the continued relevance of the Jewish message, but advocates the start of an active missionary campaign. This was in contrast to both the mood of the moment and the course of Jewish history, which had abandoned such activities sixteen hundred years earlier. Moreover, Baeck justifies his proposal on precisely the same grounds that others had shied away from it – the Holocaust – save that he saw the addition of new souls as one way of compensating for the loss of six million Jews. This, for him, was the difference between those who had a 'narrow' mindset and a great one. He also had no doubt that this was not just a matter of religious opportunism but a divine mandate. God demanded it too. It should be noted, however, that Baeck's proposal was not viewed sympathetically by many rabbis, who either felt that there were different priorities or that Jews had so often suffered from Christian attempts at mission that it would be unacceptable to unleash a campaign of their own. The plan certainly did not meet with any practical result.*

## 9.2 Andre Ungar on Discouraging Converts (1958)

*Rabbi Dr Ungar was given responsibility for producing a booklet on the beliefs, practices, and facts of Reform, showing its relevance to modern Jews. The title – 'Living Judaism' – was intended both as an assertion of the vitality of Reform and to distinguish it from other forms of Judaism which might be regarded as more tied to the past. The issue of conversion was one of many topics briefly covered.*

In general our attitude to would-be proselytes to Judaism is one of discouragement. We enquire into the applicants' motives on the basis of the true tolerance of Judaism, not on account of any exclusive racial pride.

Like our forefathers, we believe that there are more paths than one leading to God and righteousness – that a Christian or Moslem or Buddhist may be just as worthy and godly a person by practising his own faith in its noblest spirit as a Jew adhering to his ancestral rites. Our mission as Jews does not consist in trying to make all mankind Jewish, but in helping them to become God-fearing and good, each in the context of his own culture and background. On the other hand if a candidate for conversion proves that his whole soul is set on embracing Judaism, that he wants it above all other things in the world, that he desires it for its own sake, for the sake of God and for no ulterior motive, then Jewry not only may, but must, accept him as an honoured member.

Source: Andre Ungar, *Living Judaism*, p. 20.

COMMENT: *Ungar reproduces the 'yes-it-is-possible-in-special-cases-but-we-prefer-not' position that had characterized Jewish thinking for several centuries, even though there had been a much more welcoming attitude originally. He uses the fact that Judaism values other faiths as a means of justifying this negative approach, even though it is a general point that is irrelevant to the particular individuals who seek to become Jewish. Although Ungar does concede that those who are worthy may be admitted, it is noticeable that it is hedged with five conditions, which is even more off-putting when compared with the adamantly forthright opening statement of discouragement.*

## 9.3 Charles Berg on the Rabbinic Dilemma (1959)

*In the passage above, Rabbi Ungar had referred enigmatically to those seeking conversion for an 'ulterior motive'. Many would have assumed that he meant for the sake of marriage, which was regarded as a sign of insincerity. However, it was also the most common reason for applicants and posed a dilemma for rabbis which Rabbi Berg tried to address.*

In our day when religion does not play a decisive part in the lives of the majority [of non-Jews], there are few who are attracted to Judaism *meyirat shamayim* (from a fear of heaven); yet these few exist. They do not, however, constitute a special problem. The problem is created by the many who are, or intend to be, married to a Jewish partner. It is true that without this connection they would never have thought of becoming Jewish. The vast majority of such applicants are refused by the orthodox authorities. If we would act in the same way, what would be the consequences? As a child of a non-Jewish mother is not considered Jewish by traditional Law, a Jewish man who 'marries out' and his descendants would be automatically forced out of the Jewish orbit, even if they would lead a proper Jewish life. On the other hand, atheists of Jewish origin or those who attached themselves to another religion (conversion away from Judaism is not recognised in Jewish law) would still be considered Jews.

It is true that many applicants know little about Judaism when they have their first interview with the Rabbi. The decision he has to make is a difficult one. There are cases where the motive is not really genuine, where the conversion is sought for the sake of appearances (a synagogue wedding for instance) or merely to please parents or relatives. Such applicants should be refused. On the other hand, there are many who sincerely desire to accept Judaism in order to form a united and happy family and make it easier for the children to be brought up in our religion.

... We Jews take pride to point out that our religion is of an universalistic nature. This means in simple words that we are not only concerned with the spiritual and moral welfare of our own people, but care for all men. Yet the final test of an universalistic attitude is whether we are able to accept in our midst persons of a different background as members of the Jewish people.

Source: Charles Berg, 'As Regards Proselytes', *The Synagogue Review*, 33, pp. 151–3.

COMMENT: *Berg gives an honest description of the practical situation rabbis face when dealing with conversion. He is humane enough to recognize the negative personal consequences of turning away those whom the Orthodox have already rejected, while he also recognizes anomalies of Jewish status that allow completely non-practising Jews to be regarded as Jewish. Although still insisting on sincerity as a requirement for conversion, he softens the disapproval against 'ulterior motives' to permit conversion for the sake of family life and children's identity. Moreover, he appeals to the same universalist concerns that Unger had cited, but, this time, to allow conversion rather than discourage it.*

## 9.4 Michael Boyden on a More Welcoming Approach (1979)

*The extremely cautious approach towards admitting conversion began to be re-examined in the 1970s as a result of the steeply rising rate of intermarriage with non-Jews. The vast majority of the non-Jewish partners did not convert, and fears that this would lead the Jewish partners to drop out of Judaism raised serious questions as to Jewish survival. Whereas previously there had been the concern that conversion was being used to accommodate intermarriage, now it was simply being bypassed. Rabbi Boyden felt it was time to change communal attitudes.*

Obviously, a good Jewish education is vital for the survival of the Jewish people, but it will not, I believe, solve a problem which is endemic to a reasonably free and open society. You cannot send your children to the same schools as other children, have them meet others at university, work in the same establishment and have completely free social intercourse without it being inevitable that a percentage will choose their marriage partners outside of the Jewish community. In the end, we shall have to look at our relationship with those who marry out and re-examine our attitude to the convert.

Here the Reform movement has a vital contribution to make, if we can stop looking over our shoulders at what the Orthodox will say. Normally, our Beth Din accepts just over 100 converts a year. This has been true of every year for the past decade, with the exception of 1978, for which year the figure was 88 conversions. What is for sure is that intermarriage is on the increase and if our figures are remaining relatively static, this only means that we are taking in a smaller and smaller percentage in terms of those who have married out. People sometimes ask me what the size of our convert class is. When I tell them that it is a small class, they react with pleasure. 'Good', they say, 'we only have a small number converting!'. I would suggest to you that a small class is anything but good. It is bad, because it means we are failing to deal with the real problem. And so to those beleaguered congregations, particularly in the provinces, who go on accepting converts, in spite of the insults they receive, I say '*B'ruchim atem l'adonai* [ Blessed are you to God]. You fulfil a real *mitzvah*. You are at the forefront of the fight for Jewish survival'.

We need to look at our own attitudes to the proselyte. Must they always have to prove themselves in our communities? Will we never accept them as fully Jewish? Rabbi Alexander Schindler [past-President of the Union of American Hebrew Congregations] said 'Until the end of their days we refer to them as converts, if not worse. Don't think these whispers, behind their back, aren't heard and do not hurt'. We can begin by removing those 'not wanted' signs from our own hearts and making our proselytes feel fully welcome within our own communities.

Source: Michael Boyden, 'Z.P.G. and Jewish Survival', *A Rabbi's Journal*, 5, pp. 12–13.

COMMENT: *Boyden is uncompromisingly direct is his comments and exposes two areas which had virtually been taboo subjects. First, he points to the inevitability of intermarriage in a society that is receptive to Jewish participation. The Jewish community cannot expect working relationships not to develop into personal relationships. Second, he lambastes the prejudice that is often held towards converts. Even those who are formally accepted are always seen as different and unwanted.*

*Converts have to face not only initial obstacles from religious officials but social discrimination from ordinary congregants, which is more lasting and more painful. He also asserts that much of this is due to a pusillanimous*

*concern for the criticisms that Orthodoxy would otherwise make. Boyden*
*makes a powerful call for the reversal of both the entry barriers and the*
*negative attitudes, a call that is in sharp contrast with much previous*
*thinking.*

### 9.5  Lionel Blue on the Benefits of Converts (1997)

*In 1969 Rabbi Blue became Clerk to the Rabbinical Court of Beth Din of*
*the Reform Synagogues of Great Britain, a post he occupied for the next two*
*decades. During this time, his work covered various status issues, includ-*
*ing cases of adoption and divorce, but primarily concerned applications for*
*conversion. After his retirement, he reflected on his experiences:*

Converts time after time surprised us by their enthusiasm for what we
insiders had come to take for granted, the strength and reasonableness
of our own faith. We gave something to them, it is true. But they gave us
precious things as well, like self-confidence. The Jewish community had
drawn in on itself during the Holocaust. But it is dangerous to love one's
own more by loving others less. And it was a battle in those post-war
years to keep the universalist heritage of Judaism alive. In this the converts were crucial . . . A great deal depends on the individual rabbi of the
local synagogue involved. Some are welcoming, some are off-putting,
some think that conversion is one in the eye for Hitler, and some think
that it is endangering Judaism just as much. I, needless to say, am pro-
convert because they let in fresh air, and small religious worlds suffer
from claustrophobia. Also in a time when political anti-Semitism lurks
beneath the surface, becoming a Jew is as dangerous as it ever has been.
Only a fool or a believer would finally go through with it.

Source: Lionel Blue, 'Insiders and Outsiders', in Walter Homolka, Walter Jacob and
Esther Seidel (eds), *Not By Birth Alone*, pp. 131, 135.

COMMENT: *Blue adds a new dimension to the debate on conversion*
*by noting that, quite apart from adding to the size of Jewry, proselytes help*
*boost Jewish appreciation of their own faith. The fact that an outsider from*
*the majority culture wishes to join a minority group is a tremendous com-*

*pliment. This approach was shared by a growing number of Reform rabbis, whose attitude was becoming more accommodating, but whether this percolated to the congregations at large is less certain. Blue also claims that Judaism benefits from the wider perspective which converts can often bring and which prevents it from becoming too self-absorbed. However, he is right to admit that his is not a universal view and others might regard this as a regrettable dilution of Judaism.*

## 9.6 Jonathan Romain on Outreach to Potential Converts (2000)

*Despite the more positive approach that had been urged by Rabbi Boyden (and Rabbi Dr Baeck several decades earlier), little changed in practice. The number of adult conversions per year hovered around the 120 mark, while the estimated mixed-marriage rate was 1500 per annum. At a time when it was extremely difficult to convert through the Orthodox authorities, Reform was failing to attract even a tenth of the numbers to which it could aspire. It was felt by some that although not all the non-Jewish partners of such unions would wish to convert, a significant percentage might be interested if encouraged to do so.*

A convert to Christianity is greeted with delight. In Judaism it is a very different story. Rabbis tend to be much busier turning down requests for conversion and see them as an unwarranted intrusion. At worst, this is justified by an element of superiority that borders on racism, with modern whispers that 'converts can never be fully Jewish', while Rabbi Helbo was downright insulting in Talmudic times: 'Proselytes are as difficult for Israel as leprosy'. At best, the objections are based on a need to prove the sincerity of applicants, so that they reach the highest ideals of Judaism. Despite the high number of born-Jews who are non-practising, it is felt that anyone who elects to become Jewish should emulate the most dedicated of us. This is accompanied by the automatic assumption that anyone who is engaged to a Jewish partner cannot possibly be sincere. But why should coming into contact with Judaism through the Jewish family life of a fiancé/e be any less worthy than being introduced to it through a book in the library that someone single picked up?

Standards should not be lowered. Sincerity and knowledge will remain prerequisites. What should change is the way in which we apply them. We should abandon the traditional response of rejecting an enquirer three times to test their resolve. Why teach people we do not mean what we say, and why slap good people in the face three times and then expect them to come back? Why send applicants away 'to think about things for six months' when many have nurtured the idea for years before summoning up the courage to approach us? We should welcome them onto conversion courses and see how they fit into the reality of Jewish communal life. There is an even earlier stage of being pro-active and letting potential converts know we are receptive to them. Next time you read your synagogue newsletter, notice that it refers to 101 activities but never advertises the fact that there is a conversion class. How do we expect those who might be interested in conversion to know about classes if we do not mention them . . . and what message do we give out by hiding it away like an item in a shop never on display but available under the counter on request. It is time to dismantle the fences we have needlessly erected around the *Torah* .

. . . It is significant that many synagogues report that a disproportionately high number of Religion School teachers are converts. This is partly because they often know more than born-Jews, and partly because they are enthusiastic enough to give up Sunday mornings whilst others are still in bed. The rest of the community should be much more appreciative and should be much more helpful when would-be converts first approach us.

Source: Jonathan Romain, 'How are We Handling Conversion Right Now?', *Manna*, 67, pp. 12–13.

COMMENT: *The passage challenges the assumption that conversions for the sake of marriage are less worthy than those for reasons of personal spirituality. It could be argued that the latter is more meaningful, but it is also true that a person surrounded by Jewish family life will have greater involvement in the faith and be better supported in their new lifestyle. There is also criticism of the time-honoured methods of testing an applicant's sincerity. Although they do certainly achieve their object of putting off less committed candidates, they can also be highly insulting to those who have given deep thought to the matter. These methods, the passage infers, not only reflect the antipathy to admitting newcomers but do a disservice to the Jewish community by depriving it of members who could contribute greatly to synagogue life and, ironically, to the future continuity about which their detractors are so worried.*

## A Final Thought . . .

Some time ago I received the following letter:

> Dear Rabbi
>
> I would be obliged if you could help me with the following matter. A member of the United Synagogue has fallen in love with a Christian girl. In a few years' time they wish to marry, and the girl wishes to become a Jewess now. The couple's profession is hairdressing, and apparently Saturday is their busiest day. Of course the [Orthodox] *Beth Din* would not accept her application, knowing that they would not desist from work on the Sabbath. As an Orthodox Jew myself, my suggestion was to contact the *Beth Din* in the first instance, and the Reform if the *Beth Din* turned them down. I would be most obliged if you could possibly see this young man.

In reply I wrote:

> Dear Sir
>
> I must confess to not feeling too happy about what you write. If, as you seem to imply, your own *Beth Din* appears to be demanding over-stringent terms from a would-be proselyte, I would have thought that by far the most honourable thing to do in your position would have been to approach your *Beth Din* and attempt to make their attitude a little more reasonable. Or am I to assume that you, in common with so many other Orthodox Jews of your ilk, regard the Reform Synagogue as a

sort of gathering place for the pariahs of the Jewish community – a sort of Dantean Limbo for the theological throw-outs. We are neither impressed nor flattered by these obvious implications of your letter. We are a Synagogue body endeavouring to face up to the problem of leading an authentic Jewish life in the twentieth century, with all that this implies. We ourselves are proud that we at least try to tackle all our problems (however miserably we may succeed) and do not, thank God, conveniently shovel off our problems on to others. I am willing to discuss religious problems with anybody, Jew or Gentile, any day, any time. Would you be so kind to inform your Jewish friend of this and ask him to ask his fiancée to write to me personally. I shall then give the matter my serious consideration.

Source: Alan Miller, '. . . and Thy God, My God', *The Synagogue* Review, Vol. 36, 1961, p. 61.

# 10

# DIALOGUE (INTER-FAITH)

Throughout Jewish history there have been moments of inter-faith dialogue – whether directly with individuals from other religions or indirectly through access to their writings. However, these occasional instances have largely been overshadowed by the great gulf between Jews and members of other faiths, because of factors such as social hostility, missionary zeal or supremacist theology. It was only in the twentieth century that the idea of dialogue became valued by significant sectors within Judaism and in surrounding faiths, at both clerical and lay level. The multiplication of inter-faith organizations today attests to the rise of dialogue as a religious value in itself, while the fact that these organizations are invariably endorsed by the leading representatives of the different faiths indicates their respectability within the different religious hierarchies. Nevertheless, despite its great advance, religious dialogue is still a minority interest within the faiths in Britain today, including the Jewish community. There are still many Jews who regard it as a waste of time or, even worse, as a danger, because it could lead to lessening one's faith or to conversion.

## 10.1 Morris Joseph on the Religious Integrity of Non-Jews (1903)

*When the synagogue of which Reverend Joseph was minister was founded, it had deliberately named itself 'The West London Synagogue of British Jews'. It was the first one in the country to incorporate any reference to its national identity. This was partly intended to unify previous divisions over ancestral origins between Ashkenazi and Sephardi Jews, and to declare that they were no longer relevant. It was also a conscious statement of affinity with the population at large. It implied a degree of national kinship to which Joseph sought to give religious sanction.*

What of those who stand outside the religious pale? Are they denied the means of atonement and reconciliation [with God]? The answer is No. Just as Israel has no monopoly of salvation, so he has no exclusive possession of the paths that lead to it. Judaism teaches not only that the Divine love is freely offered to all men, whatever their religion may be, but their religion is itself the instrument by which they may win it . . . God judges men not by a rigid, uniform standard, but by the standard laid down for each man individually by his education and his ideals. He needs not Judaism in order to be 'saved'. There is salvation for him outside the Law. The Divine test of a man's worth is not his theology but his life.*

   . . . Other creeds also contain a large measure of religious and moral truth; but while being just to all men, the Jew will be true to himself. Benevolence towards other religions will not coexist with lukewarmness to his own creed. That is a poor tolerance which springs from indifference. What men require is not half-contemptuous sufferance, but sympathetic recognition. We Jews know the need from our own experience. And what we feel to be our right, let us freely give to others.

Source: Morris Joseph, *Judaism as Creed and Life*, pp. 154, 272–3, 486–7.

*This sentence occurs earlier in the book but is inserted here as it occurs in the same context.

COMMENT: *Joseph reinforces the traditional Jewish view that other faiths have religious validity in the eyes of God. But whereas that is predicated on them fulfilling the rabbinic concept of the seven Noachide Laws of essential ethical behaviour, he goes a step further and frees them from fulfilling Jewishly-defined standards and demands only that they live up to their own ideals. They are acceptable to God on their own terms. Joseph also adds the important rider that respect for others does not lessen commitment to one's own faith; such tolerance is much more meaningful than an attitude of religious laissez-faire.*

## 10.2 Reform Prayer Book on Interfaith Meetings (1977)

*When a new Prayer Book was produced by the Reform Synagogues of Great Britain, it attracted much attention because of its use of modern English in the translations, alternative introductory sections for services and the re-institution of several traditional elements. Less dramatic, but highly significant, was the inclusion of a prayer for inter-faith meetings. It was the first time such a prayer had appeared, and it gave both official recognition to the burgeoning moves towards dialogue and a powerful encouragement to them.*

Lord of all creation, we stand in awe before You, impelled by the visions of the harmony of man. We are children of many traditions – inheritors of shared wisdom and tragic misunderstandings, of proud hopes and humble successes. Now it is time for us to meet – in memory and truth, in courage and trust, in love and promise.

   In that which we share, let us see the common prayer of humanity; in that in which we differ, let us wonder at the freedom of man; in our unity and our differences, let us know the uniqueness that is God. May our courage match our convictions, and our integrity match our hope. May our faith in You bring us closer to each other. May our meeting with past and present bring blessing for the future. Amen.

Source: Lionel Blue and Jonathan Magonet (eds), *Forms of Prayer for Jewish Worship: Daily, Sabbath and Occasional Prayers*, p. 297.

COMMENT: *The mere fact that such a prayer was included in the formal Jewish liturgy was a pioneering development, while its content was arresting too. Rather than shy away from the awkward subject of previous hostility between the faiths, it admitted both the mistakes of the past and the differences that still remained, yet was entirely positive in its hope that a new level of understanding was both desirable and possible.*

## 10.3 Roger Pavey on Other Religions (1979)

*Rabbi Pavey was a congregational rabbi who was engaged in the doorstep realities of inter-faith dialogue. He was willing to work with members of other faiths in matters of common interest, yet also keen to establish the grounds for so doing. He felt it important to know what were the limits of tolerance, and to what extent it was right to press Judaism's special theological insights in a liberal society.*

What, in practical day to day terms, should be the attitude of Reform Jews, modern liberal-minded people, to their non-Jewish friends and fellow citizens? First and foremost, no Jew should compromise his conviction in any way? For him, as a Jew, Judaism is uniquely and absolutely true. At the same time he must recognise that this is equally the case with Christians and Muslims committed to their faiths. The solution of the paradox is in the hands of God. Second, no Jew should ever fudge differences between him and others that are honestly held and that flow from an integrated and coherent pattern of faith and practice. Common ground is interesting, but to live there is to live in a no man's land that is neither Jewish nor non-Jewish, neither *milchig* nor *fleishig* [milk and meat-based foods that should not be mixed according to Jewish law]. We have to live with the fact that we are different and accept the differences, even rejoice in them as creative tension. Third, we have to come to terms with conversion and missionary work; it is valid and legitimate. If we as Jews proclaim the *Torah* is *ets hayim*, a tree of life, then that applies to others as well; to talk about the Noachide laws is lazy because it is inapplicable to our situation.

Source: Roger Pavey, 'Reform Judaism and the World's Religions', in Dow Marmur (ed.), *A Genuine Search*, p. 218.

COMMENT: *Pavey gives a staunch defence of the uniqueness of Judaism and twice warns against any compromise of Jewish principles or identity. What is remarkable is that he also asserts the right of other faiths to be equally self-protective, even to the extent of maintaining their missionary tradition, an activity others might feel is incompatible with dialogue. He does not advance a theological framework for the mutually unique nature of the different faiths, but is content to let God resolve the issue. Some might consider unsatisfactory this avoidance of any attempt to reconcile the difficulty, but there may also be merit in simply admitting the paradox rather than trying to construct a tortuous justification for it. Believers are used to paradox and one more might be no intellectual hardship. The Laws of Noah are seven laws of civilized behaviour which Jewish tradition regards as incumbent on all people to observe; it is the mechanism through which Judaism tolerates members of other faiths that hold different beliefs but share similar ethics. Pavey rejects it as grounds for modern dialogue, because it dealt with those who were pagans, whereas modern faiths need to be not just tolerated but respected.*

## 10.4 Dow Marmur on a Common Adversary (1982)

*Rabbi Marmur was personally very active in efforts at religious dialogue and also in reconciliation work, helping to pioneer reciprocal visits of young German Christians and young British Jews. However, he was concerned that there was another issue looming that was just as pressing, although the need for all faiths to address it might also help them understand each other better.*

There are other factors that make such co-operation imperative. One of them is the reality that religionists in the Western world have had to identify as a common adversary: secularism . . . the spirit which seeks to eliminate the religious dimension from our existence. Christendom, which once dominated the West, has not yet adjusted to being in exile, and comprising only a small minority. Islam has not yet learnt how to take up the challenge; instead, in the manner of every strict orthodoxy, it has chosen to pretend that the challenge does not exist. As a result, despite the many beautiful words that have been spoken and the many interfaith meetings that have been held, very little co-operation exists. The future of Judaism, indeed of all three monotheistic religions, depends on such co-operation. There is still much talk in Christian and, particularly, in Islamic circles, of defeating and crushing the world of secularism (and, if possible, also Judaism). Judaism with its long experience of minority status, and its openness to God's world as it is, knows that religion is not capable of defeating secularism, and even if it could it should not do so. For the independent critique of all aspects of human endeavour, including religion, which our secular world has made possible, has brought light into Judaism and Christianity and, in time, will do so to Islam. Had it not been for secularism, Jews would still be in the ghetto and Judaism the sole prerogative of obscurantists.

There is, therefore, no question of battle, but of dialogue. It is a matter of deep regret and concern that the existing organisations for Jewish–Christian co-operation have not been able to promote such understanding to its full extent, largely due to apathy. The fundamental differences between the religions will and should remain. But that need not prevent the real opportunity for co-operation that also exists. Its basis is tension: tension between the monotheistic religions on the one hand and secularism on the other.

Source: Dow Marmur, *Beyond Survival*, p. 181–2.

COMMENT: *Marmur is not impressed with the results of inter-faith dialogue so far, and is dismissive of 'beautiful words' that have no practical effect. However, he sees the need to confront jointly a common enemy, the advance of secularism, as a possible way of bringing the faiths closer. It might be questioned whether faiths who, in his view, had failed until now to adjust to the new reality around them, would choose to work together rather than maintain their independent approach. He also displays a strangely ambivalent attitude to secularism, regarding it as a threat yet acknowledging how much Judaism has benefited from it.*

## 10.5 Jonathan Magonet on the Challenge of Dialogue (1995 ff.)

*Rabbi Professor Magonet was responsible for founding, and then running for over thirty-five years, an annual Bible Week at Bendorf in Germany which brought members of several faiths together to study texts. It helped inspire a whole generation of rabbis to view dialogue as an essential part of their ministry, and led to many other positive inter-faith initiatives, both within Britain itself and internationally. Magonet was well aware, how-*

*ever, that such advances could only be made if certain conditions applied, as*
*he explained in the following two passages.*

Living with religious pluralism and diversity means that we can no longer make pronouncements [about other faiths] without taking into account the sensitivity of the other we are discussing, who we have effectively invited to overhear our conversations. Those who have experienced interfaith dialogue know that from now on there is an invisible partner forever present who acts as a new kind of superego watching over our more inflated claims and dubious comparisons.

At first this seems like some kind of self-imposed censorship that may prevent genuine disagreement, but that is not actually the case. It simply means that in our internal discussions about others we become more careful and modest in our claims and we understand that such issues that divide us may only be properly addressed in the presence of the other. We come to realise that what we are conventionally doing is talking about friends behind their back and it is no longer acceptable. The strictures of the Hofetz Hayyim about gossip and slander apply no less to other religious traditions than they do to private relationships.

Precisely because we are the 'progressive' part of the Jewish world we have a particular task in the pioneering and furtherance of interfaith dialogue. Our openness and flexibility give us the freedom to work at the interface of the 'outside' world. Moreover our liberal tradition should give us certain valuable qualities we can bring to the dialogue process, particularly the kind of humility that empowers us to listen before we feel the need to speak or pass some kind of judgement on what we have heard. Our commitment to the values of enlightenment should give us the necessary detachment and clarity to create understanding where so much misinformation and confusion abound. Our lack of false pride should allow us to accept the criticism and self-criticism that inevitably have to be faced when we have an honest encounter with the other. Above all, the challenge within interfaith dialogue is to find within ourselves the inner spiritual resources to build trust, friendship and love in situations where so much fear and suspicion abound.

Source: Jonathan Magonet, 'The Challenge of Interfaith', *The Journal of Progressive Judaism*, 4, pp. 9, 11.

All who have moved into dialogue know that one effect is estrangement from one's own community and past. There is a difference between those who have moved through and beyond their prejudices in meeting the other and those who have not. There is nothing so painful as returning to your own community and encountering the prejudices that you yourself have left behind, and often the task of re-educating your own people is harder than that of the initial dialogue in the first place. But those who have experienced it cannot go back, and it may be true to say that there is slowly evolving an interfaith community. It is not one of syncretism between the members of the two or three faiths that have encountered each other, rather it is a shared openness that affects all their religious life. It means new loyalties to a truth that cannot be denied, often in the face of mistrust, conflicts, even aggression that is elsewhere the rule. There are few things as painful, yet at the same time so spiritually uplifting, as learning to see the world and oneself through the eyes of another. For the health of all our traditions at a time of increasing insecurity and retreat into conservatism and obscurantism, this sort of spiritual exposure and self-criticism that accompanies it is essential. We have armoured ourselves against the often valid critiques of the secular world, but it is less easy to hide from those that come from another faith community whose legitimacy we acknowledge – provided there is a mutuality in the exchange.

Source: Jonathan Magonet, in Lionel Blue and Jonathan Magonet (eds), *Forms of Prayer for Jewish Worship: Prayers for the Pilgrim Festivals*, p. 36.

COMMENT: *Magonet has no doubt about the benefits of dialogue, but provides an honest reminder of the sometimes difficult consequences that it can involve. This includes how one re-assesses the way one relates to other faiths as much in their absence as in their presence. It is also how one relates to one's own community in the light of that new experience. The problem of no longer feeling as much at home in one's own tradition as before is eloquently expressed by someone who has clearly experienced it himself. Yet Magonet is adamant that dialogue is a worthwhile task and that Reform Jews have a special responsibility. While he is right to emphasize the particular qualities they have for this task, there is also the danger that if dialogue is seen by the Orthodox as the special interest of the non-Orthodox, they may shy away from it. That would be counter-productive, for their participation is important too, and so the Reform must tread firmly but gently so as not to be thought of as monopolizing dialogue.*

## A Final Thought . . .

I was in Madras. I had been invited as a last-minute participant in a conference on philosophy and religion. I was due to speak one afternoon and a polite young Indian man came up to me and told me that he was especially interested in my paper on Judaism. I was delighted at this recognition accorded to my own religion given that so many were represented here. Clearly he valued the particular quality of the Jewish faith that had somehow appealed to him even in this place so far from the Jewish world that I knew. 'Yes,' he added, 'I am very interested in the minor religions.' There was no irony intended in his remark, nor any putdown. He was simply observing Judaism from his own particular perspective, and compared to the hundreds of millions of adherents to other faiths, the few million Jews on this planet were, if not insignificant, at least distinctly 'minor'.

Source: Jonathan Magonet, *The Explorer's Guide to Judaism*, p. 1.

# 11

# ETHICAL LIFE

The biblical prophets were often at pains to point out that worshipping God but then acting unethically rendered one's supplications useless. When one of the greatest teachers of Judaism, the first-century rabbi, Hillel, was asked to sum up what was most important about Judaism, he chose neither its beliefs nor its prayers nor its ritual observances but its ethics, and declared: 'What is hateful to you, do not do to your neighbour.' In similar vein, the rabbis declared that if any person says he loves God, but does not love his fellow human beings, then he is lying, because one shows one's love of God by the way one treats God's creatures. However, although Judaism has always emphasized that faith alone was not sufficient and had to be accompanied by ethical living, human history shows that it is much easier to pray piously than live piously, and so the importance of ethics has had to be constantly reinforced by each generation of rabbis.

## 11.1 David Woolf Marks on Personal Responsibility (1854 ff.)

*It was a characteristic of the early leaders of Reform Judaism in Britain and elsewhere to seek to restore a balance between the ethical and ritual components of Judaism, which they felt had become weighted too far in favour of the latter, with obsessive attention being given to the minutiae of observances. They identified strongly with the clarion call to ethical behaviour that could be found in much of the prophetical writings. It meant that such texts were often used by Reverend Professor Marks to rekindle the sense of ethical obligations incumbent on all Jews and to address the moral lapses he saw around him, which he did in the following two extracts.*

That the great end of religion is to make us holy and wise, and to bring us into close alliance with God, is a definition in which all rational men must agree. Still, many who profess themselves religious, who really believe themselves sincere in their professions, and who would be greatly mortified if the genuineness of their convictions were questioned, fail to demonstrate by the general tone of their lives, that the final aim of religion is in keeping with the above definition. The holy prophet, from whose words I am preaching ['Thus saith the Lord, The heavens are my throne and the earth is my footstool' – Isaiah 66.1] appears to account for this human inconsistency by the fact that, whilst men recognise the presence of God within the sanctuary, they are apt to ignore the important truth, that the Supreme Being is equally present without the temple, and that the immensity of His Spirit fills all space . . . I would that it were a failing less common amongst us, to approve openly what is right, and to do secretly what is wrong; to be impressed with truth, and to act in conformity with error; to manifest piety and humility within the synagogue, and to evince widely different qualities in our daily intercourse with the world . . .

On the holy Sabbath-day we devoutly pray to God 'to guard our tongues from evil, and our lips from uttering slander and deceit' and also to make us 'humble and courteous to all men'. We all feel the reasonableness of this prayer. But if, when we go forth again into the world after the service is over, we should permit ourselves to indulge in malevolent remarks on the character of our neighbour; if we should pronounce on him a hasty judgement, bearing on a case with regard to the merits of which we are but partially informed; if we should condemn him on vulgar report, or entertain a secret wish, from jealousy or rivalry, that the charge brought against him might be true; where, let me ask, would be the harmony between our prayer and our deeds, and how could we possibly escape the withering rebuke of the passage of our text?

Source: David Woolf Marks, *Lectures & Sermons*, Vol. II, pp. 40ff.

Freedom of opinion and independence of action have been amongst the demands of every epoch, because they are of intrinsic value, and constitute the inalienable privileges of rational beings. Nevertheless, in the practice of these principles there be many who depart very widely from their theory. Some there are who are too much given to subject their freedom of thought and action to human authority, whilst others are content to remain bond-slaves to custom and to precedent ...

Who can possibly estimate the amount of evil which has been inflicted upon the world by men who turn a deaf ear to the pleadings of conscience, and refrain from giving speech to their own matured convictions, so that they may go with the crowd and exhibit themselves for the time being as the idols of the thoughtless, before whose crude theories and impulsive passions they slavishly crouch? How many wars might have been prevented, and how much blood-guiltiness averted, if men, instead of hushing to silence their conscientious convictions at the bidding of party or faction, had had the honesty and the manly independence to speak out freely what course their innate sense of right prompted them to recommend and adopt? That human history is the history of progress is a truism which, within given limitations, can hardly be questioned. But it is humiliating to reflect on the interval that separates modern society from the morality of the passage of the text ['Thou shalt not follow after the multitude for evil' – Exodus 23.2] when we see men of intelligence and position, of whom a far different line of conduct might be expected, encouraging either directly by their speech, or indirectly by their silence and inaction, the prosecution of schemes which would almost resolve society into its primitive elements. They know well how delusive those schemes are, and how perilous would be the attempt to put them into practice; yet they promote what they are convinced would prove prejudicial to the general welfare, because they lack the manly courage from 'following after the multitude for evil'.

Source: David Woolf Marks, *Lectures & Sermons*, Vol. III, pp. 230, 233.

COMMENT: *Marks is able to use his rhetorical skills to good effect in lambasting those who neglect ethical imperatives. He targets in particular those who reserve their piety for the synagogue, but fail to act properly outside it. He is equally scathing on those who sin through omission and who fail to stand up for the moral course of action when they see others engaged in it or collude with it themselves.*

## 11.2 Morris Joseph on the Duty of Ethics (1893 ff.)

*For the Reverend Joseph, the moral teachings of Judaism were the most important yardstick by which the faith was to be judged. The adherence of individual Jews to such teachings determined whether or not they should be allowed to call themselves religious. It is noticeable that this was very much reflected in the titles he gave to his various books, which highlighted the ethical aspects of Judaism rather than historical themes or practical observances. The following two passages illustrate his insistence on the primacy of moral behaviour.*

Ah! let us be wise, and make a more resolute effort to win the higher life. It is within the powers of every one of us. For think not that it needs a saint to gain it. We have to provide no striking deed of self-abnegation; our duty is plain and simple and commonplace. The materials of the true life are about us, lining our worldly path, furnished by our daily work. To attain to it we have but to do common deeds nobly – so to bear ourselves in the prosaic struggle of the world as though we ever felt the eye of our Heavenly Master upon us, to take the humble clay of earth and fashion it into a vessel of divine beauty. Yes, remember this, I beseech you; for many a man and woman is deterred from entering the higher path because of its fancied impossibility. Nothing is demanded from us but what we can do. We are asked, not to realise the ideal, but only to put forth all the power we have in the attempt to reach it. We are not asked to be the best; we are asked to be better. All that we can all be, however untutored, however insignificant, however small our moral capacities. We need not be saints, but we can all be men – true men filled with the sense of what is due to our manhood, and determined to acquit ourselves of the solemn debt. To do our daily work better, more joyously, more honourably than ever, to purify our pleasures, to rob Self of more and more of its empire over our hearts – this is within the power of us all. This is life. This is joy that never fades.

Source: Morris Joseph, *The Ideal in Judaism*, pp. 108–10.

Rightly understood, the Golden Rule ['Thou shalt love thy neighbour as thyself' – Leviticus 19.18] affirms that all men have an equal claim with us to well-being. We possess no rights in this respect which we do not share with our neighbour. In modern philosophical language this is expressed by saying that no man is an individual – that is to say, a being with exclusive rights, which he may vindicate at the expense of others. Every man is a person, a man with a neighbour, with whom he shares his rights; and those rights he has accordingly to assert with an eye to the general good. Social morality, then, consists not in using our fellow-man, not in exploiting him, but in serving him, in practically recognising that he occupies a co-ordinate position with ourselves in the great republic of humanity. Thus we come back to the old Scriptural conceptions. All men are members of one great family, and all social obligation is summed up in the command to love them as oneself.

Thus the love which is enjoined upon us is seen to be, after all, but another name for justice. Forgiveness, forbearance, charity, merciful acts of every kind become the rightful due of our fellow-man, who, like ourself, is a unit of the human brotherhood. A distinction is sometimes drawn between justice and love, and the Pentateuch, which insists so strongly upon the grandeur of justice, is declared to have been properly superseded by the teaching of the Christian Scriptures which make the gentler version the exclusive ideal. But the distinction, with the argument founded upon it, is unwarranted. There is no real difference between justice and love. Love is justice. If my neighbour deserves my love, it is his due. Love, to be moral, must be justifiable – nought, that is, but justice. If people recognised this truth more clearly, they would be saved from the exaggerated and ill-considered philanthropy which works evil in the attempt to cure it. Deeds of mercy, too, would be done more mercifully. It is because charity, for example, is given so often as an act of grace, and not as a debt due to the poor, that it is given so ungraciously, and thus fails to achieve its great end – the closing of the rent that divides the social organism.

Source: Morris Joseph, *Judaism as Creed and Life*, pp. 397–8.

COMMENT: *Joseph is aware that lauding the virtues of ethical conduct may be entirely appropriate but also carries the danger of making it seem too removed from the daily reality of ordinary Jews, while Heavenly approval feels equally distant. Thus he is keen to emphasize both that moral conduct*

*is easily attainable and that it brings the immediate reward of personal satis-*
*faction. In addition, Joseph takes issue with the Christian-influenced view*
*that love operates in contradistinction to justice; instead he asserts that they*
*are inseparable: that love is the product of justice, while justice is motivated*
*by love.*


## 11.3  Leo Baeck on the Ethical Imperative (1905 ff.)

*Rabbi Dr Leo Baeck's books often had a dual purpose – an attempt to com-*
*municate the teachings of Judaism, but also to counter the negative inter-*
*pretations of the faith by some contemporary Christian writers, led by Adolf*
*Harnack. He was particularly at pains to oppose the suggestion that Juda-*
*ism should be dismissed as a maze of complex legalism or as a doctrine of*
*unforgiving retribution. For Baeck, like Reverend Joseph, the great glory*
*of Judaism was its ethical demands, and he was determined to show their*
*continuing relevance, as in the following two passages.*

But this emphasis on our neighbour's right, that which we are bound
to grant him is lifted above transitory emotional impulse and placed on
the solid ground of clear duty. One can always find warm hearts who in
a glow of emotion would like to make the whole world happy but who
have never attempted the sober experiment of bringing a real blessing to
a single human being. It is easy to revel enthusiastically in one's love of
man, but it is more difficult to do good to someone solely because he is
a human being. When we are approached by a human being demanding
his right, we cannot replace definite ethical action by mere vague good
will. How often has the mere love of one's neighbour been able to compromise and hold its peace!

Source: Leo Baeck, *Essence of Judaism*, p. 195.

The title fellow-man applies to every man. And he is our fellow-man by
God's appointment. It is not our goodwill, nor our kindness, nor is it any
social convention or legal enactment that makes him so. He is so by the
appointment of the One God, and therefore no man must deprive him
of his standing or reduce its meaning. Every human right means a claim

that our fellow-man has upon us as his birthright given to him by God. The commandment to 'do justly and love mercy' [Micah 6.8], which is announced to man and demanded from him, is to govern all behaviour towards our fellow-man. What we owe to God is to be paid first and chiefly to His children. In our relationship to them we find the sum of the duties that God has laid upon us: in our relationship to them we can manifest our love to God and our delight in His service. The appointed path to God is by way of our fellow-man. The social element is therefore an essential part of religion. To the Hebrew mind there can be no religion without our fellow-man. There is no religion in fleeing the world or separating oneself from it. The good man can be properly described only by the words 'just' and 'loving', which involve social relationship.

Source: Leo Baeck, *God and Man in Judaism*, pp. 56–7.

COMMENT: *Baeck, who elsewhere is eloquent about spiritual communion with God and its importance in Jewish life, is adamant here that there can be no meaningful relationship with the deity without a strong and active ethical base to one's life too. Moreover, whereas Baeck rarely attacks fellow-Jews in his writings, preferring to encourage rather than lambaste, it is noticeable that here he makes a powerful condemnation of those whose ethical words are never matched by ethical actions. As Werner van der Zyl – a student of Baeck and then later his colleague both in Germany and then in England – used to say: 'A man of faith has to make decisions between what is right and what is wrong, and not between what is right and what is expedient.'*

## 11.4 Harold Reinhart on Morality (1934)

*Rabbi Harold Reinhart was an assiduous editor of his synagogue's monthly newsletter, but rarely wrote for public consumption outside of it. One of his few essays for a wider readership was for a book composed of articles by Jewish and Christian religious leaders on aspects of the two faiths. Reinhart's article was on 'The Reality Of God' but he chose to begin it by emphasizing the ethical rather than spiritual consequences it held.*

Religion is still nine-tenths morality, and in human contact we humans approach God, receive God's revelations, and share His being. For whatever may be the fruits of speculative endeavour, no amount of logic will replace moral insight and ethical practice as ways of feeling the presence of God. The first mighty achievement of monotheism is that it establishes the unassailable sovereignty of the moral law. It is the discovery of the inevitability of truth, the insistence of the ideal standard through which all else derives meaning. The revelation of this standard is the self-revelation of the God of truth and love.

Source: Harold Reinhart, 'The Reality of God', in *In Spirit and in Truth: Aspects of Judaism and Christianity*, p. 41.

COMMENT: *Reinhart was renowned for his deep personal sense of God and his intense belief in the power of prayer; yet, like Baeck, he recognized that spirituality cannot exist without ethics, and that engaging in the latter is a means of achieving the former.*

## 11.5 Howard Cooper on the Precondition to Ethics (1996)

*Rabbi Cooper was a communal rabbi for some years before becoming a full-time psychotherapist. His writings combine both disciplines and often seek to explore deeper personal insights within the Jewish tradition.*

One of the most commonplace rationalizations used for ethical behaviour, even by those not consciously identifying with the Judaeo-Christian religious heritage, is the biblical command 'You shall love your neighbour as yourself' (Leviticus 19. 18). When I ask myself how I approach this in my own life, the inevitable question with which I am faced is this: Can I really love my neighbour if I don't love myself? Which means asking: if I am depressed, angry, bitter or frustrated, can I say that I love myself? And if I don't love myself – or if I go through long or short periods when I don't feel very loving towards myself – to what extent can I show love or genuine concern to anyone else? If I experience self-denigration or self-hatred, how do I move from that feeling of stuckness and resentment to the real love of self necessary for truly reaching out to others:

family, friends, colleagues, clients, congregants, neighbours? . . . [When the saintly] nineteenth-century Lithuanian rabbi, Israel Salanter writes 'our self-love comes to us naturally without any calculations, limits or aims', the rabbi within me feels moved by the theory and the sentiment behind this, and the apparent reality it possessed in and for the man who wrote it. The therapist within me questions this as a true statement for the reality of our psychological make-up . . . The ethical ideal and command 'You shall love your neighbour as yourself' becomes a possibility when I accept that 'I can love my neighbour only to the extent to which I love myself'.

. . . How often in a first encounter, or even after knowing someone for years, we feel their pain, their inner wounds, their fragility or vulnerability. Often covered over by a persona of bluff or bravado, jokes or sarcasm, aggression or seductiveness, we still sense that silent (or not-so-silent) cry of the soul: I feel hurt, I feel sad, I feel uncared for, I feel unloved. And if we do not acknowledge those feelings within ourselves we cannot really hear them in the other, or respond to them. If we cannot bear our own pain, we cannot bear to hear it in another. And then we respond only to the outer person. We cannot 'love our neighbour' truly until we know and love ourselves. And knowing oneself does mean knowing the Nazi within us as well as the Jew; the persecutor as well as the victim; the villain as well as the hero; the devil as well as God.

Source: Howard Cooper (ed.), *Soul Searching: Studies in Judaism and Psychotherapy*, pp. xx–xxv.

COMMENT: *Cooper departs from the usual interpretation of Jewish ethics – the relationship with others as a reflection of one's relationship with God – and focuses instead on each individual's self-relationship as the key to ethical behaviour. His statement that every Jew contains 'the Nazi within' may offend some, but is a dramatic reminder of the swirling range of needs, desires and faults within everyone, which must temper their response to others.*

## A Final Thought . . .

[A practical tip:] The main things you can give [to others] are your attention and consideration. Nobody ever gets enough of either. In this most people are givers not takers. Very few of us listen with all our attention or have an understanding heart. Don't worry if you are rejected. Other people are suspicious if someone else tries to help them – they've probably been rejected too many times to trust. There's that chap by the bar getting sloshed and everybody is whispering 'tut tut'. If he hasn't yet got sloshed, try to find out what's the matter. If he's an oldie, he might have come back to a place he used to enjoy with his partner but is now bereaved or divorced. He might have been used to a lot of money, and now lives on a small pension. It helps if he can talk a bit about his problems or his partner's. But do listen. Don't pretend to listen, that's easily spotted and rightly disdained.

Source: Lionel Blue and Jonathan Magonet, *Sun, Sand and Soul*, p. 102.

# 12

# EVIL AND SIN

The existence of evil in a world created by a benign God is one of the most perplexing questions that Judaism has to confront. As Judaism subscribes to a belief in an all-knowing and all-powerful God, it means that evil exists because God actively created it or allows others to develop it.

There is no notion of a hostile power that exists in opposition to God and which is responsible for humans sinning against God's will. This in turn raises questions as to why God chose to allow evil, what purpose it serves, and how humans can best respond to evil inclinations within themselves or around them.

## 12.1 David Woolf Marks on Avoiding Sin (1856)

*Reverend Professor Marks was concerned less with analysing the causes of evil and more with tackling its existence. He had no doubt that those who sinned could not escape facing dire consequences, if not in this world then in the world to come. He sought to use the fear of such punishment to establish a preventative code of behaviour.*

To approach the state that lies beyond the grave, and where all human deeds come up for judgement, with no companion but conscience, and with a self-accusing heart, is beyond question the severest penalty that can be laid upon the man of crime. Let us be heedful of the following recommendations. First, let us cultivate the habit of the Psalmist of 'communing with our hearts when we lie down on our beds' (Psalm 4.5) so that each night may admonish us of the evil things which we may have done through precipitancy or error, and remind us of the good things we may have failed to do when we had the power and opportunity to perform them. Secondly, let us enter into a rigid account with conscience before we venture to pronounce upon ourselves so partial a judgement so as to induce the supposition that no vice stains our character and no impurity defiles our heart. For when wrong-doing becomes habitual to us, conscience falls into a kind of lethargic sleep and ceases to remonstrate so long as life goes prosperously with us. Thirdly, let us fear sin for its own native deformity, and not merely because it may find us out before men, and subject us to their censure or scorn. If we be influenced by no higher motive, then the source of amendment will be dried up within us. Lastly, let it well be remembered that if a man of crime should succeed in wearing the hypocrite's mask throughout his career, there is a righteous and infallible Judge, before whom no subterfuge can avail – a Judge who will reverse all false judgements based on outward appearances and make the sin of the sinner to find him out.

Source: David Woolf Marks, *Lectures & Sermons*, Vol. II, pp. 37–9.

COMMENT: *Marks excelled as a preacher rather than a theologian, and the passage exemplifies this strength. He is utterly confident in his assertion that sin never goes undetected and his four-fold formula offers believers a path to avoid the doom he assures them is otherwise inevitable.*

## 12.2 Morris Joseph on Satan (1903)

*Reverend Joseph was very conscious that Jews were often influenced by Christian concepts of evil and sin – especially as the very name Satan appears in the Hebrew Bible. He was keen to clarify the Jewish view and differentiate it from Church teachings.*

It is true that a being called the 'Hinderer' or the 'Adversary' (in Hebrew, Satan) does mysteriously flash here and there across the pages of the Old Testament. He comes upon the scene very fitfully and for brief periods only . . . this malevolent Being is not real, but imaginary only . . . a mere personification of Evil, of the evil that is in the world and in the hearts of men . . . To believe in a devil is to degrade our conception of God. It is to depose Him from the high throne on which He sits in majestic solitude, and to make Him share His rule with a rival. It is to degrade man also. It is to deny him that absolute moral freedom which is his inalienable birthright. It is to impeach man and God together. For if man is so poor a creature as to be the sport of a malignant Power, who can make him sin and suffer in his own despite, then is the beneficent God weak indeed, seeing that He is powerless to prevent such iniquity.

Source: Morris Joseph, *Judaism as Creed and Life*, pp. 67–8.

COMMENT: *Joseph is adamant that belief in an evil force independent of God – which implies a limit to God's power – is incompatible with Jewish thinking.*

### 12.3  Tony Bayfield on Everyday Sin (1985)

*The previous passage by Reverend Joseph expressed the Reform view so comprehensively that rabbis writing on the subject in subsequent decades largely echoed his thoughts. A wider perspective was obtained in 1985, when a new edition of High Holy Day prayer book was published which included an extensive study anthology on the nature of sin and repentance. Among the numerous readings quoted was one by Rabbi Bayfield on the sin of prejudice.*

The consequences of prejudice may be so enormous and terrible that they seem far beyond the commonplace of our own lives. What has such evil to do with us? Yet the roots and mechanisms of prejudice lie all too commonly within ourselves. There is projection, the process by which we blame others for faults we do not wish to accept in ourselves: the quarrel, the upset, the accident, the recession, which is always the other man's fault. There is displacement, by which we take out on others pent-up feelings which have nothing, in reality, to do with them: the wife who suffers for a husband's bad day at work; the immigrant who is blamed for unemployment – for it would be impolitic to have a row with the boss or client, and who can punch a world economic force on its nose? Finally there is rationalisation, by which we invent respectable reasons to justify our true motives, and then forget the former and come to believe in the latter: fear, envy and greed all too easily become seductively transformed into sweet reason. It may be difficult to relate such ordinary sins to concentration camps or to street violence but who can honestly say he never projects blame, displaces anger or rationalises selfishness? And who can say that he never hurts others in the process?

Source: Tony Bayfield, in Lionel Blue and Jonathan Magonet (eds), *Forms of Prayer for Jewish Worship: Prayers for the High Holy Days*, p. 710.

COMMENT: *Bayfield's passage is significant not just because of what it says about the nature of prejudice but because of the two implications it carries: first, sin is not something awesome that only the truly evil commit but is a fault common to all in everyday life and therefore has to be recognized by everybody; second, the roots of these relatively small sins are the same as much greater ones, and so the need to guard against them occurring in oneself or society at large is ever-present.*

## 12.4  Howard Cooper on Good and Evil (1992)

*When Rabbi Cooper was asked to give a paper on Good and Evil to the Institute of Group Analysis, he felt it important to distinguish Jewish beliefs from Christian ones, and particularly to challenge the notion of evil as a phenomenon which exists autonomously of human beings.*

In a way Jewish theology has had an advantage over Christian theology with regard to preventing a radical split developing between the concepts of good and evil. I think this has to do with how the tradition symbolises God. The Hebrew Bible makes no effort to present a picture of God as good. God is portrayed as a character who is not only loving, generous, passionate and so on but also angry, jealous, perverse, whimsical, and destructive. Christian teaching saw this as evidence of the primitive, unenlightened nature of the so-called 'old' testament and, by extension, of Judaism, which was superseded by the teaching of the new testament where goodness resides in God and in Christ, and badness is split off into the devil, Satan and (in the later books) the Jews. But this kind of theological thinking actually misses the subtlety of the Hebrew Biblical thinking. In some ways it is actually a regression back into a paranoid-schizoid form of thinking, which ignores the ambivalence and paradoxes of the Hebrew world-view. When Isaiah speaks in the name of his God, he seems very aware of the need for human beings to hold the tension between opposites because this is a true *imitatio dei*: 'I form the light and create darkness, I make peace/wholeness and create evil. I am YHWH who is doing all of this' (Isaiah 45.7). The view that our aggressive and sexual energies can be sublimated – and that this might be a healthy and creative transformation of energies which can be destructive – this view enters into Jewish thought as a way of countering the instinct to polarise good and evil into mutually exclusive areas of human experience.

Source: Howard Cooper, 'Good and Evil', unpublished lecture paper sent to the author.

COMMENT: *Cooper provides a novel insight to the traditional Jewish view that there is no external evil force that exists in opposition to God. As this can be taken to mean that God therefore encompasses both good and evil, Cooper asserts that the Jewish concept of God is a much more appropriate role model for people. It can help individuals relate to the competing inclinations within themselves, and regard them as natural to the human condition. It also implies that the sin is not having evil inclinations, but pursuing them.*

## A Final Thought . . .

I remember my first trip to Germany. I was nineteen years old . . . going to a German–Jewish reconciliation meeting. The students we met were all born after the war. They also had long hair and jeans. After a short official meeting we adjourned to the local beer-house. They were all members of the New Left. The conversation flowed easily. At midnight I stood up in order to leave. I had drunk a great deal and I thought everyone was going home. 'Please,' said one of the student leaders, 'will you stay and talk to me?' 'Yes, of course,' I said, and sat down. I did not know what was coming. He began: 'You mentioned in your talk tonight that many of your family were killed in concentration camps. Do you know in which camps?'

'I am not sure exactly. Auschwitz, I think, and Treblinka.' 'Do you know in which year they died?' I had no idea why he was asking these questions. I said: 'The last news we received was in 1942, through a letter via the Red Cross.' 'In 1942,' he said, 'my father was an SS guard in Auschwitz.' Suddenly I was sober. I could not think what to say. Thoughts came rushing into my mind. I can remember them with crystal clarity. I did not want to go through this meeting. I wanted to be anywhere else in the world but not in this place with this boy. We had met before, he and I, through our families. What sort of meeting had that been? In what conditions? I stared and said nothing. I did not know his position. Did he think his father was right? He spoke again. 'I found this out three years ago. I have not spoken to my father since that day.' My initial feeling was relief. Now I knew where he stood. I sat back and tried to place myself in his position. What would it be like to discover that my father, the man who had brought me up, the man who I loved, had done such things? I could not imagine it. I could not imagine how one could live with such knowledge. It was so much easier to be the son of the victim than to be the son of the executioner.

The pause grew and became a silence. Then he said: ' I have been waiting for you to come. I want to know what I should do?' Did I think he should go back and visit his father? The following day I spoke to an older German Jew. How would he have answered the boy's question? He replied: 'I would have praised him for leaving home. He should not see his father.' I had responded differently. I had told the boy to go back to his father, to try to understand the man. It is not only that I believe that family is of prime importance. We can never escape our parents. We carry them with us. But there was also another reason. If the New Left does not try to understand what it was like to be a member of the Old Right, there is a danger that they will merely repeat the old mistakes with new labels.

Source: Daniel Smith, 'The Faith of the Fathers; the Heart of the Children', *European Judaism*, 10.2, 1976, pp. 10–11.

# 13

# GOD

Central to Judaism is its belief in God. It gave birth to monotheism and then carried that message from ancient times to modernity, inspiring Christianity and Islam in the process. Yet the Bible itself largely avoids describing what or who is God, and concentrates instead on what God does and what God expects of humanity. The opening sentence of Genesis talks of creation rather than the Creator. There is no record of the religious search by which the first Jew, Abraham, found God, because God found Abraham and started a long series of commands as to how he and his descendants should behave. It is for this reason that Judaism has often been summarized as a religion of 'deed rather than creed'. This may be simplistic, but it is not wrong. Throughout the centuries, many rabbinic writers have speculated as to the nature of God, but such attempts were vastly outnumbered by discourses on the commandments. One of the aims of Reform Judaism was to restore the importance of worship and faith in a religion that at times seemed dominated by regulations and prohibitions.

## 13.1 Morris Joseph on Knowing God (1903)

*Reverend Joseph knew that it was impossible to describe God fully using the limitations of human insights and vocabulary. Yet, as a teacher of Judaism, it was also impossible not to attempt such a description, especially as that was the great question-mark that everyone wanted answered.*

To God our existence is due, and to Him, therefore, we owe obedience. He is the potter and we are the clay. Reverence and humility, then, are the feelings with which we must regard Him. But we think of Him with other feelings too. For he is a merciful God, whose mercies claim our gratitude and affection. He is not only our King, but our Father, our Father who orders our lives lovingly. God is not the mere Force or Intelligence, which some thinkers see in the universe, and which suffices to explain to them its existence and wonders. Nor is he a far-off, soulless Being, shut up in a remote Heaven without thought or feeling for mankind. Close relations exist between God and man, and they are mutual relations . . . The Jewish Creed has always been in a fluid condition, and Judaism leaves us free to construct our own theology, so long as we do not trench upon certain easily recognised principles which could not be discarded without destroying the religion itself. To deny the existence of God, for example, or His unity or His spiritual nature, or to deny His providential government of the world in general, or the Divine appointment of Israel in particular.

. . . and though it is an unseen God who is our father, we can still love Him. For God is manifest to the subtler gaze of the soul, revealed in the illumination of prayer or in calm hours of meditation. Nor is it an unknown Being we are asked to love. We cannot look upon God's face and read His character there; but His beneficent work in nature and in our lives is before us, and from that we can learn about Him and in a measure know Him.

Source: Morris Joseph, *Judaism as Creed and Life*, pp. 6, 41–2, 335.

COMMENT: *Joseph employs traditional terms to describe God – King, Father – and the Jewish insistence that God is both awesome Creator yet also a Being with whom it is possible to have a personal relationship. Knowledge of God comes both from this intimacy and from the evidence of God's handiwork. However, he departs from many other writers by highlighting the flexibility within Jewish thinking about God and the fact that individuals 'construct our own theology' within certain parameters. Some might consider this a recipe for anarchy, but it has always been a little-publicized hallmark of Judaism that Joseph chooses to celebrate as a virtue.*

## 13.2 Morris Joseph on a Life with God (1907)

*Reverend Joseph had described the Jewish approach to God in his earlier writings quoted above. However, he had not sought to justify the very idea of belief in God. Aware that modern Jews were as likely to be influenced by the ideas of humanism as by other faiths, he now turned his attention to this issue.*

Unlike creed, which is an affair of the intellect, religion is an affair of the heart, the life. It is a life. It is the God-idea come to birth. It is not belief about God, but belief in Him – living, vitalizing, ennobling belief. It is our consciousness of His existence, of His constant contact with us, of our dependence upon Him, of our duty towards Him, in action, shaping our morality, influencing the details, the very tone of our daily lives.

This is important for man in two ways. His conduct and his happiness are both involved. To have faith in the Unseen, to live in conscious touch with it, is to have the mightiest of all impulses to righteousness. It is to feel that in our struggle after the good, we have the sympathy of the Highest, that for every throb of admiration that virtue wins from our hearts, every thrill of pain that the effort after it costs us, there is a corresponding beat of the Universal heart. Moreover to believe in God is to be happy. It is to live in an elevated and serene atmosphere where the storms of this lower life cannot reach us. It is to be fortified against the temptation not only of sin, but of pain – of our own pain or the infinitely greater pain of the world – the temptation to break with morality altogether. That it is possible to live for goodness without living for God, to be righteous without being religious, I will not attempt to deny. But as compared to the religious man you will be heavily handicapped. The support and courage which he gets from his faith you will lack. For he knows that he has God on his side. Where are the angelic helpers you have to match?

Source: Morris Joseph, *The Message of Judaism*, pp. 126–8.

COMMENT: *Joseph seeks to enthuse rather than persuade. He offers the benefits of belief in God rather than arguments proving the reality of God. This approach undoubtedly reinforces existing believers but will not necessarily win over those uncertain or opposed to faith. He is to be admired for so candidly admitting that non-believers can be equally righteous, but his lament that they lack 'angelic helpers' probably does not bother them.*

## 13.3 Leo Baeck on Life without God (1905)

*Rabbi Dr Baeck wrote extensively on the relation of the individual to God, regarding it as the characteristic feature of Judaism and extolling the positive reasons for embracing belief in God. However, he was also aware that there were other forces that led to God.*

Man seems to be bordered by loneliness on every side. He seems to stand in the midst of the world, in infinite space and in endless time. Together with this loneliness of time and space, there arises the loneliness of fleeting, finite life coerced by causality. This is the feeling of being forsaken and subject to the inevitable. Without God life is a lonely darkness, even for the man who is in the midst of many other men and even for the man who enjoys pleasures and power. It is the loneliness of the man whose soul is far from all that is real, eternal and sublime. In this forlorn state man trembles with despair when he seeks to answer those questions about life that he cannot evade.

It is precisely from this fear that there arises the yearning for that illuminating and harmonizing One who is the creator of all eternity. The man who knows this yearning is lifted out of his forlornness; his night is filled with light and his soul redeemed from despair. Whoever knows himself to be bound to the one and eternal God knows no loneliness, for his life is never solitary. No matter how intimately we may come into contact with our fellow man we still remain alone in our innermost soul, for every person is unique upon earth and loneliness is part of individuality. But in God our life finds its peace.

Source: Leo Baeck, *Essence of Judaism*, pp. 143–4.

COMMENT: *Baeck follows in the footsteps of the Psalmist who refers to his soul as 'the lonely one' (Psalms 22.21, 35.17). He recognizes that it is not just the righteous light of God that attracts individuals, but also the cold darkness of life that propels them towards God. This might apply to some people and not to others, but it also may be true of the same person at different stages in their life.*

### 13.4  Harold Reinhart on the Reality of God (1934)

*Rabbi Reinhart was renowned for being imbued with a passionate sense of God which guided him throughout his life and was one of the hallmarks of his ministry. The extract below is from an essay for Christian readers on the Jewish understanding of God, but in which his own view is apparent.*

Although we know well that the attempt to prove the existence of God is foolhardy, yet we never tire of discussing His reality and justifying the ways of God to man. This is as it should be so long as we, as 'religious' men and women, do not forget that it is with God we start. We do not prove our way to God: we are with God: and with Him we find the ways of life . . . And our sense of Divinity leaps to scale the heavens and holds communion with sweet, soft comfort from an unseen Source. What if we see through a glass darkly? We still possess that yearning which testifies to the God of eternal and unquenchable Being more eloquently than any reasoning – that yearning which mocks the rigid rationalist with 'Canst thou with searching find out God?' We still possess something of that childlike feeling-at-home in this spiritual world that enable us to say 'The nearness of God is my good' (Psalm 73.28).

And it is this religious sense, which may be said to combine humility, wonder and longing, which is the basis of our approach to the Throne of God. This is the secret of our nature which marks us as the 'sons of God', and which makes us recognise His reality because we are of His spirit. Without this we should only know about Him; because we are as we are, we know Him, and knowing Him, we can enjoy Him. That is why 'personal religion' is the only real religion. Much thought and activity which go under the name of religion because they are in keeping with a religious spirit or associated with a religious institution, good and wholesome as they may be, are not the essence. Only if we look into our souls and find there the sense of mystery and the passion to pursue that mystery, which is the meaning of worship, do we unveil the reality of our religion; just to look into our souls and discover abandonment to God is to know immortality. Though we cannot reach His Throne, he reaches down to us. His spirit in our hearts, His whisper in our conscience, His summons to our constant effort, His answer to our yearning, these are the tokens of the God who is near to every humble soul.

Source: Harold Reinhart, 'The Reality of God', in *In Spirit and in Truth: Aspects of Judaism and Christianity*, p. 41–3.

COMMENT: *Reinhart writes not so much as a teacher of Judaism but as a believer in Judaism, sharing his own deep faith. His assertion that 'personal religion is the only real religion' epitomizes his own position, and is in stark contrast to those who value Judaism for its provision of legal codes or communal structures.*

## 13.5 Andre Ungar on the Attributes of God (1958)

*When, after a long period of stagnation, the Reform synagogues began to grow in Britain in the 1950s, Rabbi Dr Ungar was charged with writing a summary of Reform beliefs and practices. Although a personal composition, it reflected the views of the Reform rabbinate as a whole.*

We believe in the One God; the God of Abraham, Isaac and Jacob; the God of Israel, of all mankind and of the whole universe. With our forefathers and all Jewish generations, we humbly acknowledge that within and beyond the visible, passing order of things there is an eternal, divine mystery – a God who is One and universal, the source of all being, truth and beauty. It is from him that our very existence derives; in Him we find life's point, programme and meaning; our purpose as well as our happiness.

In the line of perennial Jewish tradition, we regard it as vain presumption even to try to offer a rational proof of God's existence and nature. It is not by a process of logical argument, nor in the limited evidence of our bodily sense, that we seek and find the ground of our faith. Our anchorage in God is affected through the direct, deep spiritual craving of the soul, through the accumulated illumination in our tradition of the wise and saintly of many ages.

Our trembling notion of God, while not rooted in reason, is subject to the pruning of rational thought. Faith in the Divine Being on the one hand, and knowledge gained through the advance of dispassionate science on the other, must exist side by side harmoniously. Thus, sincerely as we believe all existence is, in the full sense of the word, Creation, an effect of God's will, we think it a mistake to attach literal significance to the biblical account which clashes with the findings of archaeology, history, geology and biology. Again, with regard to miracles related in our holy books, we think it a greater praise of God (and a more acceptable truth concerning Him) to hold that He maintains an ever orderly, law-abiding universe rather than one the rules of which are occasionally and arbitrarily suspended.

We are aware of the sad inadequacy of all mortal ideas and words gropingly used to comprehend or express God's being and nature. Yet we feel that the terms Power and Wisdom, Justice and Compassion can serve as vague pointers to the God we love and worship and try to obey.

Source: Andre Ungar, *Living Judaism*, pp. 2–3.

COMMENT: *Ungar's first two paragraphs hold true of the Jewish view of God in general – the God perceived and handed down by tradition. It is his third paragraph that highlights the distinctive Reform approach, which tries to reconcile the traditional view with modern insights and regards such harmonization as essential. He concludes by singling out four main attributes of God, with the implication that these are godly qualities which are best admired by being emulated in our own lives.*

## 13.6 Lionel Blue on Searching for God (1985)

*When the new liturgy for the High Holy Days was being planned in the 1980s, it was felt important that it should not only contain prayers to God, but also examine the very act of communicating with God. Whereas previous generations of Jews had often been content just to recite the set prayers,*

*this generation was less certain – or perhaps, more accurately, was prepared
to admit it was less certain – about the very issue of God.*

Meeting God can be very simple. If it is not simple, and no voice speaks
in our silence, and no hand reaches down to meet ours in trust, then we
should ask ourselves these questions, for the mistake may be ours.

Perhaps God cannot be Himself to us, because we are not ourselves,
our true selves, to Him. We have not prayed to Him as we are, but as we
feel we ought to be, or as others want us to be, or as what we think He
thinks we ought to be. This last is the most difficult to unravel because it
hides a confusion or a blasphemy.

Perhaps God meets us and we do not recognise Him. He may speak to
us in a chance remark we overhear, through a stray thought in our mind,
or by a word from the prayerbook that resonates in us. Perhaps a side
door is the only door we have left open to Him. The others we defended
and barred, so He must steal into us as a thief in the night.

Perhaps we do not like what He says, but are frightened to say so, and
so we pretend we never met Him, and indeed could not meet Him for He
is only an idea. The avoidance is natural because in the sight of God our
success can seem failure, and our ambitions dust.

Perhaps we are satisfied with our lives and do not want to meet Him.
So we chant our prayers and sing our hymns to prevent a few moments'
silence, for He speaks in the silence.

Perhaps we have not allowed God to judge us because we have already
judged Him, and anticipated His word. He may love us more than we
know; He may know us better than we know ourselves; He may still surprise us.

Perhaps we are frightened where He may lead us. He may send us
from our father's house; He may bring us to the wilderness; He may let
us wander in it for forty years; He may ask us to find our security in what
we cannot touch. Will He give us courage equal to our need if we pray?

Meeting God can be simple, but nothing can happen if we do not will
it. If we seek the Lord He can be found; He will allow us to find Him if we
seek Him with all our might.

Source: Lionel Blue and Jonathan Magonet (eds), *Forms of Prayer for Jewish Worship:
Prayers for the High Holy Days*, pp. 310–11.

COMMENT: *Blue's piece is a contemplative meditation on God rather than a theological description of God, but it is valuable for what it implies about the state of belief among most worshippers. It assumes that a high percentage of modern Jews are either hesitant believers or have convinced themselves that they need not bother coming to terms with the God question. The passage is arresting in its honesty, while its assertion that God 'must steal into us as a thief in the night' helped establish a new realism with which future rabbis were to approach the task of teaching belief in God.*

### 13.7  Howard Cooper on the God Within (1991)

*A notable feature of the Reform rabbinate in the 1980s and 1990s was that a number also became involved in psychotherapy. Rabbi Cooper was not only among them but acted as a bridge between the two disciplines, seeking to utilize the insights of each to enlighten the other.*

God's love, goodness, transcendence and imminence are some of the foundation stones of Jewish theology. But mentally wrestle as we must with these building blocks of belief, the major stumbling block for traditional notions of God is the incontrovertible human experience of suffering and evil. Something just keeps on intruding into the cosy pictures we create: our own experiences of pain, sadness, despair and meaninglessness continually threaten to undermine our theological home.

For many of those Jews who come to me as a therapist, no amount of traditional thinking can bridge the gap between what Judaism teaches about life's meaning and how life is actually experienced day-by-day.

. . . Immanuel Kant's enquiry into the process by which the human mind converts formless experience into ordered objective knowledge led him to a change of viewpoint as revolutionary as that of Copernicus. Kant saw that the mind 'does not receive objectivity: it confers it'. The principles by which we make sense of the world are not in a world above us, as Plato had suggested, but in our own heads. When that which creates order out of chaos is seen to be ourselves, this spells the end of the objective God of realist theology. When certain traditionalist images of God are seen as the mythic projections of the human mind, we enter a new world of thinking. A question here presses upon us: to what extent has Judaism really allowed in, let alone adapted itself to, the implications of this new way of thinking? Most of the time we still seem to be religious flat-earthers.

. . . If God is not 'out there' any more, if God is not 'factual' but a self-constructed ideal which gives worth to our lives, much of traditional Jewish theological speculation becomes redundant. The death of the old notions of an external God takes us into relatively uncharted religious territory. It is here that the insights of psychotherapy can become our spiritual resource. We can take back our projections onto God and recognise our personal dependence and collective interdependence on our own human capacities for love, goodness, justice and mercy – all the old attributes we ascribe to God. They are in us – and their potential is both infinite and divine. What hinders our human capacity thus hinders the divine in us. What helps deepen and develop our sense of meaning and purpose become our religious responsibility to use.

. . . We may not be able to keep our traditional God. Judaism may have to discard theism as it discarded animal sacrifices. The projection of human needs onto a deity is part of a child's needs within adult thinking. Mature religiosity has to move beyond this. The interiorisation of the divine will follow our discarding of outmoded models of an external parental God.

. . . Psychotherapeutic thinking can help religion grow up. It can suggest that living with ambivalence is a spiritual achievement. And that certainty in our thinking is not a goal but an obstacle to maturity. It can encourage religious believers to simply affirm a set of values to which they aspire, with a God image which allows religious ideals to function freely and which grows and develops as the believer struggles with the vicissitudes of life. Such a believer will be unable to make objective statements about the existence of God, merely affirm subjectively that a notion of God is being constructed – quite probably in dialogue with the tradition – as a way of creating personal meaning. This is consistent with the Jewish mission, as I understand it – to aspire to be 'Yisrael/Israel': the one who struggles with God . . . Any post-Holocaust theology must struggle by way of paradox. The psychological and spiritual journey does not fear paradox, does not try to resolve the innate tensions of human existence. To be a Jew is to live with paradox. To be a religious Jew is to celebrate paradox.

Source: Howard Cooper, 'Jewish Belief and the Health of the Jewish Soul', *Manna*, 32, Theology Supplement.

COMMENT: *Cooper proposes an understanding of God that is radically at variance with both Orthodox and Reform thinking. It contradicts the idea of an external Power that reveals moral values and demands ritual observances. It might be questioned whether Cooper's God can be separated from one's own ego, subject to personal whims and changing temperament. It is also difficult to understand how this highly individual concept of religion can provide sufficient authority for communal structures and commonly recognized standards of behaviour. However, it is a response to a sense of dissatisfaction with the traditional view of God, and the fact that it appeared in the main journal of the Reform movement – albeit without endorsement – is an acknowledgement that it deserves serious attention.*

### 13.8  Jonathan Romain on the Consequences of God (1991)

*The chapter on God in* Faith and Practice – A Guide to Reform Judaism *re-affirmed the traditional view of God as the source of creation and revelation. However, it also raised the question as to what degree such beliefs were essential to one's Jewish identity.*

The tendency amongst many Jews to describe Judaism as a way of life rather than a faith may seem to give a low priority to the importance of faith. However, it reflects the fact that it is the consequences of faith, rather than the faith itself, that are significant. Arising from belief in God, however expressed, are several statements that are also indispensable to Judaism: that the world has a purpose, that life has meaning, that all people are equal, that each individual is unique, needs to be treated with dignity, and has a role to play. In similar vein, it is the practical consequences of prayer that are as important as the act of communion itself. Thus Jews pray to God not only to praise God, but also to remind themselves how they should behave. By declaring how God cares for the living, supports the falling, heals the sick and free prisoners, one expresses appreciation of the attributes of God and also sets out a programme for one's duties as a Jew. Belief and action are inseparable in Judaism. The Reform prayer book both affirms the presence of God in daily life and proclaims the path of righteousness which the Jew is obliged to follow . . . Belief in God is central to Judaism. However one is not required to profess any particular belief as a condition of membership. Judaism has always valued personal conduct above purity of faith.

Source: Jonathan Romain, *Faith and Practice: A Guide to Reform Judaism Today*, pp. 30, 156.

COMMENT: *The passage asserts not so much that modern Jews have doubts about the nature of God, but that the issue is not critical for many of them. They are more interested in what God expects of them, than the nature of the God they believe in. Some will counter that this ignores the many theological questions that ordinary Jews do have; others will argue that one of Judaism's characteristics is a profound disinterest in theology compared to other faiths. Perhaps both views are true, which is why some Jews can feel frustrated in their religious search.*

### 13.9  Alexandra Wright on Sensing God (1997)

*In an essay on faith and spirituality Rabbi Wright surveyed the writings of various religious thinkers who suggested that it was no longer possible to believe in a personal transcendent God, However, although she understood their arguments, she felt dissatisfied at the lack of meaningful alternatives that they presented and found herself rebelling against their conclusions.*

Whether we like it or not, we are propelled towards the search for some understanding of why we are here. What is the purpose of our existence? Is there something beyond the finite? Is God merely a projection of our wish-fulfilment, or does God exist independently, objectively? There has to be something more. There has to be a mystery that exists beyond ourselves, a mystery that can inspire within each human breast a feeling of awe and reverence. I know that there does exist some reality beyond the temporal and spatial reality which you and I experience every day. I know, too, that it is possible to touch that reality, or to encounter it, perhaps only for a split second, and to see oneself as one really is in the universe, infinitesimally small and insignificant, but at the same time a magnificent creature of creation.

If you have seen a new moon appear from behind a cloud at night, or watched a blood red sun drop slowly into the ocean, or stood in your community listening to the prayers being sung by the people. If you have walked along Jerusalem's streets for the first time, marvelling at the people and their language and their ancient faith, or stood alone at Masada in darkness before the sun has even appeared. If you have watched the faces of children by the Sabbath candles, or comforted a widow in her grief and sorrow, or witnessed the struggling victim of abuse come to terms with the harm inflicted and re-invest herself with dignity and grace. If you have lost your temper and persecuted some poor hapless victim standing near you, or cried when Rabin and Arafat shook hands for a second time and wished the broken world would mend itself for pity's sake, then you would know that there is a God, more than the sum total of our human values, more than [Mordecai] Kaplan's mental construct. We wait for those brief moments to experience something of this wondrous reality, we wait and we will continue to wait, as the Psalmist says: 'My soul waits for the Eternal One.' We may not be Moses on Mount Sinai, or Isaiah caught up in the Temple. But ordinary men and women that we are, we each know that we have known in the past moments of heightened awareness and a perception of another reality which I would like to name God.

Source: Alexandra Wright, 'Barefoot by the Bush', *Manna*, 56, Theology Supplement.

COMMENT: *Wright puts her case for God on an unashamedly emotional basis, the instinct of the soul, and as the only possible conclusion to the wonder of life. There may be many counter-arguments, especially from those whose lives are characterized by suffering and deprivation, but Wright's response will no doubt strike a chord in the hearts of many, even if their minds still contain question marks.*

## A Final Thought . . .

A man was going from village to village, everywhere asking the same question, 'Where can I find God?' He journeyed from rabbi to rabbi, and nowhere was he satisfied with the answers he received, so quickly he would pack his bags, and hurry on to the next village. Some of the rabbis replied, 'Pray, my son, and you shall find Him.' But the man had tried to pray, and knew that he could not. And some replied, 'Study, my child and you shall find Him.' But the more he read, the more confused he became, and the further he seemed from God. And some replied 'Forget your quest, my child, God is within you.' But the man had tried to find God within himself, and failed.

One day, the man arrived wearily at a very small village set in the middle of a forest. He went up to a woman who was minding some chickens, and she asked whom he could be looking for in such a small place, but she did not seem surprised when he told her that he was looking for God. She showed him to the rabbi's house.

When he went in, the rabbi was studying. He waited for a moment, but he was impatient to be off to the next village, if he could not be satisfied. Then he interrupted, 'Rabbi – how do I find God?' The rabbi paused, and the man wondered which of the many answers he had already received he would be told this time. But the rabbi simply said, 'You have come to the right place, my child, God is in this village. Why don't you stay a few days; you might meet Him.'

The man was puzzled, he did not understand what the rabbi could mean. But the answer was unusual, and so he stayed. For two or three days, he strode round and round, asking all the villagers where God was that morning, but they would only smile and ask him to have a meal with them. Gradually, he got to know them, and even helped with some of the village work. Every now and then he would see the rabbi by chance, and the rabbi would ask him, 'Have you met God yet, my son?' And the man would smile, and sometimes he understood and sometimes he did not understand. For months he stayed in the village, and then for years. He became part of the village and shared in all its life. He went with the men to the synagogue on Friday and prayed with the rest of them, and sometimes he knew why he prayed, and sometimes he didn't. And sometimes he really said prayers, and sometimes only words. And then he would return with one of the men for a Friday night meal, and when they talked about God, he was always assured that God was in the village, though he wasn't quite sure where or when He could be found. Gradually, too, he began to believe that God was in the village, though he wasn't quite sure where. He knew, however, that sometimes he had met Him.

One day, for the first time, the rabbi came to him and said, 'You have met God now, have you not?' And the man said, 'Thank you, Rabbi, I think that I have. But I am not sure why I met Him, or how or when. Or why is He in this village only?'

So the rabbi replied, 'God is not a person, my child, nor a thing. You cannot meet Him in that way. When you came to our village, you were so worried by your question that you could not recognize an answer when you heard it. Nor could you recognize God when you met Him, because you were not really looking for Him. Now that you have stopped persecuting God, you have found Him, and now you can return to your town if you wish'.

So, the man went back to his town, and God went with him. And the man enjoyed studying and praying, and he knew that God was within himself and within other people. And other people knew it too, and sometimes they would ask him, 'Where can we find God?' And the man would always answer, 'You have come to the right spot. God is in this place.'

Source: Jeffrey Newman, in Lionel Blue and Jonathan Magonet (eds), *Forms of Prayer for Jewish Worship: Prayers for the High Holy Days*, pp. 16–18.

# 14

# HOLOCAUST

The Holocaust not only involved the murder of six million Jews and the destruction of countless, once thriving communities, but traumatized Jewish theology. It challenged once assured notions of human progress, and it also led many to ask how an all-powerful God could allow such massive atrocities to take place. Where was God at Auschwitz? Could one even speak of God anymore after Auschwitz? It was certainly impossible for anyone writing after the Holocaust to ignore it, whether immediately afterwards or several decades later.

## 14.1 Ignaz Maybaum on the Need for Self-Accusation (1944)

*Rabbi Dr Maybaum had come to England from Berlin in 1939 while in the midst of a successful career there as communal rabbi and teacher of Jewish philosophy. He had seen the rise of Nazism at first hand, and had suffered imprisonment by the Gestapo for making anti-Hitler comments. The passage below comes from a book he wrote during the course of the war, when the extent of the Holocaust was not appreciated fully but questions as to its significance were already surfacing.*

Hitler has destroyed the Synagogues of the European continent. The Jews whom Hitler persecutes, tortures, murders have no conceivable guilt which they and other reasonable persons can find to justify this martyrdom. It is the most pious, the most Jewish Jewry whom Hitler's hangmen have struck against in Poland. We are as guiltless of what Hitler does to us as we were guiltless when the Babylonians destroyed the Temple in Jerusalem and led our fathers into captivity in Babylon.

This comparison between our lot in this epoch of Hitler, with the lot of our fathers, reminds us how they reacted. The Prophets of those days, beginning with Ezekiel, went through all past history, and they had only one explanation for the calamities which had come upon Israel: God is just, and we are guilty. Israel has forgotten the teaching of Moses. This is the reason for our suffering. The realistic historian will say that this explanation is unjust and exaggerated. But it saved Israel. No one can live with an accusation against God in his heart. We can only live praising God, His justice and His love.

The destroyed Synagogues stand before us. Who destroyed them? Who is this Hitler? God is the Lord of history. Can we say that the Synagogues which Hitler destroyed were what Synagogues should be? They were not what that history which begins with the Tabernacle and leads to the Pharisaic Synagogue required. If we have the strength to give this answer, if we react to this catastrophe which has come upon us as our fathers reacted to the catastrophe of their time 'God is just and we are guilty', then a new chapter begins, a new day dawns. Then our people will live. It will in its Synagogues praise God who lets the tree felled by the axe grow again.

Source: Ignaz Maybaum, *Synagogue and Society*, pp. 162–3.

COMMENT: *Despite his modern credentials, Maybaum reverts to a traditional response when trying to make sense of the tragedy occurring around him. It is not clear how he reconciles his statements that the Jews of Europe 'have no conceivable guilt' yet are suffering for their sins, unless he implies a collective guilt or one built up over several generations. He seems certain, however, that such an approach not only has theoretical integrity but practical validity, as it has helped Jews survive past traumas and will do so again. It allows him to end on a surprisingly optimistic note for one writing in mid-1943.*

## 14.2 Ignaz Maybaum on Hitler as God's Servant (1965)

*The Holocaust was to dominate Rabbi Dr Maybaum's writings for the next thirty years, although the passage of time did little to alter his original thesis that it occurred with God's knowledge and compliance. It was a theme he took to its most radical conclusion in the passage below.*

The catastrophe which befell Jewry in the years 1933–1945 is now called the third *churban*. The first *churban* destroyed the Temple of Solomon, the second *churban* the Temple of Herod. The meaning of *churban* is that of a catastrophe which makes an end to an old era and creates a new era. The *churban* is progress achieved through sacrifice. The medieval society which had survived in Europe is crushed today. Hitler, Lenin and Stalin did what should have been done by kinder, wiser men but, alas was not done by them . . . After every *churban*, the Jewish people made a decisive progress and mankind progressed with us. After the first *churban* we became the people of the diaspora proving to the gentiles that a people can survive without the heathen attachment to its land. After the second *churban* we made worship dependent on the spoken word alone. After the third *churban*, the Jewish diaspora is no longer limited to Ashkenazi and Sephardi regions, but has become a world-diaspora. The medieval organisation outside which God was not supposed to be found has been destroyed. You can be a Jew outside the *din* [Jewish Law], outside the religious organisation defined in the codes. The Middle Ages have come to an end. The sins of a stagnant Europe, the sins of an isolationist America, the sins of the democracies failing to progress towards the solutions of the new problems gave birth to Hitler. Of Nebuchadnezzar, the destroyer of Jerusalem, the word of God says in the Book of Jeremiah: 'Nebuchadnezzar, My servant' (27.6). Of Ashur who destroyed Samaria, Isaiah says that God himself called him to come. Would it shock you if I were to imitate the prophetic style and formulate the phrase ; Hitler, My Servant!? Hitler was an instrument, in itself unworthy and contemptible. But God used this instrument to cleanse, to purify, to punish a sinful world; the six million Jews, they died an innocent death; they died because of the sins of others. Western man must, in repentance, say of the Jew what Isaiah says of the Servant of God: 'Surely our diseases he did bear, and our pain he carried . . . he was wounded because of our transgressions, he was crushed because of our iniquities' (53.4–5).

Source: Ignaz Maybaum, *The Face of God after Auschwitz*, pp. 33–4, 66–7.

COMMENT: *Maybaum's description of Hitler as the servant of God is shocking yet, as he points out, not alien to traditional thinking. As someone who lost his two sisters in Auschwitz, it might be considered that he is one of those who have the personal qualifications to make such a statement. Some might consider the thought blasphemous, and others object to the morality behind the supposed divine method of achieving progress and consider it far too high a price to pay. However, it is one way of re-asserting divine control over an apparently ungodly world. It is also the ultimate insult to Hitler that he, the worst anti-semite of all times, was merely carrying out the will of the Jewish God.*

## 14.3 Arthur Herman on Absolving God of Blame (1973)

*Rabbi Herman was a congregational minister when he wrote the essay below, but the special empathy he felt with victims of the Holocaust led him eventually to specialize in working full-time with survivors and their families.*

In my humility I join the long list of post-Holocaust sufferers. God lives yet, that I know deep in my heart. Around me I see a world where God seems to have turned His back, closed His eye or perhaps is not being listened to. The problem before me is that of including in my belief an episode in human history that is not worthy even of animal life. But I begin with a positive approach. Fundamentally, I trust in the morality of God's direction of the universe because of my absolute belief that, unless there is religious content in the ways and habits of mankind, what has happened to six million Jews can happen to the whole human race. It is possible for a group of human people to elevate themselves to the status of gods and bring violence and death to all others.

What happened in Europe, when the image of God in which man was created was defaced, was done by men, by creatures of God. But this only proves man's need for a closer relationship with God. For only when man severs himself completely from God, and that which God requires of him, does he lose his humanity and sink to the level of an indiscriminate extermination of other human beings.

. . . After Auschwitz, Sobibor, Treblinka and many other shrines to the pagan gods of totalitarianism the world is no more as it was. Man is changed but God is changed too. We have lived through a bitter night of demons and would-be gods, and come through realizing that man can break the image of God in which he was fashioned, but will thus also shatter the image of God who fashioned him.

Only God is eternal. Man comes and goes but God remains. Man destroys but God survives man's worst destruction. It is not God that dies but god. The feather-bed faith in a god who can be smashed through terror is itself shattered. God rules still; it is just that, in the struggle against God, man has torn the man from Man and the god from God . . . If we intend to put the blame for some things on to God, and utilize Him as an excuse for our own shortcomings. then we are dishonest with ourselves and with Him. For since the night of doubt and the darkness of disbelief God the crutch, God the excuse for non-action, is no more.

Source: A. S. Herman, 'The Holocaust and Reform Judaism', in Dow Marmur (ed.), *Reform Judaism*, pp. 230–4.

COMMENT: *Herman – in contrast to Maybaum – has no doubt that human hands were responsible for the Holocaust, not a divine one. This leads him to affirm God's presence, not to question it, although asserting that a more refined understanding of God has emerged: the real God rather than the man-made god. Only the latter has died. Herman is confident that this new awareness of God will inspire humans to act differently in future – although whether he is justified or not is open to question.*

## 14.4 Albert Friedlander on Awareness (1977)

*Rabbi Dr Friedlander had been a child refugee from Nazi Germany, and he began his rabbinic studies after the war. He saw his task as not only being to explain the Holocaust, but to ensure that the world learnt from whatever lessons arose, so that its terrible history would not be repeated.*

One of the causes of Auschwitz was – technology. Our actions now have effects which are beyond our awareness. This conflict between man and his technology, the concept of alienation, has been assimilated into modern life. A new dimension is here, a growing darkness. In the last century, man suffered from a lack of knowledge; in our time, man suffers from too much knowledge, from intentionally producing false knowledge. And if our intellect is insufficient or misdirected, this also applies to our feelings. All of us know this. The death of an infant moves us; the death of six million people simply stuns our senses.

We are Eichmann's sons, removed from the consequences of our actions. The fine edge of our sensibilities has been worn away by the monstrosities of our age. The six o'clock news is the most brutal programme on our televisions – and we do not even turn it off. Each day, murder and destruction flicker across the screen as part of our home life. Is it any wonder that we have learned to live comfortably with the knowledge of the death of the six million? We can keep a body count of our own, right in the privacy of our living-room.

Yet there are moments in every life when we break out of the structure, when we are no longer controlled but, suddenly, are in control. And then we can be human beings. We can be humane. We can reach out towards our fellowman. And our shared suffering and our shame can be a bridge and can cease to be a barrier. Auschwitz – remembered within the community of human fellowship – can then become a question addressed to God. Then. But not until then.

Source: Albert Friedlander, in Lionel Blue and Jonathan Magonet (eds), *Forms of Prayer for Jewish Worship: Daily, Sabbath and Occasional Prayers*, p. 391.

COMMENT: *Friedlander highlights the danger that the shock of the Holocaust is increasingly blunted by constant exposure to the latest tragedy to occur. The greater problem is that by becoming conditioned to Auschwitz, we fail to act towards others in the light of it. God may still have questions to answer, but only when humanity has shown it too has responded.*

## 14.5 Albert Friedlander on Forgiveness (1985)

*By the 1980s a less awe-struck attitude to the Holocaust began to emerge, especially among non-Jews. This was partly the result of the passage of time and the rise of a generation unfamiliar with its horrors; and partly because the State of Israel attracted much criticism through its policies towards the Palestinians, which was interpreted by some as lessening the guilt that Western countries needed to feel at their past. Rabbi Dr Friedlander sought to address the changing climate of opinion.*

The Holocaust must not be forgotten . . . and yet, the world wants to forget. The anniversaries are not intended to conjure up the past, but to exorcise it. Europe is weary of the revenant shades who point to evils. 'The Holocaust?' 'Let us forgive and forget' is a central thought within our society, but addressed mainly to the Jews. 'Why not let go?' Jews are asked. 'Must you be grim and unforgiving? Must we continue to mourn your six million when so many more have died since then? There have been more recent genocides, in Asia, in Africa. In Ethiopia, millions are dying of starvation. We have enough upon our conscience. Why not forgive and forget, like the rest of us?

. . . Can we forgive? Who are we to usurp God's rule? Some years ago, speaking at a German Kirchentag (church conference) in Nuremberg, I talked about the anguish of Auschwitz. A young girl rushed up to me after the lecture, Rabbi', she said, 'I wasn't there, but can you forgive me?' and we embraced and cried together. Then an older man approached me. 'Rabbi,' he said 'I was a guard at a concentration camp. Can you forgive me?' I looked at him. 'No,' I said, 'I cannot forgive. It is not the function of rabbis to give absolutions, to be pardoners. In Judaism, there is a ten day period for penitence, between the New Year and the Day of Atonement, when we try to go to any person whom we have wronged, and ask for forgiveness. But you cannot go to the six million. They are dead, and I cannot speak for them. Nor can I speak for God. But you are here at a church conference. God's forgiving grace may touch you.'

Source: Albert H. Friedlander, 'The Holocaust must not be Forgotten', *European Judaism*, 19.1, pp. 5–6.

COMMENT: *Friedlander's double 'no' to the question 'can Jews forget and forgive?' will not satisfy everyone nor represent all Jewish opinion, but it is shared by many Jews, certainly with regard to not forgetting. Some, however, would argue that it is only by forgiving – even on behalf of the dead – that the living can free themselves of a burden, as well as move closer to their non-Jewish neighbours.*

## 14.6 Barbara Borts on Goodness as a Form of Revenge (1995)

*The new prayer book for the Pilgrim Festivals issued in 1995 contained an anthology of readings on appropriate themes. Among those in the section on Sukkot [Tabernacles] was one on 'Values' by Rabbi Borts which sought to invest the ancient festival with new meaning in the light of the experiences of modern Jews.*

What is clear to me is that, in order to connect past, present and future, we need to find a cause which liberates us from crippling grief and bitterness and shows the way to hope and life. We have focused too much on the despair, and not enough on the hope and, dare I say it, redemption. We have pursued Nazis and neglected the rescuers. In this work lies the most sacred task for the future.

We need to find the resisters, the good, the altruistic, and put them on trial – expose them and their goodness to the world. We need to hear open testimony about their courage and merit. We need to teach the world a lesson about the possibility of virtue and righteousness in a world of hatred, prejudice, racism and anti-Semitism; a world which, despite the Holocaust, still tolerates state-sponsored torture, murder and genocide. We have to be part of what has been called 'The Conspiracy of Goodness'. I believe that it is here that the real revenge on the Nazis might take place – to create a world that believes that goodness is natural and which will work towards the eradication of all blind hatred.

Source: Barbara Borts, in Lionel Blue and Jonathan Magonet (eds), *Forms of Prayer for Jewish Worship: Prayers for the Pilgrim Festivals*, pp. 796–7.

COMMENT: *Many commentators have spoken of examples of courage or moments of hope arising from the ashes of the Holocaust, but Borts goes further than these fleeting instances by proposing the development of a new perspective which actively seeks and celebrates goodness.*

## A Final Thought . . .

There are several kinds of faith and there is probably an appropriate time for all of them. There is faith through which a man accepts his lot; there is a simple faith in divine providence, or reliance on authority. There is also faith which is a compound of trust and hope. No matter what to-day may be like or the odds – this faith urges that there is a partnership between the divine and the human – and that salvation or redemption in this world – in the here and now, is possible and not merely a pious pipe-dream.

I learned this lesson not in theological college, but in a miserable little concentration camp grotesquely called Lieberose (lovely rose) in German Silesia. It was the cold winter of 1944 and although we had nothing like calendars, my father, who was my fellow-prisoner there, took me and some of our friends to a corner in our barrack – announced that it was the eve of *Chanukah*, produced a curious-shaped clay bowl, and began to light a wick immersed in his precious, but now melted, margarine ration. Before he could recite the blessing – I protested at this waste of food. He looked at me – then at the lamp – and finally said – 'You and I have seen that it is possible to live up to three weeks without food, and we once lived almost three days without water, but you cannot live properly for three minute without hope.'

Source: Hugo Gryn, 'A Modern Miracle', *Living Judaism*, Autumn 1985, pp. 15–16.

# 15

# INDIVIDUALS

Judaism is a communal religion. Jews are assumed to be part of a group, whether the smaller unit of the family or the larger unit of the congregation. Many rituals assume a family structure, such as the Sabbath eve or the Passover meal. Jews are expected to pray together, with a minimum quorum for the full service and most prayers written in the plural. Compared to some other faiths, there is much less emphasis on personal spirituality within Judaism, yet it is not absent and the individual is valued too. Each person has their own choices to make, and responsibilities they must fulfil.

## 15.1 Morris Joseph on Individual Values (1930)

*The early Reform leaders often sought to highlight the ethical demands of Judaism, which they felt had sometimes been obscured by the welter of ritual laws. Reverend Joseph often preached and wrote about the moral standards to which the Jewish community as a whole should aspire, but here addresses the role of the individual in three particular areas.*

Human Dignity: To bow down before wealth is to get our moral values wrong almost throughout the whole scale. We take over the rich man's conception of rectitude, faulty though it may be; we forgo our opinion for his; we are obsequious, servile, and immorally humble. We part with our one source of dignity – the only true source of dignity that any man has, and which the most ignorant and the poorest share with the most gifted and the richest – the righteousness, and the fineness of soul, which makes us sons of God, created in his image.

Moral Independence: General laxity of courage or opinion, far from lulling us into acquiescence, ought to sting us into protest. If the world condones certain deviations from the path of old-fashioned rectitude, it has left off condemning dubious business methods, detraction and backbiting, loose living, the unhealthy play, the unclean novel, then it is for us to say 'I will clear myself of all complicity in such abominations, though in doing so I stand alone, and have to pay the price in derision and worldly loss'.

Optimism: The optimist also sees the dark side of life, but, unlike the pessimist, he sees the bright side too, and that encourages him to believe that the bright side is the right, the winning side; it encourages him to work, and prove it to be the winning side. For optimism is not the ignoring of evil, but the courageous determination to look it steadily in the face and to quell it with that very courage.

Source: Morris Joseph, *The Spirit of Judaism*, pp. 38, 113, 261.

COMMENT: *Joseph discusses highly practical issues but imbues them with spiritual values. His hope is that this will reinforce individuals in the everyday challenges they face.*

## 15.2 Leo Baeck on Struggling with Infinity (1947)

*Rabbi Dr Baeck regarded the people of Israel as having a sacred role as a community, but that applied also to each individual. Caught between his own mortality and the immortality he sensed around him, the internal struggle of each individual was, for Baeck, a supremely religious act.*

The constant preoccupation with the path and the future, with duty and destiny – this constant tension is what is asserted to be the meaning of life. It is in this that the soul conceives its essence. Man here experiences the fact that he belongs to an infinity. Infinity besets him whether he goes into himself or beyond himself. He lives in a space without end, part of it, in a time without conclusion, a piece of it. World and eternity are one word. In this infinity man lives. His realm is the opposite of the merely circumscribed and delimited place, his day is the opposite of a fixed and unchanging fate . . . Man is surrounded by endless space and endless time, but they neither crush him nor allow him to become absorbed in himself. In every act that is demanded on him, man experiences the commandment, full of divine restlessness and sacred movement. He is never finished, his peace is never the peace of final fulfillment . . . Man desires infinity; he realizes it. He, the finite, who has comes forth from infinity and eternity, now is active within it . . . Inherent in this will to infinity is the struggle for it, the struggle with the eternal. He masters infinity by living it, by introducing it into his life, by making God's commandments an inner acquisition. He brings the beyond down to this world, he brings it down from heaven to earth and thus 'conquers' God, as it were, he makes God come closer and closer to this world. All moral heroism, as well as moral patience, is in this struggle with the infinite. Mankind took a step forward when one man allowed infinity to enter his life, when he 'conquered' God. It is a victory that signified the overcoming of the tension, that creates life out of the tension. It is the greatest victory in human life.

Source: Leo Baeck, *The Pharisees and other Essays*, pp. 137–42.

COMMENT: *Baeck describes the individual not in prosaic terms of everyday tasks but in a majestic vision of a soul capable of soaring to and fro between the finite and infinite. It is based on the fact that the Hebrew word 'olam' can mean both 'world' and 'eternity'. His portrayal is uplifting, but also has the danger of being so far divorced from day to day realities that not all may be able to identify with it.*

## 15.3  Howard Cooper on the Divided Self (1985)

Yom Kippur *is the festival that, more than any other time in the Jewish calendar, encourages self-analysis, with the liturgy forcing every individual to reflect on their inner nature. In a study passage included in the High Holy Day prayer book, Rabbi Cooper addresses the competing forces within each person.*

I could say that I am suffering from a split consciousness. There are two forces inside of me, each seeking to dominate the other. One I experience as a masculine, assertive force. I am manipulative and egocentric, and I have an urge to be dominating and authoritarian. My intellect enjoys having answers, possessing truths. Mind, will and logic dominate. That part of me is pulled to *halachah* and order, argument and debate, looking for a fixed and secure Jewish framework in which to orientate my daily life. This force within me endlessly seeks an anthology of traditional practice in which I can anchor myself against the rootlessness and the superficial truths which pervade my Western life. When it is overemphasized, however, I experience it as destructive. It is ambitious and greedy: it enjoys judging, owning, using. It has to be right. It wants its own way. It is often detached and aloof.

The other force is not concerned with having and using. It is concerned with feeling and sensitivity, dreams, creativity, fantasy, *aggadah*. It is intuitive, gentle and strong. It allows me to be receptive, allowing and accepting. When I live from this still centre I do not need to manipulate people and events to suit my own needs. I experience this force as a powerful feminine one, in which my ego submits to a power greater than myself. Its concern is my growth, development and change as a human being. It is the force of *rachamim*, which as the Biblical root *rechem* (womb) suggests, is the creative force acting as a gestation process, and working towards my gradual emergence as a being living in harmony with God's will rather than my own. I have come to identify that place of inner calm as my own soul, where God dwells.

Source: Howard Cooper, in Lionel Blue and Jonathan Magonet (eds), *Forms of Prayer for Jewish Worship: Prayers for the High Holy Days*, p. 352.

COMMENT: *Cooper anticipates the move towards inclusive language in later editions of the liturgy by describing how each individual embraces both masculine and feminine elements to their character. He perhaps does a disservice to his cause by largely portraying the masculine side as negative and feminine side as positive, whereas both have strengths and weaknesses and complement each other. Nevertheless, the idea of a male – and a rabbi – acknowledging and praising his feminine aspect was groundbreaking and no doubt many found it a liberating concept.*

## 15.4 Elizabeth Tikvah Sarah on Accepting Individuality (1999)

*Rabbi Sarah earned a reputation for being outspoken on a variety of issues, especially feminism and gay rights, and was passionate in the cause of permitting diversity and promoting individuality. In the article below, she considers how they should interact with Jewish institutional life.*

In theory Progressive Judaism is the daughter of the Enlightenment and Emancipation, an age which liberated the individual from absolute communal power. In practice, many progressive communities – i.e. both 'Reform' and 'Liberal' in the British context – have become very set in their ways. Progressive congregations may not attempt to control what members do in their own homes, but how easy is it for members to attempt to modify established synagogue practices? Within most progressive communities as with orthodox ones, the individual member is expected to conform to 'the way we do it here'. Very few progressive synagogues seem able to create an environment in which individuals may contribute their gifts and express their individuality within the context of community activities and religious services.

Concern for the individual is not a modern invention. The *Torah's* laws concerning the just treatment of people, all refer to the individual: the neighbour, the stranger, the poor, the worker, the widow, the orphan, the elderly person, the deaf, the blind. But recognising the rights of individuals to just treatment is one thing, incorporating the needs of individuals within the community is very difficult. And then right now in the closing days of the twentieth century, a huge reaction against excessive 'individualism' seems to be taking place. Many institutions have begun to stress the primacy of community over the needs of the individual.

Individual responsibility without individual rights is highly dangerous. So the challenge is to create forms of community which include individuals and the differences individuals bring. But how? By getting away from the idea, in the first instance, that community is only about what we share in common, that it necessarily involves everyone conforming to a mono-culture. Once a community agrees on its core values – mutual respect, compassion, peace, integrity, equality, justice, lifetime learning – and each individual member agrees to express and act on those values, it should be possible to devise ways of facilitating individuals to contribute their unique qualities, gifts and interests to the life of the community. If the synagogue building is alive with people on a Sabbath morning, does it matter that they are engaged in a variety of activities, from dance to social action – including different forms of service? And even within an individual service, once we get way from the notion that 'we've always done it this way' or 'it has to be like this', isn't it possible to create a format for services which incorporates variations and makes space for creativity, meditation and individual preferences?

Source: Elizabeth Tikvah Sarah, 'Creating Community', *Manna*, 64, Theology Supplement.

COMMENT: *Sarah highlights the fact that even Progressive congregations can be resistant to change, and that the process of institutionalization can stifle the creativity of individuals. Her proposal is to loosen the need for conformity within community. It would suggest that Reform Judaism, which frequently calls for pluralism within the Jewish world at large, cannot do so with any integrity unless it also permits pluralism within its own ranks.*

## A Final Thought . . .

[On his fifty-sixth birthday, and seeing an old photograph of his family containing various relatives and himself] And then there was me, a child looking speculatively out of the picture, curious as to what kind of life lay beyond the frame. I hadn't noticed that child for years. I'd never considered him or thought of him. But now I suddenly wanted to speak to him as if there were some kind of unfinished business between us. So I sat on, sucking a pencil, laboriously composing a letter just as I used to long ago.

Dear child (I wrote)

I don't know how we are related, if we are, for not one cell of your body lives in mine. I know you tried to imagine me once or twice as you gazed into the future, but you wouldn't recognise me now. I don't know if I've been your friend or foe, for there was a lot of niceness in you I never allowed to grow, but I didn't have much choice. It is of course your birthday too, and I remember the presents you longed for – a cup cake at the Corner House, meeting a millionaire who would give dad a job. But I cannot reach through the glass and can give you nothing. I can't even pass on some knowledge which would make your life easier. That sort of knowledge, as you'll learn later, always comes too late, after events not before them. But as I look at you, your image gazes into me and I see myself without the rucksack of anger and reproaches I've got used to carrying on my back. I wonder what it would be like to let it go. I know from your face that it wasn't always there. Perhaps I can, because as I get older I am closer to being a child again, second time round, and I become free from grown-up hopes and fears.

I can't continue this letter – it is too personal. But from it comes this advice. When you try to reconcile yourself to God and to love your neighbours, spare some love for the child who lives within you – whom you haven't thought about for years. He has a present to give you, though you can give him nothing in return.

Source: Lionel Blue, *Blue Heaven*, pp. 20–1.

# 16

# ISRAEL

The Land of Israel is central to the events of the Bible and the subsequent history of the Jewish people. Even after exile, there was a constant awareness of the importance of the land, with daily prayers calling for the restoration of Zion and the ingathering of the exiles. Every year, the Passover liturgy expressed the hope that next year the participants would be back in Jerusalem. Israel was regarded as the true home of the Jews and there was every expectation that they would return, even if such a move seemed destined not to occur until the messianic era.

## 16.1 David Woolf Marks on the Ingathering of the Jewish People (1843)

*The calls for a return of all Jews to the Land of Israel may have been heartfelt in times when Jews suffered oppression in their host country, but did not feel appropriate in nineteenth-century Britain where Jews were integrated into society at large, enjoyed rights and prosperity, and were pressing for full political emancipation. Reverend Professor Marks sought to reconcile the ancient hope with subsequent reservations.*

The final ingathering of the Jewish people is not to be accomplished by the ordinary means adopted by mortals for colonising any particular district; it is to be effected by the wonder-working hand of the Lord . . . Spiritually considered, the doctrine ought to have great influence on our thoughts and our actions. Without a future restoration the problem of the continued identity of the Hebrew people would almost be incapable of being solved; we should have no connection with the past or with the future, but should appear like a community which had been the sport of chance, and in regard to which Providence had no fixed design. But entertaining a full belief in this doctrine, we are enabled to discover why the Lord has so peculiarly dealt with our fathers and with us ... We connect our restoration with the establishment of the Messianic kingdom – when the roar of the canon will no longer be heard, when harmony and love will universally prevail – and we should conduct ourselves towards God and man, as to be accounted worthy of the spiritual agency which the Arbiter of the Universe has committed to the race of Abraham. On our actual social and political relations, however, the doctrine of our final ingathering does not exercise the slightest possible influence, because that event points to a time when the Lord will annul the political constitution of every empire of the world. Though we confidently hope for the fulfillment of the prophecies because of the universal blessings which the predicted age will diffuse; still the sentiments which we cherish for our native land, as Englishmen and citizens are no more affected by the doctrine of restoration, than are the sentiments of the large body of our non-Jewish compatriots by the doctrine which many of them maintain of the millennium. The believers in both doctrines may cherish their conscientious convictions, without suffering these varying articles of faith to weaken in the slightest degree their affection for their common country, or to diminish the ardent zeal which it becomes us to manifest for our monarchial and other national institutions, and for the prosperity and glory of the British empire ... We do not live according to our ancient local and political laws; we do have not, nor do we desire to have, our own Jewish magistrates; and we have no political longings save those which we can gratify in the land of our birth. In no single thing do we consider ourselves apart from our compatriots, except in our religious beliefs and worship.

Source: David Woolf Marks, *Lectures & Sermons*, Vol. I, pp. 203, 205–7, 271.

COMMENT: *Marks deftly separates the competing claims of Jewish and British identities, by declaring the former to be spiritual only and therefore of no immediate consequence to the everyday realities in which the latter applies. He also distinguishes them in terms of time and action, with the former postponed until a time far in the future and of God's making rather than the result of human effort. British Jews may pray for the restoration of Jerusalem, but their real gaze was directed to the Queen and Parliament.*

## 16.2 Morris Joseph on the New Jewish Order (1930)

*The establishment of the British Mandate by the League of Nations in 1920 placed the Land of Israel under the control of Britain and turned the idea of an independent Jewish homeland from a religious dream into a practical issue. At the same time Zionism was growing as an active political movement among many Jews. Whereas, in previous decades, Jewish nationalism was effectively dismissed by being relegated to the messianic era, now it had to be confronted. It posed a particular dilemma for Reform Jews, who were among those most integrated into British society.*

Even for us Reform Jews, Palestine is still a holy land, one fraught for us with sacred memories, dearer to us than any other country save the land of our birth. We still retain some of the old love for it, still pray for the peace of Jerusalem ... What destiny, then, do we desire for it? I would say that the less political the new Jewish order in Palestine proves to be the nearer it will approach the ideal one. If we except the age of Solomon, it would be true to say that never has Israel been politically great among the nations. His greatness was to be of another kind; it was to be the unique greatness achieved by a people living for the God-idea and striving to enthrone it in the hearts of mankind at large ... Palestine must become more Jewish. There must be more Jews in it, enjoying a better social status, speaking their ancient language as their everyday tongue, and finding their highest purpose in the development and dissemination of those characteristics which, taking their rise in the Bible, and informing the later literature, have come to be included in the term 'Jewish Culture' ... [But] to make Palestine truly Jewish [politically] might conceivably imperil the position of Jews elsewhere. With a land of his own, he might come more plausibly than ever to be regarded as an alien in the land of his birth. There is no doubt that anti-Jewish prejudice does linger on in the most civilised countries, and it is possible that the realisation of the cry of 'Palestine for the Jews' will strengthen it.

Source: Morris Joseph, *The Spirit of Judaism*, pp. 66–8.

COMMENT: *Joseph is sympathetic to those attempting to restore Jewish life and culture to the Land of Israel, and so, unlike some of his contemporaries, he is not antagonistic to all of the Zionist aspirations. However, he does emphasize that the chief goal of Jews is spiritual. He also openly voices fears of the anti-semitism that Zionism could unleash, and which would undermine the status in English society that Jews had striven so hard to secure. Some might feel that this has applied to more recent periods too.*

## 16.3 Ignaz Maybaum on Palestinian Provincialism (1944)

*The rise of the Nazis shook the confidence of many who had believed in the onward progress of European civilization, with Jews being immersed in its values and culture, secure within it and contributing to it. The nightmare that was unleashed also raised the urgent need of a safe haven for Jews fleeing persecution. It gave added weight to both the philosophy of Zionism and practical steps to further its political goals. This in turn called for a reassessment of the largely negative attitudes of Reform rabbis. As a refugee from Nazi Germany, and writing during the war, Rabbi Dr Maybaum was acutely aware of the new reality, yet also of potential dangers.*

Nationalism is a dangerous explosive in Palestine and a menace to the Jewish political life which is evolving there. Zionism may accept the secular nationalist idea. But it must not subordinate itself to it. If the Jewish people grows to be itself an absolute, setting aside the absoluteness of God, if Jewish history is to begin with Theodor Herzl, and Herzl's teachings are to replace the teachings of Moses, if Jewish nationalism repeats the mistakes, or, rather, the sins of European nationalism, then protest is inevitable . . . The Hebrew Renaissance as a preliminary to the religious revival of Judaism is the most important event in recent Jewish history. But if this Hebrew Renaissance is to degenerate into a Palestinian provincialism, then we stand at the grave of a great hope . . . Zionism must not become the programme of Jews who have abandoned their belief in the victory of truth and justice, the victory of humanity, and have turned wearily from Europe, proclaiming the ideals of Western civilisation dead. We belong – in Palestine and in the Diaspora – to Western civilisation, and we look to Europe, more than ever in these sad times . . . Zionism must be so formulated that it will not merely be a political conception, of importance to one section of the Jewish people and not to another. Zionism cannot change the Diaspora-destiny of Judaism, and the Jew in the Diaspora and the Jew in Palestine are both the Jewish people.

Source: Ignaz Maybaum, *Synagogue and Society*, pp. 34–5, 42–3.

COMMENT: *For Maybaum, it is not European culture that has a fatal flaw but European nationalism, and this leads him both to retain his trust in it and warn Zionists not to imitate the same mistakes. While he is still firmly wedded to the 'Diaspora-destiny' of Jews, he does at least imply that there is a role to play for those in the Land of Israel, and a relationship between the two groups.*

## 16.4 Harold Reinhart on a Jewish National Disaster (1945)

*Not all Reform rabbis were prepared to concede some role to those seeking to build a Jewish homeland, as did Rabbi Dr Maybaum. Rabbi Reinhart epitomized those who were aghast at the consequences of such activity, fearing its impact not so much on non-Jewish attitudes but on Jewish life itself.*

The term 'Jewish National Home' bristles with difficulties. The tacit assumptions of most users of the term nowadays are that the Jews are a nation like other nations, and that Palestine is rightly, or at least should be, the home of that nation, just as Belgium is the land of the Belgians and Greece the land of the Greeks. Against this assumption and this theory, we believe that the Jews constitute, not a nation like other nations, but a world-wide community of believers, a universal people who possess a common religious tradition and a common spiritual destiny, and who are in the truest sense of the word nationals of their respective fatherlands. Their rights and their obligations as such are their inescapable concern. As such they are not seekers of a 'national home' . . . [Some] might rejoin that the potential Jewish nationals will come from those countries from which anti-semitism drives Jews. The alacrity with which this opinion is often voiced suggests a disbelief in the future emancipation and democracy which is depressing . . . As to the desirability of world-wide Jewish concentration of effort on the project of a home in Palestine, it is largely a question of proportion and emphasis. The centre of our interest and the burden of our desire is the building of a living creative Judaism for ourselves here in our own land. The destiny of Israel lies in the wide, wide world. *Torah* is the bond that unites us all. The creation of a new Jewish nationalism we deem a disaster.

Source: Harold Reinhart, 'Q. and A.', *The Synagogue Review*, Vol. 19, No. 5, pp. 34–5.

COMMENT: *Reinhart sees Judaism as a faith only, to which land and borders are irrelevant. Any attempt to introduce a racial or national element to Judaism is, for him, a perversion of its spiritual nature. While the view is perfectly legitimate, the fact that it was written in January 1945 when millions of Jews were being murdered in what they had previously considered their fatherland, makes his stance seem uncompromisingly doctrinaire.*

### 16.5 Lionel Blue on the Arab Problem (1968)

*The establishment of the State of Israel in 1948 ended the religious debate as to the merits or otherwise of a Jewish homeland. Most Jewish groups – including Reform synagogues – accepted the new reality that had emerged. However, statehood brought new questions with it, including the relationship between Jews and Arabs. These became even more acute after the Six Day War of 1967 when Israeli victories led to the sudden acquisition of territories with a large Arab population. One of the early voices to raise concerns was Rabbi Blue.*

Israel has solved every problem except the Arab problem, and that is the only important problem now worth solving. A dialogue with the Islamic world is long overdue. The political solutions, the so-called 'realistic' solutions lead one way only – to tragedy. There is, however, one hope. Israel and Arabs are political entities. Behind them stand two other and greater beings – Judaism and Islam. It is possible that the goodness inherent in them can achieve what the politicians cannot. In the past too many guns have been blessed by too many religious establishments. Too many 'rousing' sermons have been given to 'inspire' congregations to new heights of national folly. The Christians fell for the trick first, we have learnt it from them, and the Arabs have learnt it too. It was a murderous trap. It looked so innocent, and so easy, and led millions to death and murder. Of course it is easy to see it in others, but difficult to recognise it in ourselves. The golden calf is more obvious than the still small voice. God is being buried under the relics we peddle – bottles of Jordan water, plastic bags of real Holy Land earth, and now a wall! The memories and symbols of the Jewish past were not meant for this. The Israel problem poses a crucial test for Judaism itself. Organised religion has in the past been so spiritually poor that it has no credit left. It has preferred to win popularity and risk losing its soul. It will end, of course, by losing both. If there is no religious initiative the result will be a syndrome of violence.

Many years ago a way was shown by people such as Judah Magnes. In the short term it did not seem to be realistic, and most Progressive Jews deserted it. They wanted to be in the establishment, not in the opposition – a lonely place. It is curious that just as that wish is near fulfillment, when the old policies are dying and the forgotten ideas and ideals of binationalism again appear, we are not there to articulate them. I hope that the leaders of Progressive Judaism will not jump on the wrong bandwagon once again.

Source: Lionel Blue, 'Jews and Arabs', *Living Judaism*, Autumn 1968, pp. 111–13.

COMMENT: *Blue's comments caused a considerable stir when they were made, as they went against the prevailing mood of triumphalism in the period after the stunning military successes in the Six Day War. Moreover, his criticism offended both political and religious circles. Today, however, his remarks appear prophetic, and themselves count as the still small voice drowned out by the cacophony around the golden calf.*

## 16.6 Charles Berg on Supporting Israel (1973)

*Amid the warnings about divided allegiance, the excesses of nationalism and concern for Arab rights, there were also many for whom the State of Israel was wholeheartedly welcomed, whether as the renewal of an ancient promise or as a haven for Jews suffering persecution anywhere else in the world. The comments of Rabbi Berg, who had come to England before the war to escape Nazi oppression and who now ministered to a suburban congregation, typified that support.*

In our days it is an important *mitsvah* to support our brethren in the State of Israel. Even those of us who think of their future as being in the lands of the diaspora and consider themselves loyal citizens of the country in which they live are, emotionally, deeply involved in the wellbeing of our brethren in the Holy Land. Those who were not, until recently, fully aware of this involvement realized it at the moment when the threat to the very existence of Israel forced our brethren to fight for their lives and everything which was dear to them. Israel passed this stern test but she will need our help for many years to come. It is our duty to give her our unflinching moral and material support.

Source: Charles Berg, 'Revelation, *Halachah* and *Mitsvah*', in Dow Marmur (ed.), *Reform Judaism*, p.108.

COMMENT: *This apparently simple passage is highly significant. It reflects the transition of the Reform leadership from a position of outright hostility to Zionism to open support; reference to the State of Israel – the political reality – now takes precedence over mention of the Holy Land – religious identification – a term which is rarely used again after this period. The awareness of the vulnerability of the fledgling State led to major practical steps at Israel-education, fundraising and even encouraging emigration there. Another consequence was that the call for 'unflinching' support became re-interpreted as totally uncritical support. It began a period in which the pendulum swung the other way in Reform circles, with reservations about developments in Israel being stifled.*

### 16.7 Dow Marmur on the Wisdom of Insecurity (1982)

*The Israel-consciousness that had enveloped the Reform movement in Britain led not only to policy changes, but to the need for a theological reassessment. Rabbi Marmur, whose deep-seated belief in the centrality of*

*Israel was to lead to his own eventual settlement there, sought to provide a religious perspective.*

There is a heavy price to be paid for living with insecurity, and after the Holocaust it became quite obvious that we Jews could not go on paying it without, at least, a respite, The creation of the State of Israel was absolutely necessary for our continued existence. Its creation, and the sovereignty that came with it, gave Jews access to power. There seemed no longer the same urgency to wait for the heavenly Jerusalem, because the earthly Jerusalem was within reach. Insecurity was no longer the heritage of Israel because the soldiers of the State that bore its name could provide security.

The Hebrew word, *bittachon,* now used as the term for military 'security', started off as a theological term and meant 'trust'. It sought to express the feelings that the Biblical Isaac had towards his father on their way to Moriah, as a reflection of the feeling that Abraham had for God. It is the secularization of this word which epitomizes the burden of contemporary Jewry. We are not entitled to castigate the Israelis for having changed the meaning. History forced it upon them, upon us all. Without their valiant defence of the Jewish homeland, few Jews would have wished to continue to live, let alone to believe. Nevertheless, without the return to its original connotation – but not, God forbid, by jeopardizing the security of the State of Israel – the future of Judaism seems, to say the least, improbable. Judaism was founded on trust; therefore it can never exist on mere security.

The mixture of martyrdom and heroism that has been characteristic of Jews in this century appears to have made us invincible. We responded to the massacre of the Nazis and the machinations of the Arabs with determination and amazing strength. However, in order to be victorious we cannot rely merely on our own resources; for that, trust in God is needed. The way to such trust is linked to the wisdom that comes from insecurity. The State of Israel presents us Jews with great opportunities, but it also brings with it great dangers: the real risk that the new generation of Jews, in Israel and elsewhere, will confuse security with trust and, worse still, abandon the latter. Events in recent years in Israel suggest that the risks can be contained and that the religious heritage need not be squandered. To strengthen all forces which work on behalf of, and in the spirit of, trust has become a priority for all Jews.

Source: Dow Marmur, *Beyond Survival*, pp.190–1.

COMMENT: *Marmur makes the bold assessment that Judaism would have been at a crisis point after the war had not the State of Israel arisen. Its arrival provided a vital new impetus to belief in a Jewish purpose and a reason for Jewish continuity as doers rather than victims. However, he is equally adamant that Judaism cannot survive by the State of Israel alone: it must re-discover the spiritual dynamism that has propelled it this far.*

## 16.8 Hugo Gryn on Jewish Power (2000)

*By the turn of the millennium, Israel was over fifty years old and British Reform's attitude toward it had matured into a more measured relationship, neither overly negative or adulatory, but aware of both its on-going precariousness and its unique status. This mixture of hope and fear was expressed by Rabbi Gryn.*

To people like me Israel is very special. It is the Jewish monument to the spirit of man who wants to live and not to die, to build and not to destroy. It is the place where Jews exercise sovereignty. It turns out that it is still vulnerable, but it has got tremendous determination to do well. I believe that ultimately the test of any morality is what you do when you have power. For a very long time the Jews – as Jews – were actually powerless, but now there is some Jewish power and it is going to be a very interesting time to see what happens. I like to think that eventually history will come to judge us as having dealt responsibly and morally with the bit of power that we have. Israel has an awful responsibility on its shoulders. It must redeem land, which they have done in spectacular fashion. They must redeem people, which they are doing and who become, in an amazingly short time, productive, creative, responsible members of society. But there is also an expectation for Israel to redeem history. And that is very difficult.

Source: Hugo Gryn, *Chasing Shadows*, p. 258.

COMMENT: *When Gryn writes 'history will come to judge us', he displays the almost total identification of most Reform Jews with Israel. The State has become a standard-bearer for Jewish destiny, both for its own citizens and for Jews living elsewhere in the world.*

## A Final Thought . . .

I have a vivid memory of sitting in a room of Arabs and Jews and being totally unable to distinguish who was who! The room belonged to Saida Nusseibeh, the woman who more than anyone else in Britain had laboured to bring together the two peoples. Her guests were mainly British, including Diaspora Jews, and some Israelis and a similar mix of Palestinians, many of whom had been born and brought up in the West.

I was astonished. There were the same semitic faces, and since the evening was for discussion and non-confrontational, what people said heightened my sense of confusion. Surely that man speaking of the Jewish pain and suffering in the Holocaust must be Jewish – but just now he seemed to have an intimate understanding of Palestinian politics. Maybe he's an Israeli journalist – but, on the other hand . . .

I realized that I could introduce many of the Arabs – many but not all of whom were Palestinians – to my community, and they would be indistinguishable from my own members. Equally, their attitudes ranged from hard-line and intransigent to deeply empathetic.

Source: Jeffrey Newman, 'Jews and Arabs: Can We Make Our Enemies Our Friends', in Jonathan Romain (ed.), *Renewing the Vision: Rabbis Speak Out on Modern Jewish Issues,* p. 210.

# 17

# JUDAISM

What does it mean to be a Jew? Those outside the faith have often held views that range from one extreme to another, with Jews either being the incarnation of evil who threaten those around them or God's elect who have survived against every expectation. Feared or admired, they are a mystery, separate from those around them yet influencing the society in which they live. Jews themselves have also been divided as to the exact nature of their identity, whether they are a race or a religion. They are equally divided as to their purpose, whether it is to be a people pursuing their own destiny or servants of God who act as a light to the nations.

## 17.1 Leo Baeck on Jewish Optimism (1905)

*When Rabbi Dr Baeck sought to describe the distinctiveness of Judaism, he held that its belief in God and its ethical affirmation made it a religion of optimism. It was not a superficial optimism, blind to the sufferings of the world, but a deep faith in the goodness of God and the goals of humanity.*

In Judaism this optimism becomes a demand for the heroism of man, for his moral will to struggle. It is an optimism which strives to realize morality in practice. It is not a doctrine of joy and sorrow, putting questions to destiny and waiting for answers, but rather a doctrine of the good which puts its questions to man and gives him an unerring answer in its 'thou shalt'. Not the contentment of the spectator in his cloistered peace, but the ethical will of one who, certain in his God, initiates and creates in order to mould men and renew the world – this is Jewish optimism. It lacks, no doubt, the classical calm, but instead it attains the peace born of the struggle for God. In this heroic optimism – often voiced in the prophetic 'And yet!' was created the great style of ethics and life.

The optimism in Judaism consists in the belief in God, and consequently also a belief in man, who is able to realize in himself the good that first finds its reality in God. From this optimism all the ideas of Judaism can be derived. Thereby a three-fold relationship is established. First the belief in oneself: one's soul is created in the image of God and is therefore capable of purity and freedom; the soul is the arena in which reconciliation with God is always possible. Secondly, the belief in one's neighbour: every human being has the same individuality that I have; his soul with its possible purity and freedom also derives from God; and he is at bottom akin to me and is therefore my neighbour and my brother. Thirdly, the belief in mankind: all men are children of God; hence they are welded together by a common task. To know the spirituality of one's own life, of the life of our neighbours and of the life of humanity as a whole as they are grounded in the common reality of God – this is the expression of Jewish optimism.

Source: Leo Baeck, *Essence of Judaism*, pp. 86–7.

COMMENT: *It was always to be expected that Baeck would define Judaism by its spirituality, but what is surprising is that he prefers to emphasize the fundamental optimism of Judaism rather than commandment or covenant, both of which appear frequently in his writings. It is also noticeable that, for Baeck, one of the key characteristics of this optimism is its universalism. Judaism demands that Jews are citizens of the world at large.*

## 17.2 Vivian Simmons on the Material and Spiritual (1928)

*For many years Reverend Simmons was one of the ministers at West London Synagogue, a congregation that not only served its own membership but acted as an exemplar of Reform Judaism to wider society. It was as much to this audience that Simmons addressed his remarks below.*

Foremost among Jewish characteristics has ever been the ability to sanctify the material and the physical. The Jew has never despised the physical needs and activities of the material world. He has glorified them all. Our most common and most sacred ceremonial is not mystical but practical. But out of the material things man has woven a pattern of beauty, goodness and truth. He has added something of the spirit. As a great modern preacher has said: He adds love to a house and calls it a home. He adds righteousness to a city and calls it a community. He adds religion to a building and calls it a sanctuary.

But because all men are by nature so much concerned with the earthly life, the Jew has always sought to clothe the spirit with a form. Saving only God himself who is above any kind of form, the Jew has found the actual in the ideal, and the ideal in the actual. There has never been any word in Hebrew for 'religion'. For the very good reason that all life is religion, and by no means a mere department of it.

Source: Vivian Simmons, in Lionel Blue and Jonathan Magonet (eds), *Forms of Prayer for Jewish Worship: Prayers for the Pilgrim Festivals*, p. 775.

COMMENT: *Simmons sums up the way in which Judaism has never seen everyday matters as a contrast to spiritual ones or a barrier to attaining them, but as a path towards them. Most Jews occupy the realm of the mundane and Judaism has made its home there too.*

## 17.3  Ignaz Maybaum on the Jewish Experiment (1962)

*The utterings of the pagan seer, Balaam, in the Book of Numbers provide a rare external perspective of the Israelites in Bible times. His declaration that 'Blessed be everyone that blesses you, and cursed be everyone that curses you' (24. 9) led Rabbi Dr Maybaum to consider the role of Jews in the world at large.*

The Jewish Diaspora is God's experiment with the gentiles who are on trial. There is among them a nation without power. If their civilisation bids them establish a law which safeguards the rights of the powerless, they are blessed and can endure as a civilisation. If they treat the powerless with the lawlessness of intolerance and persecution, they are cursed with the moral sickness that leads to the decline and fall of the mightiest civilisation. The history of the Jewish Diaspora shows clearly that we can only live in a civilisation which has absorbed elements of Judaism. This is the case with Western civilisation which has three elements: the Greek, the Jewish and the Christian. This Jewish element makes Western civilisation a place where the Jewish Diaspora can settle with the prospect of upholding Judaism whilst participating loyally and constructively in the task of this civilisation. Furthermore, the fact that Jews live in the realm of Western civilisation and can uphold their Judaism in the countries of Western civilisation gives hope for this civilisation itself. While it has Jews living and worshipping God this civilisation can guarantee its escape from the deadly inevitability of decline and fall. The theory that each civilisation has its day and that it is a short day of spring and summer after which autumn and winter with its death arrives, threatens and paralyses civilised man. But there is no need to fear. There is hope. There is evidence of eternity. Western civilisation need not sink into the oblivion which has already devoured more than twenty civilisations since man awakened 6,000 years ago to the maturity of civilised man. Western civilisation will last. With the Jewish Diaspora the nations are on trial, and Western civilisation, with Jewish existence possible in it, is aware of the Judge who condemns or pardons the nations in this trial in which Balaam's word about Israel is the final and eternal judgement: 'Blessed be everyone that blesses you, and cursed be everyone that curses you.'

Source: Ignaz Maybaum, *The Faith of the Jewish Diaspora*, p. 155–6.

COMMENT: *For Maybaum, Jews have a purpose far beyond themselves. Their fate among the nations acts as a yardstick by which God judges those nations. They are a barometer of the moral health of any society in which they live, and also an indicator of its longevity.*

## 17.4 Jonathan Magonet on Jewish Schizophrenia (1988)

*In writing a guide to Judaism for non-Jews, Rabbi Professor Magonet endeavoured not only to describe how Judaism has developed over the centuries, but what it means to be a Jew today. While lauding the many benefits it offers, he was careful to also record the dilemmas it poses.*

I am by intuition and experience a religious believer but at the same time

I am intellectually secular and critical. I am the child of two thousand years of Jewish rabbinic tradition, and an even older biblical one, but I am equally the child of two centuries of the Enlightenment. To deny the truths of that Jewish religious tradition and the martyrdom of the Jewish people to preserve it, would be for me a great betrayal. But it would be no less a betrayal to deny the intellectual and scientific insights of the past couple of hundred years, including the critical challenges they raise to the foundations of Jewish tradition. In this sense I am deeply schizophrenic. But I think that all of us committed to Jewish life today are schizophrenic in the same way – it is just that we find different strategies for coping with this deep inner conflict.

I cannot be an open-minded intellectual seeker in my professional or academic life, and switch off a part of my mind when I enter Jewish studies. I cannot be a liberal democrat in my social and political life, yet accept autocracy and authoritarianism in my Jewish religious life. I cannot live in a society which claims to be open, pluralist and multicultural and yet at the same time reduce that pluralist Jewish world that I know and experience to a narrow monolithic one, whether the label is 'Orthodox' or 'Progressive'. To quote Dr Leo Baeck, Judaism is my home not my prison. As a man, I cannot value the things I have learnt from the struggles of the women's movement, and then deny these hard-earned perceptions in my Jewish life. I cannot set aside the insights of a century of depth psychology into the nature of prejudice and projection, into the sexual fears and insecurities of human beings, and then shrug off the attitudes to secular and social minorities in our own tradition. I cannot celebrate the Passover and support Jewish causes, yet ignore the sufferings of Palestinians at the hands of Jewish power. I cannot ignore the enormous religious growth I have experienced through interfaith dialogue, with Christians and with Muslims, over much of my adult life, and then accept the narrowness and even prejudice against others I find in many parts of the Jewish world today, my own no less than others'. I may be schizophrenic but at least I can try to be consistent.

Source: Jonathan Magonet, *The Explorer's Guide to Judaism*, pp. 218–19.

COMMENT: *Magonet articulates the conflicting influences that affect Jews of all denominations, save for those who totally cut themselves off from wider society. The religious acrobatics demanded of most Jews today can lead some to give up the balancing act and seek comfort in tradition, others to abandon Judaism entirely, and others to walk the tightrope of faith and reason as the only way forward.*

## A Final Thought . . .

My mother was a role model, a truly religious woman. Not that she attended synagogue regularly. Nor did she engage in theological debate. I remember, when I was about fifteen, helping her hang up the washing and trying to engage her in a debate on the nature of God. 'What do you want of me?' she asked, 'There's a God. There is nothing else to say.' But she was religious in the deepest sense of the word. Where people suffered, she rushed to help. Whether it was the simple things that were needed, the apple pies, or the more demanding things, a shoulder, or teaching deaf children to read, or teaching new immigrants to speak English, she was always there. She was utterly honest in all her dealings. She had no need to define God; she just knew the ethical demands imposed on us by the one God. And she taught those values to us, her children.

Source: Jacqueline Tabick, 'I Did Not Want to be the First', *Manna*, 70, 2001, Theology Supplement.

# 18

# THE MESSIAH

Ever since Isaiah predicted a time when the lion would lie down with the lamb and swords become ploughshares, Judaism has been associated with the powerful belief in a world radically better in character than the existing version. It was a message reinforced by subsequent prophets and endorsed by rabbinic literature, but with the details left tantalizingly vague. When would that time arrive? Was it in human control to bring it nearer, or dependent on God's decision alone? Would the messiah be the final seal on a the world that was on the brink of perfection, or would the messiah arrive to rescue a world on the brink of destruction? Over the centuries many possible answers were offered, but none were accepted as definitive. It is remarkable that such a vision should be both so strong and yet surrounded by so many question-marks. It was against this conundrum that Reform rabbis sought to add their perspective.

## 18.1 David Woolf Marks on the Messianic Conditions (1858)

*If one issue divides Jews and Christians, it is that of the messiah. Has the messiah come? What effect will the messiah have? Will the messiah be an ordinary human being to be admired or a divine character to be worshipped? Such questions are posed not just by Christians, but by Jews themselves, both because of the influence of surrounding Christian culture and because Jewish tradition contains different viewpoints as to the exact nature and timing of the messiah. Reverend Professor Marks sought to provide a Reform response.*

It is impossible to recognise, in the present comparatively imperfect state of human progress, the realization of that blessed condition, which the prophet Isaiah associates with the era when the Messiah is to appear. And as our Hebrew scriptures speak of one Messianic advent only, and not of two advents; and as the inspired book does not preach the Messiah's kingdom as a matter of faith, but distinctly identifies it with matters of fact which are to be made evident to the senses, we cling to the plain inference to be drawn from the text of the Bible, and we deny that the Messiah has yet appeared on the following grounds.

First. Because of the three distinctive facts which the inspired seer of Judah inseparably connects with the advent of the Messiah, viz.: the cessation of war and the uninterrupted reign of peace, the prevalence of a perfect concord of opinion on all matters bearing on the One and only God, and the ingathering of the remnant of Judah and of the dispersed ten tribes of Israel – not one has, up to the present time, been accomplished.

Secondly. We dissent from the proposition that Jesus of Nazareth is the Messiah announced by the prophets, because the Church which he founded, and which his successors developed, has offered, during a succession of centuries, a most singular contrast to what is described by the Hebrew Scriptures, as the immediate consequences of the Messiah's advent, and of his glorious kingdom. The prophet Isaiah declared that when the Messiah appears, peace, love and union will be permanently established; and every candid man must admit that the world has not yet realized the accomplishment of this prophecy . . . [while] it is very certain, that since the appearance of him whom our Christian brethren believe to be the Messiah, mankind has been split into more hostile divisions on the grounds of religious belief, and more antagonistic sects have sprung up, than in any historic age before Christianity was preached.

As Jews, we maintain that the promised Messiah has not yet appeared . . . but what it [Jewish tradition] does especially behove us to bear in mind is, first, that the prophets identify the Messianic advent with an *age* when brute force shall have come to an end; and, secondly, that this important work of the regeneration of mankind is to be brought about by the instrumentality of the Jewish people, if not some remarkable individual born of that race.

Source: David Woolf Marks, *Lectures & Sermons*, Vol. II, pp. 86–8.

COMMENT: *Marks makes clear the Jewish grounds for refuting Jesus as the messiah: that he failed to fulfil the conditions of such a role – in Jewish eyes, at least – and has not brought real and lasting peace to the world. Marks also highlights the Jewish preference to speak of the messianic age rather than the messiah, and to emphasize the it is the era of peace that is important, not the person who helps usher it in.*

## 18.2 Morris Joseph on the Messianic Idea (1903)

*Reverend Joseph was writing at a time when, as a result of the Zionist movement, the physical ingathering of the Jews to the Land of Israel – one of the events that would accompany the messianic age – was no longer a religious ideal but a political programme. How did this affect the messianic doctrine?*

The question whether a Messiah is to be one of the figures of the Messianic Age, or Israel is to be a nation once more and the Temple in Jerusalem the religious centre of the whole world, is not a vital question. We can be equally good Jews whatever view we hold on these points. They are details on which freedom of thought can be tolerated without injury to the Faith. But the same cannot be said of the Messianic Idea. That is one of the essentials of our creed, without which Judaism would have neither meaning nor life. If there is no Golden Age in store for the world, which the Jew is to bring nearer by his belief and his example, if Israel is never to behold the triumph of the great principles to which he has borne such pathetic witness, then Judaism is vain. To despair of that triumph is to confess that Judaism has no purpose to fulfill in God's scheme. It is to deny its truth. If the dogma of the Divine Unity is the foundation of our religion, the Messianic Age is its coping-stone.

Source: Morris Joseph, *Judaism as Creed and Life*, pp. 171–2.

COMMENT: *When Joseph avoids answering the question as to the exact form of the messianic age, it is not just a reflection of his diplomacy but also of the ability of Judaism to permit different viewpoints – both here and in other areas – without the need to label them as truth or heresy. Actions and commandments may be regulated, but not matters of belief in what may or may not come to pass. He does assert, however, that what is essential is the very idea of the messianic era, which holds that a better version of the world is possible and that Jews have a purpose in bringing it nearer.*

## 18.3 Leo Baeck on the Messianic Demand (1905)

*Rabbi Dr Baeck was concerned that reference to the messianic era was seen as mere escapism, a distraction from the realities of the world. He was keen to emphasize that it had an immediacy that should not be forgotten or under-estimated.*

There is no sentimentality in the messianic message. Since it is a message of commandment, it brings suffering as well as consolation. There is here no mere dreaming about the future; for the man who dreams about the future does nothing about the present. There is a driving, compelling element in this idea of peace that is well-nigh revolutionary. Every great idea, every conception thought out to the messianic end, means opposition; a commandment is paramount to a protest because it is not only concerned with the alleviation of the needs of the hour but also demands the days to come and the whole man. Those few who live for the sake of mankind contradict the many, repudiating and demanding in the midst of mankind. Because there is an element of the unconditional and the absolute in the messianic idea, it implies an attack on all indolence and self-sufficiency, an onslaught on the notion that whatever is, is right.

Every grown civilization claims to be complete and worthy of acceptance by all. But the messianic idea stands in constant opposition to the self-satisfaction of civilization, against which it asserts its denying, radical, revolutionary outlook. Messianism is a leaven in history. The religion of Israel began of old with this revolutionizing trend, with this demand to choose the new road and to be different.

. . . Messianic conviction is an ethical treasure in which suffering and consolation, the will to fight and the confidence of peace, are reconciled. Here we can see the contrast to Buddhism, which knows neither hope for the future nor the goal of the kingdom of God. Its attitude towards the days to come is simply one of resignation. This is the same deficiency that afflicts Greek humanist philosophy which lacks enthusiasm and yearning, the faith and expectation of those who know they have been entrusted with a mission.

Judaism's messianic conception may also be contrasted with that of Christianity. Judaism stresses the kingdom of God not as something already accomplished but as something yet to be achieved, not as a religious possession of the elect but as the moral task of all. In Judaism man sanctifies the world by sanctifying God and by overcoming evil and realizing good. For Judaism, the whole of mankind is chosen; God's covenant was made with all men.

Source: Leo Baeck, *Essence of Judaism*, pp. 250–2.

COMMENT: *Baeck is adamant that messianism should be an active force and implies that it should be a constant thorn in the political process, protesting against the ills or follies of society. It is a message to which not all Jews have paid attention, but of which those in power have often been aware, and hence the fear of religious movements which they felt had allegiance to a higher vision. Baeck also lauds the superiority of Jewish messianism over that of other faiths, in a manner that would probably not be expressed in today's climate of inter-faith mutual appreciation. Moreover, it stands out all the more starkly because of the contrast to his next sentence, in which he attempts to reverse the notion of the Jews as the chosen people by declaring that all mankind is chosen.*

## 18.4 Jonathan Romain on the Messianic Task (1991)

*The authors cited above had fashioned their views on the concept of the messiah partly from Jewish tradition and partly from the prevailing belief in the on-going progress of civilization. Those writing after 1945 could no longer take the latter for granted.*

Despite Judaism's firm belief that there will be a Messianic Age, there is no definitive opinion as to when it will occur. Indeed, two opposing traditions have developed: according to one, it will be when the world has sunk into total depravity and only the Messiah's coming will save it from destruction; according to the other, it will be when the world is on the brink of perfection and the Messiah's arrival will be the final seal. Reform thinking prefers the latter interpretation because it avoids the danger of personality cult and instead emphasises the duty of all people to work towards the coming of the Messianic era. Rather than denying responsibility for the state of the world or claiming that individuals lack the ability to have any effect, it is the task of every person to contribute to its betterment. The saying of Rabbi Tarphon has taken on the status of a motto in Reform circles – 'It is not your duty to complete the work, but neither are you free to desist from it' (Pirke Avot 2.16). *Tikkun olam* ('repairing the world') has become a key phrase that reinforces the importance of collective effort to achieve a better society. The small success of each individual can gradually build up and bring even closer the Messianic Age. It is accepted that the coming may not be imminent, and Reform does not have a messianic timetable. Indeed, after the Holocaust some consider the notion of a world free of fear and hurt to be an impossible dream. The transformation required in human nature defies imagination. Nevertheless, resignation and despair are not the answer; maintaining the vision of perfection is essential and striving towards it is fundamental to Jewish existence.

Source: Jonathan Romain, *Faith and Practice: A Guide to Reform Judaism Today*, p. 32.

COMMENT: *The passage highlights the fact that, for Reform, one of the key consequences of belief in a messianic world is the need for personal participation. It is an idea that can raise the importance of small actions and can give cosmic significance to individual efforts.*

## A Final Thought . . .

[Finding Godliness often] becomes a practical not an academic question . . . it took place in the waiting room at the end of a hospital ward. The doctors were doing their rounds, so I sat waiting with two women. One woman fumbled with her handbag, the other smoked cigarette after cigarette. They weren't aware of each other. The Sister poked her head in and beckoned to Cigarette. 'You can see your husband now. I'm afraid you'll find him rather sleepy.' Cigarette went out and returned ten minutes later. She hesitated and then went over to Handbag, which intrigued me, and impulsively tapped her on the arm. 'Your turn now. No, I won't come in with you. See him alone.' Handbag, looking astonished, scuttled out, while Cigarette sat on motionless. Something significant had happened. But what? Later on I learnt that the man was dying. Cigarette was his wife, Handbag his mistress. I'd witnessed an act of spontaneous generosity. Cigarette had let God get into the act as well as her rival, and I don't think she would ever regret it. The glow certainly remained with me for months.

Source: Lionel Blue and Jonathan Magonet, *How To Get Up When Life Gets You Down*, pp. 21–2.

# 19

# MISSION

The concept of 'the Chosen People' originates in the Bible, where Israel is told that 'the Lord your God has chosen you to be His own treasure out of all the peoples that are on the face of the earth' (Deuteronomy 7.6). It has always been understood within Jewish tradition not as a mark of superiority but as a job description, with the children of Israel and their descendants being chosen for a task by God. The nature of that task has generally been defined as being a living witness both to the existence of God and to God's ethical demands for humanity as a whole, which are summarized in the seven Noachide Laws. The emergence of other faiths such as Christianity and Islam – both of which correspond to ethical monotheism – has been seen not as a setback but as a stage in the further-ance of that mission. The object is not so much a world that is Jewish, but a world that is God-fearing.

## 19.1 Morris Joseph on the Election of Israel (1893)

*The concept of mission was central to Jewish thinking, but also suffered from accusations by those outside the faith that it was a sign of Jewish elitism. This posed a problem for Jews in general, but particularly for Reform Jews who were more integrated in wider society and were both keen to uphold the tenets of their faith yet not be regarded unfavourably because of them. In addition, having suffered from centuries of Christian missionary activity, Jews did not wish to be labelled as guilty of claiming a monopoly of the truth themselves. It was these dilemmas that Reverend Joseph sought to address.*

Already in the far-off days of Sinai, when Israel's religion was still young, he received his charter from the Divine hand: 'You shall be to me a kingdom of priests and a holy nation' (Exodus 20.6). Surely, the ideal the words shadowed forth was something higher than mere self-contained sanctity. A kingdom of priests pre-supposes a congregation to minister to – a world-wide congregation whom they are to imbue with the truths they themselves have learnt from God's own lips. They are to be a holy nation; but their sanctity is to leap from them like a flame from a central fire, until it has kindled the whole world.

And, in saying so, I have not forgotten there are many to whom it is a stumbling block. To call ourselves the chosen people – to assert that God has revealed Himself especially to us – savours, it is said, of arrogance. But where is the arrogance? If we did not believe this we should deny the superiority of our own creed, and our allegiance to Judaism would be unfounded. Why am I a Jew, if it be not because I think that Israel's religion is the purest expression of theological truth and embodiment of the noblest ideals of duty that have ever been given to the world? Every religionist would make the same claim on behalf of his own system. If we are guilty of arrogance on such grounds, we share the guilt with every conscientious religious thinker under the sun.

Or are we arrogant because we speak of ourselves as a favoured race. With what have we been favoured? Spiritual servitude and worldly dis-advantage . . . a troubled life lasting through the centuries. Perpetual unrest, woe almost without surcease, gloom brightened by merely pass-ing gleams – this has been Israel's lot from the day he became God's own to this day. In the material sense, we have gained nothing by being the favourites of Heaven save what other men would reject – the pain of self-conquest and the suffering inflicted by a hostile world.

. . . And what of the present? Is our mandate exhausted? Is that mis-sion still in our keeping, or has it been transferred to other hands? . . . Religion is being purged, it is true, of superstition and error, and slowly and painfully the world is climbing to its moral regeneration. But the spiritual darkness that covers the earth is still thick enough to need the holy light that Judaism sheds, and our example may yet be helpful to many a brother in his toilsome ascent to perfection.

Source: Morris Joseph, *The Ideal in Judaism*, pp. 22–9.

COMMENT: *Joseph acknowledges the criticism that the idea of mission has brought but brushes them aside. He does not minimize the importance of being chosen or even the superiority this gives the Jewish people, but instead argues that it is a theme common to all faiths, while also highlighting the disadvantages it entails. He is equally adamant that the role is on-going and is not limited to the past.*

## 19.2 Leo Baeck on the Task of Israel (1905)

*When writing his critique of Judaism, Rabbi Dr Baeck described the Prophetic vision in which the people of Israel would bring the rest of the world to the mountain of the Lord and establish God's kingdom on earth. But what role was left when exile and then Christian supremacy made missionary activity impossible? Did loss of land and power make mission redundant?*

Often it seems that the special task of Judaism is to express the idea of the community standing alone, the ethical principle of the minority. Judaism bears witness to the power of the idea as against the power of mere numbers and worldly success; it stands for the enduring protest of those who seek to be true to their own selves, who assert their right to be different to the crushing pressure of the vicious and the levelling. This too is a way of constant preaching to the world.

By its mere existence Judaism is never a silent protest against the assumption of the multitude that force is superior to truth. So long as Judaism exists, nobody is able to say that the soul of man has surrendered. Its very existence through the ages is proof that conviction cannot be mastered by numbers. The mere fact that Judaism exists proves the invincibility of the spirit, and though it may sometimes assume the appearance of an extinct volcano – Judaism has often been depicted in that image – there yet dwells a power in it which quietly renews itself and stirs it to fresh activity. From the few, who remain so for the sake of God, there emanates the great and decisive tendencies in history. With regard to this fact alone one is often tempted to adapt a well-known phrase by saying: 'If Judaism did not exist, we should have to invent it'. Without minorities there can be no world-historic goal.

Source: Leo Baeck, *Essence of Judaism*, p. 273.

COMMENT: *Baeck turns the apparent failure of Judaism into its true strength and insists that it serves its historic purpose precisely through being a minority. Through its isolation, Israel plays a universal role. It could be argued that, in theological terms, this is making a virtue out of necessity, but it does provide both a powerful continuation of Judaism's task and one that is possible to fulfil in its difficult circumstances*

## 19.3  Andre Ungar on the Chosen People (1958)

*When Rabbi Dr Ungar published his pamphlet summing up the beliefs and practices of Reform Judaism, the growth in inter-faith relations meant that there was a very different religious climate from the time of previous writers. Did the Jewish sense of mission still operate in this new context, and if so, what form did it take?*

We believe that we are a Chosen People. This belief in no way conflicts with our assertion of the equal dignity and worth of all human groups or nations. Our being chosen does not imply additional glory or honour for Jewry, it is no sign of any innate or acquired superiority, either intellectual or even spiritual. It means no more and no less than that, because of the will of God, historic conditions and the willingness of our forefathers, the House of Israel has accepted a special responsibility.

'Chosen people' really means 'choosing people'. The task that our forefathers accepted (and every generation of Jews must accept anew) is a challenge that was, and is, open to everyone. It is to become a messenger of God's will to his fellows on earth, a teacher of true piety and morality to the world, by example as well as by precept. History shows that in past ages Jewry rose to its opportunities. That a small band of nomadic tribesmen managed to irradiate with its insight the lives of several hundred million people (Moslems and Christians as well as Jews) is a proud proof of the sense of mission that animated our ancestors, and of the value of the content of that message. The man born to be a Jew and the one who freely embraces Judaism faces this same historic and religious challenge.

Perhaps it sounds odd to say that we are a people with a mission but not a missionary people. Our aim is not to convert the Gentile world to

Judaism, but to help to realise true godliness and human decency within their own national, cultural and religious frameworks. And, likewise, we wish to maintain the distinctness and the distinctiveness of the Jewish community and Jewish life. Judaism is a subtle blend of universalism and particularism.

Source: Andre Ungar, *Living Judaism*, pp. 4–5.

COMMENT: *Unlike Reverend Joseph sixty-five years earlier, Ungar is keen to emphasize that Judaism does not make any claims to superiority over other faiths. Moreover, by suggesting that it is a 'choosing people' rather than a chosen one, he softens the notion of Jews being hand-picked by God, although still retaining the idea of a sense of mission. Nevertheless, the mission itself – bearing witness to God – is essentially the same.*

### 19.4 Dow Marmur on Chosenness (1982)

*Rabbi Marmur felt the idea of a Jewish mission was under threat from two sources: the increase in secularization meant a lessening of religious belief and thus also of the special role of the Jews; at the same time the political turmoils in Israel led many to opine that Jews were no different from any other nation. There was a danger that Jews themselves would come to believe that the existence and future of Judaism was irrelevant, a view that Marmur sought to combat by explaining what chosenness still signified.*

The decision cannot be made on the basis of exegesis. Both the Bible and Rabbinic literature say so many things about what it means to be 'a peculiar people' that almost any view will find its support in the sources. We are, therefore, not really in a position to decide which is the authentic interpretation. Let us instead attempt to state what ought to be the Jewish view of election in the light of the challenge of the coming years and decades. The limitations of Orthodox extremism, Reform liberalism and Zionist rejection are obvious: the first, implying Jewish superiority, leads to fundamentalist exclusivity; the second, based on a notion of mission to the Gentiles, is a manifestation of a sense of superiority no less objectionable than the one propounded by Orthodoxy; the third, insisting that Jews are no different from other nations, is unrealistic and untrue.

Chosenness, in the last resort, is an affirmation: 'that the Lord is your God, that you will walk in His ways, that you will observe His laws and commandments . . . a holy people to the Lord your God' (Deut. 26.17–19). To be chosen means to choose by declaring one's allegiance. It does not begin with God who chooses us, but with us who choose God. The chosen are those who are prepared to take upon themselves the commandments as understood by tradition. It is written, 'You will observe His laws'. It does not say all of them! Not only those who observe everything are entitled to regard themselves as chosen, but all who declare their commitment to the Jewish way of life.

Chosenness is thus not a matter of divine initiative but of human endeavour. It is man's affirmation of God by doing His commands that evokes God's response and makes the individual a part of His people. Election is not based on birth but on commitment. It need not imply that every individual has to make it for himself; being part of a tradition implicates him in the endeavours of the collective.

Source: Dow Marmur, *Beyond Survival*, pp. 176–7.

COMMENT: *Marmur follows the trend of viewing chosenness as self-initiated rather than divinely appointed. This serves both to lessen the claim to favouritism which has proved such a source of criticism, and to emphasize the need for individuals to earn their right to a special role.*

## A Final Thought . . .

During my studies at Leo Baeck College a well-known Jewish bookshop, Shapiro-Valentine, in the East End closed down. When I visited the sale, the bookseller, the historian Professor Chimen Abramsky in another guise, persuaded me to buy a couple of volumes of *Midrash* (traditional biblical Jewish exegesis). When I purchased them, even without being able to read, let alone understand, their content, I felt a sudden burden of responsibility to ensure that the tradition they incorporated did not end in this ignominious way, but that I, I alone if necessary, had to some-how teach and hand them on. Though I have never taught those exact texts, I think that the desire to communicate the content of the Hebrew Bible and the rich tradition of Jewish scholarship, has been a primary motivating force in my subsequent career.

Source: Jonathan Magonet, 'Reading Our Sacred Texts Today', in Tony Bayfield, Sidney Brichto and Eugene Fisher (eds), *He Kissed Him and They Wept*, p. 111.

# 20

# PEACE

The Hebrew word that is perhaps the most commonly known worldwide is 'shalom' – 'peace'. The vision of peace dominates the Bible and permeates Jewish liturgy. The culmination of the Aaronic blessing, which originated in Numbers 6.26 and became a regular feature in services, is the blessing of peace. The very name of Jerusalem – 'ir shalom'/'city of peace' – expresses the hope that an ideal world will be characterized by an era of harmony. Moreover, the Hebrew concept of 'shalom' is not just the absence of war and strife, but a positive value in itself. It carries associations of wholeness and completeness, both individually and generally, with each person being at ease with him/herself, and with society at large being at one with itself.

## 20.1 Morris Joseph on the Goal of Peace (1903)

*Despite the ideals of Judaism, the realities of human existence mean that peace is often more talked about than experienced, especially between nations. Should Jews – small elements in wider society – be expected to oppose national trends? What effect could individuals have on the ways of the world? Reverend Joseph was adamant that the answer had to be affirmative.*

Peace ought to be not only a personal, but a national ideal. There are, doubtless, occasions when war is defensible as a lesser evil than a disastrous and dishonourable peace. But they are less numerous than is usually supposed. And it should be the aim of a people to make their number as small as possible. War is so terrible a calamity, so dark a blot on our civilisation, that the greatest sacrifices should be made to avert it There are worse things, it is true, than war; but the worst of them is the belief that war is essential to national vigour, that there are international quarrels which cannot be settled without it, that its entire abolition is impossible. Such a belief is fatal to the ultimate establishment of universal peace. Nor should such an idea as glory be any longer associated with war. Only that nation should be deemed glorious which has made the greatest efforts, and submitted to the heaviest sacrifices, in order to preserve peace. Every good citizen will earnestly strive to keep this truth before him and to win others for it. He will also uphold the principle of international arbitration, and to do his utmost to extend his rulers' recourse to it. This fine expedient must not be kept for minor differences only. It must be recognised as the normal, the only natural and becoming method of settling disputes between civilised nations.

The Jew who is true to himself will labour with especial energy in the cause of peace; he will strive to bring about that change of temper in men, that juster attitude to the question of War and Peace, which alone will permanently put an end to international strife. Never can he consistently belong to a war party. His religion, his history, his mission, all pledge him to a policy of peace, as a citizen as well as an individual. The war-loving Jew is a contradiction in terms. The 'man of sorrows' must beware of helping, however remotely, to heap sorrows upon others. His history forbids it; but so, too, does his vocation. His task is to sow not strife, but brotherly love, among men; he has been called in order to bring not a sword, but peace.

Source: Morris Joseph, *Judaism as Creed and Life*, pp. 453–5.

COMMENT: *Joseph argues not just that war is wrong, but so is the very attitude of mind that considers it an option for solving any problem. He admits that armed conflict is sometimes necessary, but his aim is to alter the perception of war and thereby make it unacceptable as an instrument of policy. Jews should be in the forefront of such a campaign, both because of their given mission and because of their own experience when bloodshed prevailed over reason.*

## 20.2 Harold Reinhart on International Peace (1968)

*Rabbi Reinhart was a staunch pacifist throughout his life. He accepted the necessity of war to defeat the evils of Nazism, but remained a passionate anti-war campaigner and a strong advocate of the United Nations. In the 1960s, the Vietnam War begged the question of whether military action was also justified in the conflict between the proponents of capitalism and communism.*

I believe that international peace is the most fundamental practical problem, and that the attainment of peace is the most urgent challenge, before man today. I hold it to be the duty of every thoughtful person to declare his concern for peace, and to manifest that concern in word and deed. It is not to be wondered at that most people are inactive in this context. They are confused and bewildered by the complexity of the problem, and inhibited and frustrated by the concentration of governments and organized society generally on 'progress', 'national advantage' and 'security' – all in large measure euphemisms for the competitive war machines. 'What can I do?' 'What good is some puny peep against all the powers of the world?' Such is the counsel of despair.

Lip service to the ideal of peace is not enough. As a first step every citizen can identify himself with bodies actively concerned for peace. He can take some part in communication, study, and practical projects in the name of peace. He can witness to an attitude other than the prevailing one of floating with the tide, a tide of cold wars, hot wars, and threats of wars which is drawing mankind steadily to the brink of doom.

At present, peace societies are feeble instruments. But the mightiest movements in history have all had small beginnings. And still the nagging doubt: may not all the peace workers fail utterly? No man can say. But let everyone who loves life, who believes in humanity and is stout of heart, declare himself an advocate of peace, a seeker of the ways of peace, and a champion in heroic effort to achieve it. The result is in the hands of Heaven.

Source: Harold Reinhart, 'Peace', quoted in Lewis and Jacqueline Golden, *Harold Reinhart: A Memorial Volume*, pp. 219–20.

COMMENT: *Reinhart's description of both the problem and a possible solution to achieving peace holds true today as much as when it was first written. He provides a practical programme of action based on the rabbinic imperative that one may not be able to complete the task, but neither is one free to desist from it (Pirke Avot 2.16)*

## 20.3 Hugo Gryn on the Vision of Peace (2000)

*As a teenager, Rabbi Gryn had been sent to the Nazi extermination camp, Auschwitz. There were many different reactions among those that survived. Some emerged embittered and full of despair. Others simply wished to forget and concentrate on rebuilding their own lives. Some put their energy into establishing a Jewish homeland. Gryn derived a different message.*

When I think about the summer of 1945, when through a chance I cannot fathom, I was free and still in life, and filled with so many uncertainties, there was one certainty for me: that when the world saw and understood what unspeakable atrocities had been committed in the name of racism born of long-festering prejudice, intolerance and the deafening silence of decent by-standers – why, I was sure that never again would there be anti-semitism, or race-hatreds of any kind and that nothing would ever again erode the Divine image imprinted in every human being and the dignity of individual men and women. The sad truth is that tyranny and race-hatred did not end when the Second World war ended, as we then hoped and believed, but the vision for peace did not die.

Source: Hugo Gryn, *Chasing Shadows*, p. 256.

COMMENT: *For Gryn, the Holocaust did not lessen his vision of peace, but reinforced it. It was a modern equivalent of the principle behind the injunction to the Israelites in the Book of Exodus not to oppress the stranger because they themselves had experienced being strangers in the land of Egypt. Contemporary Jews, who had suffered from the terrible consequences of the absence of peace, were all the more obliged to work for it.*

# 21

# REFORM JUDAISM

As its name suggests, Reform Judaism was an attempt to amend and find a more relevant expression of Judaism to that prevailing at the time. By what authority was such a change introduced? What determined its arrival in 1840 rather than some earlier or later period? Was it seen as rejuvenation of Judaism, restoring a by-then stagnant faith to its former dynamism, or was it regarded as a modernisation of Judaism, implementing radical changes to accommodate new realities? Did the Reformers see themselves as the true heirs of the Judaism of old, or were they consciously creating a new branch of their religion?

## 21.1 David Woolf Marks on the Need for Reform (1842)

*The West London Synagogue – the first Reform congregation in Britain – was founded by a group of lay leaders. However, it was their first minister, Reverend Professor Marks, who both shaped and gave expression to the new ethos of Reform Judaism.*

We must not confound the form with the substance; we must not regard an infinity of ceremonials as the final aim of religion – viewing as secondary all that is moral, all that is spiritual, all that embraces the eternal salvation of man. Now since, in the progress of time, it has been the misfortune of our people to fall into this particular error, we, who purpose to rectify the evil, declare at the very outset of our career, that it is not a desire for innovation, not a want of respect for those institutions which our more immediate ancestors obeyed, but a paramount obligation, a deep sense of right that impels us to those measures which, in our inmost hearts, we consider the only means of arousing our brethren from that indifference to spiritual matters into which they have unhappily sunk; and of preserving our sacred religion from the blight of infidelity, to say nothing of apostasy, which is making inroads amongst us.

... We must solemnly deny that a belief in the divinity of the traditions contained in the Mishna, and the Jerusalem and Babylonian Talmuds, is of equal obligation to the Israelite with the faith in the divinity of the Law of Moses. We know that these books are human compositions; and though we are content to accept with reverence from our post-biblical ancestors advice and instruction, we cannot unconditionally accept their laws. For Israelites, there is but One immutable Law – the sacred volume of the Scriptures, commanded by God to be written down for the unerring guidance of his people until the end of time.

... On all hands it is conceded, that an absolute necessity exists for the modification of our worship; but no sooner is any important improvement proposed, than we are assured of the sad fact that there is not at present any competent authority to judge in such matters for the whole House of Israel. Does it not follow, as a necessity, that every Hebrew congregation must be authorised to take such measures as we shall bring the divine service into consonance with the will of the Almighty, as explained to us in the Law and in the Prophets?

... We are, happily, emerging from the darkness into which persecutions of unparalleled intensity and duration had banished us; our domestic, social, and political life is assuming a brightness which we feel assured will continue to become even more cheering. Shall then the life of the Synagogue alone remain darkened by the shadows of deepest mourning and despair? We feel that the time has arrived when we must do our utmost to make our religion respected, not only in the sight of the world at large, but, which is of far greater concern, in the sight of our rising community, who will not rest satisfied with the insignificant assurance that a practice must be revered because it has sprung into existence in countries and under circumstances totally different from those under the influence of which we live.

Source: David Woolf Marks, *Lectures & Sermons*, Vol. I, pp. 5–12.

COMMENT: *Marks is forthright about the need for change and the obli-gation to do so both to restore the original spirit of Judaism that has suffered from neglect, and to answer the needs of a new generation of Jews living under different conditions from the past. He also sees Reform as a response to the twin attacks of missionary activity and assimilation.*

*These factors are, to his mind, of sufficient authority to justify change. However, his insistence on the abiding and immutable role of the Penta-teuch is highly puzzling, given the fact that he himself would have admitted that many parts were either irrelevant, such as the sacrificial system, or unacceptable, such as stoning a rebellious child. It indicates astonishing inconsistency in his thinking. While Marks has a pioneering role as the first Reform rabbi in Britain, he did not produce a coherent Reform theology.*

### 21.2  David Woolf Marks on the Dangers of Reform (1884)

*By the 1880s, the West London Synagogue had grown to such an extent that it had not only survived an initial ban of excommunication by the Ortho-dox authorities but had moved three times to larger premises. Two other Reform synagogues had been established elsewhere in the country. How-ever, Reverend Professor Marks was also aware of potential pitfalls and felt obliged to alert the new movement to them.*

No body of men can undertake a task like that on which promoters of this synagogue engaged more than forty years ago without incurring a serious risk. There are sufficient reasons for apprehending that when men set themselves free from the control of what others of the same community recognise as spiritual authority, they may be betrayed into extreme changes, and that having ignored some post-Biblical ordinances and modified others, they may be led on to treat lightly ceremonial dis-ciplines in general, heedless of the grave truth, that the very spirit of religion would wither, just as the fruit-kernel would perish, if deprived of its outward coating.

Be cautious, be diffident, of introducing further changes into your public worship, unless they be for the purpose of removing what may tend to interrupt the devotion and solemnity proper to the House of

God. If the ritual – an element which is so indispensable to practical Judaism – is to command veneration, it is in the last degree essential that it be invested with a certain fixedness of character, and it must not be tampered with by sentimentalism, nor by a feverish desire for change for mere change's sake.

Source: David Woolf Marks, *Lectures & Sermons*, Vol. III, pp. 50–1.

COMMENT: *Like anyone who had led revolutionary changes in his particular field, Marks had become aware of the thin dividing line between reformation and anarchy. Hence his plea for caution over further reforms that might dissipate the faith altogether. However, it is also common for reformers to wish to preserve the changes they have made but deny to others the same right to change that they themselves had claimed. Marks could be accused of stultifying the innovative spirit of Reform Judaism, and this may be one of the reasons why it failed to grow greatly for the next half-century.*

### 21.3 Morris Joseph on Reform and Tradition (1903)

*Reverend Joseph had no doubt about the towering role of Reverend Professor Marks in founding and developing Reform Judaism in Britain. However, he was equally convinced that some of the principles Marks had formulated were difficult to uphold and needed to be re-assessed.*

It has been deemed the characteristic function of progressive Judaism to reject the traditional view [on the binding authority of the Talmud], and to keep Judaism strictly within the four corners of the Bible, a position which is clearly self-contradictory, seeing that no religion can be progressive which is identified only with certain phases of it. Moreover, this view has proved to be impossible in practice. Its advocates have inconsistently to fall back upon the Rabbinical citron at Tabernacles and the traditional ram's horn at New Year. They borrow the Feast of Dedication from post-Biblical ordinances, and the whole framework of their liturgy from Talmudic and post-Talmudic sources.

Still more significant is it that Traditionalism, far from being a synonym for religious stagnation, as is commonly supposed, is necessarily the authoritative licence for religious progress. The interpretation which is to elucidate the Divine Word is itself mutable; it responds to the ever-changing needs of the human mind. The Oral Law is not fixed, but fluid; its growth does not belong to any one age, but continues indefinitely. Thus the Rabbins could declare that to Moses every ordinance was revealed that was to be instituted in after times, however remote, and that the doctrine of any teacher, however obscure he might be, was to be venerated in the same degree as if it had been taught by the Prophets or even by Moses himself. In other words, new conditions call for new interpretations and new ordinances, and these are sacred. If at certain periods that theory has made for rigidity and apparent narrowness, it provides at other times for elasticity and growth.

Source: Morris Joseph, *Judaism as Creed and Life*, pp. 33–4.

COMMENT: *Joseph openly distances himself from Marks's reliance solely on the Bible and his professed exclusion of rabbinic teachings. This is both because it is untenable practically, as seen in the examples he quotes, and because he holds that the rabbinic tradition (the Oral Law) is intrinsically flexible and open to change. Thus, in his eyes, Reform is effectively a continuation of the progressive interpretation within Judaism that had become stagnant.*

## 21.4 Harold Reinhart on Reform and Radicalism (1930)

*When Rabbi Reinhart became Senior Minister of West London Synagogue in 1929, he found a community that had long ago lost its reforming zeal and that could be described as conventional and complacent. Coming from an American Reform background that was much more highly charged, Reinhart was determined to rekindle the radical spirit of Reform Judaism in Britain.*

I wish to reject unequivocally for the use by our Synagogue the term that has lately found favour among a few: 'the middle way'. There is a sense in which the use of this phrase might be good and helpful; it might suggest moderation and careful judgement. But I submit that this is not the sense in which it is understood within and without our Synagogue: that we are to march in the safe and sheltered middle, accepting what is proved and tried by others and can be accepted without fear of too much condemnation by those who are still further behind in the march, a constant halting between two opinions, failure to believe in the old, but lack of sufficient spirit and power to seek the new. Doubtless there are some who would be satisfied with such a policy as this. But it is totally unworthy of our historic congregation. 'Safety first' is no worthy goal for us. We must emphasize anew that we stand for a definite point of view in Jewish life. We assert the right and the duty to change and adapt. We lay a different emphasis upon past revelation as opposed to present than do our orthodox brothers. For us the teachings of the past have authority in so far as they are able to convince us and to find justification in our own conscience. But the authority for ultimate decision is the voice of God in our own hearts. 'To thine own self be true,' say we, and not only, 'thou canst not then be false to any man,' but also, thou canst not then be false to God. Orthodoxy with its completed code and its lack of living authority sufficient to deal with any matter of radical significance, must exalt conformity into the place of prime importance. We may respect this attitude. But it is not ours. And those who would use the cloak of orthodoxy to cover a policy of continuous vacillation, compromise and timidity, merit the contempt of earnest men. Reform means a frank and free facing of the religious situation and the willingness to follow where the logic of that situation demands. Ours the task to revive the creative side of Jewish faith and practice. Ours to hew the channels through which may flow the waters of a new and freshening faith.

Source: Harold Reinhart, 'The Senior Minister's First Year', *The Synagogue Review*, Vol. IV, No. 8, pp. 117–18.

COMMENT: *Reinhart is distinctive by his forthrightness. This applies both to his scorn for the conformism of Orthodoxy and to his passion for the mission of Reform. The passage signals his departure from the middle way associated with Joseph, who preferred compromise to extremes. Notable, too, is his insistence that a higher authority than both the Bible and Rabbinic Literature is 'the voice of God in our own hearts' – although some might*

*consider it far too subjective to provide real guidance for an organized faith.*
*He also takes the radical step of reversing the burden of proof: declaring not*
*that tradition is to be automatically accepted unless proven inappropriate,*
*but that it is only to be accepted if it concurs with modern sensibilities.*

## 21.5  Arthur Katz on Re-assessing Reform (1958)

*The 1940s and 1950s brought cataclysmic new factors into Jewish life and*
*thinking. For many Jews, the Holocaust destroyed their belief in the uni-*
*versal progress of humanity, while the birth of the State of Israel provided a*
*form of vicarious Jewish identity for many non-religious Jews. Yet Reform*
*Judaism had changed little in character since the 1840s. Rabbi Dr Katz*
*argued that it had to adapt to the changing climate.*

Let us look back at what happened in Reform Judaism in those early
days.

Early Reform was convinced that young people would be drawn to
Judaism by its sheer logic. They devoted all their time and attention to
the ethical and moral precepts of universal Judaism; reason rather than
ritual was their technique of piety. We, the third and fourth generation,
have learnt that Classical Reform made the mistake in 'reforming too
far', in intellectualizing religion and thus sundering Judaism from the
Jewish people. Judaism has much to it that is of the mind, but Jewishness
is of the heart, and a religion must be saturated with emotion, it must
have symbols, around which to rally feeling and sentiment, and Judaism
needs both mind and heart to be nourished.

What a paradox, that Judaism having preached pure ethical Universalism in its early days, brought up a generation on a religion so reasonable
that there did not seem to be much to teach and thus slowly lost interest.
Still their sons and daughters found their place in Jewish affairs, but not
as religious Jews, but rather by their Jewishness, by their identification as
Jews whose Jewish feelings were whipped up by Hitler's frenzy or compounded by the struggle to establish the State of Israel.

Indeed it is hard to be a Jew. But it is harder to be a Reform Jew than
an Orthodox Jew. Anyone can adhere to Orthodox Judaism by following
the prescribed rules of Talmud and Poskim [subsequent legislators], but

it is much harder to be a Reform Jew, for he must decide by himself on the basis of study and guidance what to retain and what to reform.

Source: Arthur Katz, 'Looking Ahead', *The Synagogue Review*, Vol. 32, No. 6, p. 154.

COMMENT: *Katz articulates the desire felt by many at that time that Reform Judaism was itself in need of reform. The emphasis on the ethical rather than the ritual aspects that Marks had championed had to be redressed and greater balance restored. This was both a response to changing circumstances and also a requisite if Reform was to attract newcomers, who would largely come from more traditional backgrounds and not feel at home in the 'cold' atmosphere often associated with Reform synagogues. Katz also alludes to the heavy responsibility that freedom of choice brings, although he seems prepared to trust that all Reform Jews will undertake sufficient 'study and guidance'.*

## 21.6 Werner van der Zyl on the Tradition of Reform (1963)

*Following the Second World War, Reform Judaism in Britain had begun to grow in membership and synagogues. This was partly because of the influx of Continental refugees from Reform communities there, and partly because of members of Orthodox synagogues changing to Reform. One result was that Reform was seen as a threat by the Orthodox establishment, who started to launch attacks on its validity in the 1960s. By way of response, Rabbi Dr van der Zyl – himself one of the refugee rabbis – both mapped out the need for Reform and defended its Jewish credentials.*

It is the duty of Jewish people in every generation to interpret, through knowledge and guidance from the past, the meaning of the divine will for their own age. Rabbis for today must be responsible for a true interpretation of Jewish values for today, both in principle and practice. It is not possible for our generation to live by the law merely by referring to the opinions of authorities centuries ago, of a bygone age when our forefathers lived in a different world. Two thousand years ago was the time of the rabbis, today is the time of modern science when man conquers space. To the modern man, earth and sky and universe have taken on a different meaning – we are no longer able to equate 'sky and earth' with 'heaven and earth'. Many forms we use have thus become meaningless and need a re-interpretation in line with the thoughts of a new age.

Reform in Judaism is nothing new. In the times of the prophets and the Men of the Great Synagogue, progressive interpretation was always maintained, otherwise no authority could have abolished the principle of 'an eye for an eye', mentioned in the *Torah*, or have permitted war on *Shabbat*. Hillel, when he found that the law in Deuteronomy that cancelled debts in the Sabbatical year proved to be detrimental to the poor, introduced the *prosbul* permitting their collection afterwards – a change in the Law of *Torah*, in true pursuance of the principle by not adhering to the letter. And there are many similar cases . . . When Maimonides, who though much ahead of his time, faced a similar problem in the 12th century, he gave answers which startled the people of his day – and some orthodox rabbis banned his 'Guide for the Perplexed'.

In the past Jewish law had been the dominant factor in the life of a Jew. In our age science and philosophy gradually deprived the *Torah* of its overriding role. In the conflict between science and religion Judaism in its old interpretation could not always give satisfactory answers to problems which confused the Jews, and many Jews began to think Judaism inferior to the thought of the new age. But all this does not mean that Judaism must surrender to the new age. In so far as principles or ideas are still pagan, we have to oppose them . . . As Jews we have a unique experience. As Reform Jews we believe in the renaissance of Judaism in our own time.

Source: Werner van der Zyl, *The Synagogue Review*, Vol. 37, No. 5, pp. 102–3.

COMMENT: *Van der Zyl justifies Reform both as a necessary response to modern conditions and as a continuation of the reforming trend that has always existed within Judaism. Reform is not a new development but the latest manifestation of a long-established process.*

## 21.7 Collective Theological Essay on Living Within Two Cultures (1990)

*The essay was the result of informal discussions among rabbis and communal leaders over a long period. Its intention was to be a position paper, outlining what Reform Judaism – albeit labelled Progressive Judaism – stood for at that point. It did not claim to be authoritative – merely representative of those who had contributed to it, and it was then edited by Rabbi Bayfield.*

Progressive Judaism is the response our teachers and teaching have made to the ideas of the modern Western world. Such cross-fertilisation is by no means unique in the Jewish experience; it has always occurred and has always revitalised Judaism in each epoch. There are many aspects of the modern Western world which distress us – its dethronement of God and enthronement of humanity, its uncritical faith in science and scientific knowledge, its abuse of technology as an instrument of human torture and destruction, its ruthless exploitation of human and natural resources solely for economic gain, its elevation of self-interest as the main determinant of human relations. There are, however, many aspects which we gladly embrace – its scholarship, its enunciation of individual human rights, its cultural pluralism, its psychological insights, its advances in many scientific and technological areas which offer an enhanced level to the quality of human life. Whatever our ambivalence, the present is with us and we acknowledge that it forms a starting point.

We recognise that modernity has brought both good and bad to the world. Judaism believes that it is essential to live in the world, adopting a stance described as one of 'creative maladjustment'. The meeting between Judaism and the world has not always been positive for Jewish life. Nevertheless, we Progressive Jews do not believe we can fulfill our obligations as Jews by turning our back on it and seeking our survival through isolation. We value our difference and distinctiveness, but do not wish to preserve it by separating ourselves from the wider community. We choose freely to live simultaneously within two cultures, holding Jerusalem as our highest joy, whilst doing justice to Athens.

We understand that truth, which we equate with the divine Reality and the divine will for the world, is multi-faceted and that no single expression of Judaism or of any religion can encompass all truth. We therefore acknowledge that any form of religion is, in a sense, provisional: that no one expression of Judaism can accommodate all Jews in all places at all times; that Judaism does not possess a monopoly on truth; that truth may be found in other religious traditions; that truth is also to be found through teachers and disciplines which may have no formal religious label.

We recognise that a significant level of religious doubt is endemic to modern thinking. The search has been continuous ever since Abraham and Sarah set off on their religious journey. This emphasis on search is a healthy antidote to the certainties which each generation so frequently holds about truth and a corrective to the plague of fanaticism which defaces the religious world of our time. Nevertheless, we acknowledge that many Jews today are less certain than we imagine preceding generations to have been about belief in God. Such doubt and skepticism are part of a contemporary Jewish reality which it is our duty to face.

Source: Tony Bayfield, 'Progressive Judaism, a Collective Theological Essay and Discussion Paper', *Manna*, 27, Theology Supplement A. 1–4.

COMMENT: *The essay is remarkable for its humility. It lauds neither the supremacy of Judaism in general nor the path of Reform in particular. Instead it acknowledges the merit, where appropriate, of both modern secularism and other faiths. It also hints that they too may contain aspects of God's revelation. It emphasizes how Reform must seek an accommodation with them, and be unafraid either to reject what is harmful or to adopt what is beneficial. The essay also admits that religious doubt is a prevalent factor in Jewish life, even for those who consider themselves religious, and suggests that no serious expression of Judaism today can afford to ignore it.*

### 21.8 Dow Marmur on Reform and Jewish Law (1999)

*As Reform Judaism became more popular and more mainstream, the question of defining its relationship with Jewish Law became more pressing. This became more urgent with the birth of the Masorti/Conservative movement in Britain in 1985, which accepted the binding force of Jewish law but was willing to use its principles to sanction change. Where did Reform Judaism stand and what parameters did it accept?*

A non-dramatic, incremental quiet revolution has taken place in Reform Judaism. [It] reflects the truth that we are neither *halakhic* Jews seeking to follow the law in all its minutiae – as invented by what today is known as Orthodox Judaism – nor those who seek to circumvent it while claiming its authenticity, Conservative-style. And we are not anti-*halakhic*, classical Reform-style. Mercifully we no longer maintain that anything that smacks of Orthodox Judaism has no place in our movement. Just look at the way even *tefillin* have become options in Reform worship, or consider the dietary discipline and home observance adopted by an ever growing number of Reform Jews.

We are neither *halakhic* nor anti-*halakhic*. We are post-*halakhic*. We have moved beyond artificial legalism – *halakhah*, time-bound and unjustifiably restrictive, yet petrified and petrifying – towards the affirmation of *mitzvah* the sense of obligation that comes from Sinai, hallowed, and often defined and refined, by hundreds of generations that have gone before us.

We are trying to follow in the footsteps of these generations, not by imitating their mores but by adopting their values. In doing so, we believe that we have done precisely what they have done in their endeavour to live as Jews and to celebrate the presence of God in their lives. But because our situation is different from theirs, our way of expressing these values must differ, too. Jewish history suggests that this has always been the case. By being who we are, we see ourselves as authentic exponents of normative Judaism.

Because we are sensitive to history and to the needs of those whom we serve, we have changed very much in the almost two centuries of our existence. We continue to change. The notion of Reform as a dynamic verb – not a static noun or adjective – remains true.

Source: Dow Marmur, 'Duck Creeds, Try Deeds', *Manna*, 63, p. 3.

COMMENT: *Marmur lifts the debate regarding Reform and Jewish Law beyond the previous confines of 'for' or 'against', and asserts that the reality of modern Jewish life can no longer be defined in those terms. Not law, but commandment and covenant are the new indices of Jewish life, although the actual method of decision-making is left vague. He does make clear, however, that Reform Judaism is part of an ever-changing process – a verb rather than a noun – and so no system should be adopted that is constrictive. Sinai is both the focal point and the start of a process of Progressive Revelation that is on-going in each generation.*

## A Final Thought . . .

I passionately believe in Reform Judaism with all my heart:

- because of the young man due to be married who came to me. His father had married a non-Jewish lady and she had died soon after he was born. He went to live with his Jewish grandmother, who brought him up in an Orthodox Jewish manner. He went to Jewish youth clubs, in an Orthodox synagogue, and was *barmitzvah* there, believing he was Jewish. When he came to be married, it was discovered that he was not Jewish. I recommended him to our *Beth Din* who examined him and declared he was Jewish. He was married in our synagogue.
- because of the lady to whom I spoke. She married during the war, had two children, and at the end of the war her husband was killed. She recently met a man whom she wanted to marry, but she was told that because she had not seen the body of her husband she could not remarry in an Orthodox synagogue. She did so in ours.
- because while we do not agree with inter-marriage, we do know that it exists, and rather than drive away members from the community, if there is sincerity and conviction, we believe it is better to bring them into the fold after showing proof of their sincerity and knowledge.
- because of the lady who divorced her husband in the civil courts. She told me that she wanted to remarry but obviously needed a *get* [document of religious divorce] first. This can only be given by her husband, and in this case he refused to give it to her unless she paid him a sum of money. The Orthodox authorities advised her to pay. She was allowed to remarry in our synagogue – without paying her husband.

Source: Percy Selvin Goldberg, 'Why I Believe in Judaism', *The Jewish Telegraph*, 19 July 1963, p. 3.

# 22

## SOCIAL ACTION

The term social action may be a modern one but it is rooted in the mission of the Prophets in the Bible, who protested against the social and political evils of their day. They attacked the monarchy for its abuse of power (Isaiah 1.23), railed against the malpractices of the business community (Amos 8.4–6) and criticized the neglect of human rights in society (Amos 5.7–11). However, not all subsequent Jewish leaders shared their courage or were as concerned with the wider issues of society at large. Many considered that the role of the synagogue or rabbinate was to be occupied solely with internal Jewish affairs. It was a view reinforced by the legacy of centuries of separation between the Jewish community and the rest of society. Reform Judaism, by contrast, saw itself as restoring the spirit of Prophetic Judaism to a faith that had become dominated by the minutiae of rabbinic legislation. It also viewed public life as the natural habitat of modern Jews.

### 22.1 Morris Joseph on Political Responsibilities (1903)

*At the same time as West London Synagogue was founded in 1840, the Jewish community was fighting for full political emancipation, with the right to be elected to local government and Parliament. Many of the early Reform lay leaders were active in this struggle, their desire for political reform matching their desire for religious reform. Sixty years later, with those political rights long gained, Reverend Joseph reminded their heirs of the responsibilities that accompanied them.*

The suffrage is a sacred trust and the good citizen will so regard it. He will give his vote conscientiously, after patiently endeavouring, as far as his intelligence and his opportunities permit, to understand and weigh the issues involved. The franchise may be his right, but every right carries with it a corresponding responsibility. To have a vote and use it thoughtlessly, or to be too indolent to use it, is to show oneself unworthy of its possession. Nor may we discriminate and say, 'I will vote at Parliamentary elections, which involve national issues, but it is not worth troubling to vote for the County or the Borough Council.' This attitude is answerable for many of the shortcomings that disfigure the work of such public bodies, and for the difficulty that is experienced in remedying them.

The suffrage, moreover, must be used for the promotion of the general good, as we conceive of it, and not for our own personal ends. To give our vote, for example, to a candidate for Parliament merely because he has promised to support a Bill for the making of a new street that will increase the value of our property, is to abuse the trust confided in us. In politics we must be guided by political considerations only, by principles which we sincerely believe to make for the Welfare of the State. All thoughts of self must be discarded. But our political principles must be ethically sound. The good of the State, like the good of the individual, can never grow out of moral evil. Patriotism is the supreme duty of the citizen, but our conception of patriotism must be based upon reverence for righteousness. 'My country, right or wrong' is the utterance not of the patriot, but of the fanatic.

Source: Morris Joseph, *Judaism as Creed and Life*, pp. 491–?.

COMMENT: *The simple way in which Joseph outlines the moral concerns that should guide political involvement is very effective. It is clear, however, from his need to speak out in this way, that he is trying to combat the twin-evils of indifference and self-interest that often characterize people's attitudes to politics, in whatever century they live.*

## 22.2 Solomon Starrels on Taking a Stand (1932)

*The 1920s had seen Britain reeling from the effect of economic depression and mass unemployment. The membership of Reform synagogues tended to come from the more affluent strata of society, some of whom felt that the function of a synagogue was to teach about one's relationship with God. It should avoid economic and political matters. For some this was a matter of principle, for others it arose either from fear of them becoming divisive issues, or because of worries as how any stand would be perceived in non-Jewish circles. Rabbi Starrels was committed to the opposite approach.*

For myself, I prefer a spirit of abandon in the Synagogue. I don't want the Synagogue to be too cautious or too hesitant. I don't want it to wait until a battle is virtually won before committing itself. I don't want it to leave to secular agencies the leadership in moral struggles, and for the rabbinate to follow at a safe distance. I would prefer that the Synagogue should occasionally make a solid mistake, or sometimes espouse a cause that should later prove fallacious, than that it should be everlastingly cautious and hesitant and timid and respectable. For if the Synagogue is to hold its place in the modern world, it must come to grips with the greatest living issues and speak out in unmistakable terms.

What are these burning issues with which the Synagogue must deal? They are of course many, but the three I have chosen are among the most urgent. The first is the problem of poverty. Whenever there is vast wealth and dire poverty existing side by side, we have not only an economic problem but a religious one as well. Last year in our own Midlands whole fields of cabbage were destroyed in order to manipulate the market price – and all this while children are undernourished and there is widespread destitution. The Synagogue is free to speak out because it is not committed to any economic system and has no political axe to grind. True to its historical role as champion of the poor, it must take the lead in the struggle to eliminate in a world teeming with abundance, the shame of poverty.

A second great task to which the Synagogue must address itself is on behalf of human brotherhood. At the centre of our faith is the admonition 'Love your neighbour as yourself'; and yet we find the world ridden with class and caste and racial discrimination. The whole democratic structure of the Synagogue collapses unless we hold fast to the absolute equality of all men and the supreme worth of every individual . . . A third problem is that of war. In Europe today there are more men under arms than in 1914, and there is more bitterness and suspicion and seeds of war than in that fateful year . . . It is in keeping with the highest interpretation of Judaism to refuse to sanction war or to have anything to do with it. I have been taught that Israel's mission is peace, and I believe it, and I feel that the time has come for us to show that we really mean it.

Source: Solomon E. Starrels, 'The Function of the Synagogue Today', *West London Synagogue Magazine*, Vol. I, No. 6, pp. 83–4.

COMMENT: *Starrels speaks out on the subjects of poverty, democracy and war, but more important is his clear assertion that it is both appropriate and necessary for the Synagogue to involve itself in all matters that concern the life of the nation as a whole. In his eyes, the risk of occasionally making a mistake is far outweighed by the twin dangers of ignoring moral imperatives or being irrelevant to everyday life.*

## 22.3 Gerhard Graf on Ethics in Judaism (1970)

*The growth of inter-faith dialogue and religious pluralism brought many benefits, including the awareness that most major faiths shared a common ethical value system, as did those who were humanists or secularists. This also presented the danger that ethics became seen as divorced from any one religion, and that the key element of any faith was its distinctive practices and beliefs. Rabbi Graf felt the need to counter such assumptions.*

Jewish action naturally includes ritual, but it also includes an emphasis on the pursuit of Jewish ethics. I often hear it said that ethics is 'something universal' and need not be specially emphasized by us. What terrible darkness has descended upon us! What ignorance! Are we to leave ethical pronouncements and ethical action to another religion? Are we to leave its claim to secular humanism? Are we to pedal softly when nationalism and racism lift their heads? Are we to remain silent as long as it does not concern us and we are not in danger? Does all this not belong to the task of our synagogues? Does not this impel us to protest openly, strongly, uncompromisingly and act accordingly *l'shem shamayim*, for the sake of heaven?

We are inclined always to look inwardly and not outwardly. Do not many of our actions betray the loftiest concepts of Jewish teaching? Are

only 'the others' wicked nationalists and racialists? Have we not assimilated into our system the most ghastly characteristics of the masses? Why
are there 'Reform' synagogues who want to keep the non-Jew from
joining our faith forgetting that ours was the first missionary faith in
the world? Shame on those who count the number of converts in their
midst. Indeed they need the Day of Atonement. Shame on all those who
look down on the coloured man. We miss the cosmopolitan spirit in
many a Jewish fellowman.

Judaism is a mixture of particularism and universalism. We have
assimilated ourselves to the particularism which plays such an over-
whelming role all over the world at present, forgetting the universal side
of Judaism. Let us be 'different' in this respect also that in our synagogues
we again propagate a little more universalism.

Source: Gerhard Graf, 'More Light Needed', *Living Judaism*, Vol. 4, No. 2, p. 40.

COMMENT: *Graf effectively reminds his readers that ethical action is
an essential component of Judaism, and that opposing racism is as Jewish
as lighting candles.*

## 22.4 Tony Bayfield on the Ethics of Action (1988)

*In the 1980s there was much greater emphasis on Social Action as a active
part of the work of Reform Judaism. It was no longer seen as the particular cause of individual rabbis, but the general responsibility of the Reform
movement as a whole. Some were nervous that this would be seen as endors-
ing certain political groups or becoming allied with controversial campaigns.
Rabbi Bayfield argued the case for publicly engaging in social issues.*

It is simply not possible for a Jew, rooted in tradition, to ignore blatant
inequalities within society and the suffering of the weak, to turn away
from the implications of unemployment, homelessness and poverty. It
is inconceivable that believing Jews should see starvation and famine
abroad and shrug. To disregard issues of war and peace, of our treatment
of the environment, of racial and religious oppression is to disregard
the very core of how Judaism conceives of religion. To be sure these are

political issues but they are also religious issues. Religion may indeed be about our solitariness but if it is only about our solitariness, it is an indulgence that humanity cannot afford and God cannot bear.

How to eradicate famine will confront us with a number of possible strategies; how to combat oppression will lead us to the choices offered by opposing political parties. Religion does not always tell us which course of action will be the most effective, but religion does demand that we act. Judaism would be ill-advised to wed itself too closely to any one party political programme but Judaism is, inevitably, political, since politics deals with how people organize themselves in society – justly or unjustly, oppressively or in a manner which liberates.

Judaism demands social action, not social isolation. The proponents of a particular course of action may sometimes confuse their particular strategy as the only strategy. At least as great a danger are the excuses and rationalisations many more offer for inaction. All the grain we send to Ethiopia may well not get through to the starving, but to send no grain at all is to pronounce the most terrible of verdicts. Religion defines the goals and values; the strategies are for discussion. But only a murderer could have asked 'Am I my brother's keeper?' Religion without inwardness will be fake. Religion which is only inwardness, which shrinks from the inevitable political implications, renounces the very essence of Jewish tradition.

Source: Tony Bayfield, 'Rekindle the Light to the Nations', *Manna*, 18, p. 1.

COMMENT: *Bayfield asserts that it is impossible to be Jewish and avoid being political; nor is there any problem with the latter, so long as it is the cause which drives one's actions rather than party politics.*

## 22.5 Dow Marmur on a Theology of Social Action (1988)

*Social action may have been advocated by the leadership of Reform Judaism, but it was not always welcomed by the membership, which was suspicious of too much identification with what was seen as radical issues, such as homelessness and race relations. Moreover, in reaction to a growing public climate of anti-Zionism – often perceived as a cloak for anti-semitism – many felt that Jewish efforts should be directed towards internal needs rather than external causes. Rabbi Marmur sought to provide a religious justification for social action that would counter such instincts.*

Instead of being overwhelmed by the tendency to social isolationism in our midst, we must seek to counteract it. To do so we need not only enthusiasm and tenacity but also a theoretical basis, a theology of social action. Let me offer only two sets of reasons: historic and mystical.

The historic reason for social action is best expressed by the many statements in Scripture to the effect that we have to behave well to the downtrodden – whoever and wherever they may be – because we were slaves in Egypt. Whereas psychology may suggest that the downtrodden oppress others as soon as they get a chance to do so, our theology insists that, because we have suffered, we must alleviate the suffering of others as soon as we are given the means to do that. Such action cannot be a matter of discretion. It is a question of duty. It is not charity but justice.

The second reason for social action is mystical. In the Jewish mystical tradition much is made of the idea that the world is incomplete and our task as human beings is to complete it, often described as *tikkun olam*, mending the world. We are doing things, performing *mitzvot*, as one way of helping to make the world a better place, of mending it. We have been created by God for this task. God has revealed His will to humanity through the people of Israel to tell us how to do it. When we are doing what our Creator revealed to us we are working towards the redemption of the world.

. . . Now it is possible that some, or many, Reform Jews who are engaged in this work do it almost as a substitute for Judaism and as an *Ersatz* for spirituality. The Jewish answer to this would be: so what? Our religious heritage is very cautious about judging motives. It is much more interested in results.

Source: Dow Marmur, 'Social Action and Reform Judaism', *Manna*, 21, pp. 22–3.

COMMENT: *Marmur sidesteps the usual appeal to the Prophetic tradition to justify social action. His use of mystical concepts is a major departure for Reform thinking, which had always equated mysticism with obscurantism, and regarded it as contrary to the rational, scientific approach upon which much of Reform was based.*

## 22.6  Barbara Borts on Repairing the World (1996)

*The command to be concerned for society at large was well-established within Judaism and had been highlighted by the rabbis above. However, Rabbi Borts was worried that the vastly improved status and security of Western Jews compared to former times could dull their sense of social responsibility. She sought to alert them to the divine imperative that still remained in force.*

There is a hoary sociological truism that one changes one's affiliations – religious, political, social and even recreational – as one becomes empowered by money or status. In England, the United States and elsewhere, Jews have made it. Our income and careers, our levels of education and our pre-eminence in many important endeavours, has established us as a well-off, well-educated, articulate and powerful force in British and North American life . . . We Jews are now a middle-class people, but is the God to whom we pray a middle-class God? Or is the fact that we were once slaves and were delivered, and then enjoined to love our neighbour and take heed of the rules of fair treatment of others, not a sign to us that this God asks more of us than our seeing to our own comfort? We may not need economic liberation because we are not poor peasants in South America. But we need other kinds of liberation from that which we have brought upon ourselves by our way of life and skewed values, and we have to realize that our neighbour must now include that poor Brazilian peasant, whose destiny is our destiny, and whose liberation is linked to our liberations.

Radical Christianity portrays God as suffering the pain of the world through the body of Christ. One does not, however, need an incarnation to portray God as a sufferer, nor in fact does one need an incarnation as a proclamation of human solidarity. The fact that Genesis proclaims that we are created 'in the divine image' and that God has breathed 'the spirit of life' into us shows that we are all children of God and partake of God's essence – the point of Judaism is not how to make the Divine human so that the Divine participates in human suffering, but how to encounter the Divine in each human so as to create the bonds of kinship which will cause us to work to eradicate suffering . . . Judaism has always emphasized this life, and hope as a central aspect. We are in effect prisoners of hope, of a sort of pessimistic optimism. A God who requires woman and man to become partners in creating the world cannot be anything but a force toward perfection. It is a task for Jews, with our image of God, with our historical suffering, with our understanding of life on the boundary, to develop and deepen the idea of *Tikkun olam* [repairing the world], to answer yes to the world and to the God who awaits our response.

Source: Barbara Borts, 'Repairing the World – a Task for Jews?', in Jonathan Romain (ed.), *Renewing the Vision: Rabbis Speak Out on Modern Jewish Issues*, pp. 194, 199–202.

COMMENT: *Borts highlights the radical strain in Judaism and the duty not to preserve the status quo but to constantly find ways of improving it. It is a messianic task but neither theoretical nor postponed till the fullness of time, but one with a practical agenda and an urgent timetable.*

## A Final Thought . . .

I am desperately concerned that the issue of asylum seeking and the authorities' mean-spirited response to it are part of a process which is the hardening of the caring arteries. There is such a process going on at the end of the twentieth century here in civilised Europe. It is an abomination, but it is happening. A civilised society has a responsibility for shielding and protecting life. In biblical times, places of refuge were a guard against the miscarriage of justice and the arbitrary use of power. Any society that wants to call itself a civilised society must have in it these areas of refuge. I believe that future historians will call the twentieth century not only the century of the great wars, but also the century of the refugee. Almost nobody at the end of the century is where they were at the beginning of it. It has been an extraordinary period of movement and upheavals. There are so many scars that need mending and healing that it seems to me imperative that we proclaim that asylum issues are an index of our spiritual and moral civilisation. How you are with the one to whom you owe nothing, that is a grave test. I always think that the real offenders at the half-way mark of the century were the bystanders, all those people who let things happen because it didn't affect them directly. I believe that the line our society will take on how you are to people to whom you owe nothing is a critical signal that we give to our young, and I hope and pray that it is a test we shall not fail.

Source: Hugo Gryn, *A Moral and Spiritual Index*, p. 2.

# 23

# SOCIETY

Ever since Jews have lived outside the land of Israel, there has always been the question of how far they should be part of their host society and to what extent separate from it. When Jeremiah wrote a letter of advice to the Jews exiled in Babylon, he urged them to work for the good of the society in which they lived, yet also warned them not to be beguiled by its values (29.7–8). The problem of assimilation leading to total loss of identity is well-recorded, yet isolation can be equally dangerous, resulting in both religious claustrophobia and being viewed as alien by others. The very existence of Reform Judaism, which saw itself as proudly rooted in Jewish tradition yet actively part of wider society, was an attempt to achieve a balanced solution.

## 23.1 David Woolf Marks on Jews' Role in Society (1857)

*The early Reform Jews felt they had a twofold task: to indicate to their co-religionists that they had not abandoned or compromised their Jewish identity in any way, and also to persuade society at large that they were as attached to British values as they were to their Jewish roots, and without any incompatibility between the two. As the first Reform minister in Britain, Reverend Professor Marks was anxious to reinforce this dual message, particularly in the light of intense criticism from Orthodox authorities and the attainment of political emancipation from the civil authorities.*

It is true that we have deep religious associations with the land of the Patriarchs, and that, in conformity with the promises of prophetic Scripture we maintain the belief that Israel will be restored to that land at the period of Messiah's advent, when all existing political relations will be adapted to the glorious events consequent upon the coming of the regenerator of the human race. But until that period arrives – a period of which no account is taken by Israelites in any of their relations as citizens – the political Jerusalem of every Jew is the land of his birth, the land where he is a citizen among citizens, in fine, his native land, whose welfare and prosperity are identified with the dearest affections of his soul.

... As the object of the Passover was to proclaim liberty as the birthright of man, let us avail ourselves of the means which our newly acquired civil rights confer upon us, to stand forth in every instance, as the staunch advocates of freedom, as the friends of all who are oppressed, and as the earnest supporters of every measure that tends to promote knowledge and to secure the well-being of all classes of our fellow-countrymen. As the Passover was the signal of the banishment of darkness, and for the diffusion of light; let our civil emancipation encourage us to labour assiduously in the cause of education, so that the generation now advancing to manhood may take their place, not merely in the bar or in the senate, but in every walk of life where Jews mingle with their Christian fellow-citizens, as equals at least, in science, in arts, in letters, and in every branch of useful knowledge.

Now that the barrier of exclusiveness is thrown down and an opportunity is afforded to us to exhibit practical Judaism in relation to the several duties of a citizen in a free state, it would ill become us to put aside any part of our ritual ordinances that are peculiar to us as Jews, in order to give more prominence to those features of our religion which might appear to mark more distinctively the cosmopolite citizen or politician. We have nothing to add, nothing to diminish. The maxim which we have always maintained amongst ourselves and indoctrinated into our children is, that the principles of Judaism harmonize completely with all the duties proper to a good subject and a worthy citizen.

Source: David Woolf Marks, *Lectures & Sermons*, Vol. II, pp. 159, 235–6.

COMMENT: *Marks has no doubt that Jews can play a full role in society, emphasizing that they should do so as Jews – both in the sense that it is in keeping with their Jewish heritage to be active in society, and that their Jewish traditions should accompany them. His assertion that 'We have nothing to add, nothing to diminish' echoes the command of Moses (Deuteronomy 4.2), and appears to dismiss the possibility that engagement with society will produce changes within Jewish life.*

## 23.2 Morris Joseph on Jewish Separatism (1903)

*The beliefs and practices that were unique to Judaism may have had their own intrinsic value, but they also had the effect of separating Jews from other people. As Jews became more integrated into society, questions arose as to what extent this distinctiveness should be maintained and in which areas it could be relaxed. Some insisted that nothing be changed, but Reverend Joseph suggests a different perspective.*

To maintain the identity of Judaism is the Jews' first duty, which is the same as saying that his first duty is to maintain Jewish separateness. What the nature of that separateness is to be constitutes the great problem for the faithful Jew of these times. Creed alone cannot be a sufficient barrier, for it must needs be lowered at the invitation of Theism. We must rely, it is clear, upon the old safeguards, upon distinctive practices. But this is not to admit that the entire ceremonial system which has been slowly built into Judaism in the course of centuries ought to be preserved. That a law or observance tends to keep up Jewish separateness is by itself no valid argument for its retention. To justify its continued existence it must show that it still serves a moral and religious purpose, that its spiritual vitality is unexhausted. Mere separateness ought not to be cherished as an ideal. Rightly conceived it is but a means to an end, and that end is the effectiveness of the Jew as a religious instrument. If it fail to secure that end, it is an unmixed evil.

It is possible to imagine an undesirable Jewish survival, to picture an Israel with a corporate life springing exclusively from a blind and ignorant adherence to superstitious customs. Gratuitous self-isolation gets no support from Jewish teaching. If the Israelite of the biblical age was warned against intercourse with the surrounding tribes, it was exclusively because of the religious and moral dangers which threatened him. In later times, if the Jew became anti-social, it was because society would have none of him. The Ghetto was not of his making. The Jew, therefore, who avoids intercourse with his neighbours, or refuses to conform to the customs of the country in which he lives, condemns his religion and does it harm.

Source: Morris Joseph, *Judaism as Creed and Life*, pp. 186–8.

COMMENT: *Joseph not only defends the right to introduce reforms to accommodate living in modern society, but shifts the emphasis from defending change to defending tradition. Rituals, however long-standing, should not be self-perpetuating. If their continued observance cannot be justified, they will be subject to alteration in the light of new needs.*

### 23.3 Ignaz Maybaum on the Value of Assimilation (1960)

*The debate over Jewish participation in society at large virtually always focused on two issues: the benefits from civil involvement that Jews could enjoy and the potential threat to Jewish identity. For Rabbi Dr Maybaum, there was an entirely different aspect that needed attention.*

Judaisation as humanisation, as the educational transformation of man and his institutions, is bound up with assimilation. The teacher who does not speak the language of the pupil is a failure. The priest cannot serve the people if his separation from the people results in alienation. Both teacher and pupil have the obligation of assimilation.

. . . The Nazis were right: to become Judaised *(verjudet)* meant, as they realised, that the predatory instincts disappeared and merciful man made his appearance. The assimilated Jew, remaining truly a Jew, is well fitted to transform clannishness, coldness, cruelty and adolescent enjoyment of fighting and war into human behaviour. Assimilation can be a process in which the Jew establishes himself in the civilisation of his Gentile neighbour and remains a faithful Jew, a person who has something to give to the Gentiles. But to become aware of this creative side in the process of assimilation implies the recognition that Jews have something to give which the Gentiles do not possess, that Jews can be – as the prophet formulates it – a 'light of the Gentiles' (Isaiah 42.6).

The whole history of the Jewish people from biblical days to our present time can be seen as a history of assimilation. But the question is: Was it an assimilation in which we lost ourselves or in which we succeeded in eliminating from the Gentile material cruelty, superstition and despair, planting kindness and belief in God and hope on the wild tree? Innumerable may be those Jews and Jewesses whom we lost through assimilation throughout the millennia of Jewish history. The Gentile nations grow by expansion, we by subtraction: 'in the stock of the felled tree is the holy seed' (Isaiah 6. 13). Jewish history is the victorious history of the remnant. The remnant remained the master even in the process of assimilation.

Source: Ignaz Maybaum, *Jewish Existence*, pp. 175–7.

COMMENT: *Maybaum differs from most Jewish commentators by considering how Jewish assimilation will affect the rest of society. It leads him to regard assimilation as beneficial, and so much so that it is worth the cost of partial Jewish losses. Moreover, he sees assimilation as the best way of fulfilling the Jewish mission and so, for him, it is in Jewish self-interest.*

### 23.4 Jonathan Romain on Integration (1991)

*By 1990 – a century and a half after the arrival of Reform Judaism in Britain – the issue was no longer that of Jews taking part in society but Jews remaining Jews. Nearly half of all Jews contracting marriages were doing so with non-Jewish partners. This often, though not always, resulted in a loss of Jewish involvement, while many Jewish-Jewish couples were opting out of Jewish life. At the same time, Orthodoxy was experiencing a minor revival, with some younger lapsed Jews becoming 'born again' – hozrim b'teshuvah – and intensifying their observance. Caught between these opposing trends, what role did Reform now have?*

The dilemma is particularly acute today where the welcome presented by an open society is so powerful that it not only allows assimilation by those who seek it, but also encourages assimilatory trends amongst those who value their Jewish identity. One response, favoured in ultra-Orthodox circles, has been to turn one's back on general society and to recreate both a physical and mental Jewish ghetto. Reform rejects this attitude as much as it opposes that of the assimilationists. It believes that it is possible to be loyal to one's Jewish heritage yet also participate in British life. More than that, Reform considers it the desirable and right course to pursue. Modernity has many faults but it has much to commend it as well: to dismiss both aspects together would be a gross lack of discrimination. It would also be doing a disservice to Judaism to deprive it of the artistic creativity, psychological insights and scientific advances that have resulted from contemporary life. At the same time, energy is needed to resist its less desirable features, such as its materialism, destructive capacity and many forms of personal abuse. Given such caveats, there is no reason why modern Jews cannot be modern and Jewish, enjoying both cultures that they inhabit, and bringing them into harmony. The key word is 'integration', whereby one's roots and lifestyle are firmly Jewish, but without precluding other involvements . . . Reform Judaism is very far from being 'convenient' as some critics allege; instead, it epitomises the literal meaning of the word Israel ('one who wrestles with God') and is a constant attempt to combine the highest ideals with everyday mundanities, whilst living Jewishly in society at large.

Source: Jonathan Romain, *Faith and Practice: A Guide to Reform Judaism Today*, pp.123–4.

COMMENT: *The passage acknowledges the problems facing those committed to both Judaism and modernity but is adamant that it is possible to harmonize them and that the struggle involved is central to being Jewish. It is equally insistent that modernity has positive aspects, and to ignore them would be to diminish Jewish life.*

## A Final Thought . . .

On my visit to [my home town of] Berehovo I could not help but think that although Jews there were involved in the community over such a long time and although, particularly in the Czech period, they really had full legal equality, the fact is that while Jews and non-Jews depended on each other for many of the essentials in life, and we lived in the same society, we were not really part of the same community. There was hardly any visiting, sharing or gossiping. I realize now that of Berehovo's three big and beautiful churches, I had never been inside any of them, and the chances are that none of the Christians ever set foot in our synagogues. And when the chips were down, I do not know of a single instance of a Jew from Berehovo being saved or hidden by a non-Jew. That I spend much of my time working for better understanding between religious groups and fighting racism as hard as I can, is partly because I know that you can only be safe and secure in a society that practises tolerance, cherishes harmony and can celebrate difference.

Source: Hugo Gryn, *Chasing Shadows*, p. 257.

# 24

# SUFFERING

The reason as to why people suffer has long occupied Jewish thinkers. Does suffering have a purpose? Is it always deserved? Why do apparently blameless individuals endure misery? Some rabbis sought to provide answers, feeling that a definite response was necessary to make sense of the seemingly senseless, and to enforce the view that God was in control of events even if humanity did not always appreciate the divine plan. Other rabbis felt that poor answers only compounded the problem and that it was better to admit that they did not know and accept that there were aspects of life that were a mystery and beyond human comprehension.

## 24.1 Morris Joseph on Reasons for Suffering (1893)

*As a leading writer and exponent of Judaism, Reverend Joseph was faced with the question of suffering. As a congregational rabbi, he could not give an academic answer that satisfied theologians but left others baffled. He sought to provide a response that carried meaning for those who turned to him in the midst of their suffering.*

Undeserved suffering is discernible in every stratum of the animal world, where one species lives only by preying upon the other, and in human life, where wholesale destruction often involves the righteous and the sinner in a common death. It is a riddle that neither Theology nor any other system of thought holds the key. But, on the other hand, it is well to be on our guard against exaggerating the proportions of the problem.

The mystery of suffering is not so impenetrable as we sometimes think it. Much undeserved suffering there seems to be, but it does not follow that it is aimless. Pain does not necessarily show a want of beneficence in God. It is a sign that some physical law has been broken – a danger-signal which smites us with its intense light, but warns and saves us. Does it not tell of disease which would otherwise remain undiscovered, to cause at last still greater agony, which could be ended only by death? Suffering is the very condition of life . . . Man has only learnt because his wits have been sharpened by the hard grindstone of painful experience. He has progressed because he has suffered. His contest with the forces of Nature, with the earth he has subdued, with the brute over which he has had dominion, has raised him from savagery to civilisation. It has been the nursing-mother of science . . . It is the same with sin, the twin-mystery with pain. For how has society risen in the moral scale if not through repeated experience of the futility of sin, of the certainty of retribution, and finally through fear of sin itself, through a horror of the degradation of the evil-doer. Righteousness has been evolved from transgression.

If I am asked why it should be in the nature of things that evil and suffering are the indispensable forerunners of goodness and progress, why God should seem cruel in order to be kind, I answer that I cannot tell. Nor does my inability to solve the difficulty give me any great concern. It is enough for me that what seemed to be chaos, proves to be order when the light of knowledge is turned upon it, that what in my ignorance I thought to be evidence that the world is swayed by a malignant power, or is the sport of blind chance, is in reality a testimony to the Divine love. If I cannot see the orb of love in the distant sky, shall I not say that it is because of my limited vision, not because there is no such orb? Must God disclose all his credentials to men in order to be trusted? Are there not moments when we weak mortals may fittingly pay tribute to the Divine scheme 'the homage of silence'?

. . . The truth is that when we rail at life it is only because we have ceased to be reasonable. We allow the memory of our woes to colour our judgements, and forget altogether the many blessings we enjoy. Because there is a cloud in the sky we ignore its general brightness, and declare that it is all black. More than half of our troubles are our own handiwork, directly traceable to our own folly; and yet we lay them at the door of a malicious fate, as though it were the business of fate to work a miracle, and forcibly avert the natural consequences of human actions. The truly brave man will frankly admit that he is author of much of his misery, and resolutely set himself to prevent its recurrence by strengthening the weak points in his character that have caused it.

Source: Morris Joseph, *The Ideal in Judaism*, pp. 124–30.

COMMENT: *Joseph seeks to minimize the problem of suffering by a variety of methods: declaring first, it is a natural part of life; second, that it prompts mankind to better itself; thirdly, that though we may lack explanation for it, this does not lessen God's love for us; fourthly, that there is sometimes a direct cause from our own behaviour. This is a very detailed response from someone who claims 'Nor does my inability to solve the difficulty give me any great concern'. It is surprising that he leaves until last situations in which suffering is the result of human actions, which might have been expected at the beginning of his argument, with the other three points then addressing situations that are without obvious human cause. His intention is clearly to end on a positive note, encouraging individuals to effect as much as they can and engendering a sense of optimism in their ability to ameliorate life.*

## 24.2 Leo Baeck on Responding to Suffering (1905)

*When Rabbi Dr Baeck first wrote about suffering, it was for a German Jewish readership that was largely prosperous and assimilated. It might have been taken more as an academic excursus rather than, as it was to become forty years later, a matter of personal urgency.*

Human sufferings are a religious possession to the extent and in so far as they can become a religious duty. We are not only to suffer pains – it would turn them into the saddest of misfortunes if we only knew to bear suffering – but we must actively carry them, we must meet their tests with all of our strength. We should not deny pain and persecutions by sinking ourselves into God and explaining all suffering as deceitful appearances; we must affirm suffering with secure certainty by turning it into an ethical imperative. Do your duty and the worst will have to become good for you; all the masters and teachers of Israel are agreed upon this. The question of theodicy is answered – or eliminated – for them since life is viewed as a body. It is not a present that it should be or is given to us, but a task to be fulfilled; and therefore it is worthwhile to be lived.

Source: Leo Baeck, *Essence of Judaism*, p. 75.

COMMENT: *Baeck is less interested in the causes behind suffering than in the way humans respond to it. He regards it as an example of how free will can have transforming powers and can enable individuals to overcome their afflictions. It was a perspective that was to stand the test of the Theresienstadt concentration camp in which he himself was placed. His own personal conduct there – teaching and lecturing amid the murderous brutality – demonstrated how suffering could be faced and conquered.*

## 24.3 Ignaz Maybaum on Jewish Suffering (1941)

*Shortly after his arrival in England, Rabbi Dr Maybaum was asked to lead services for fellow refugees from Nazi Europe. His sermons, delivered in German but then published in English, addressed those who had just experienced many levels of suffering, including maltreatment, emotional trauma and the murder of relatives. For them, suffering was not a concept but a reality.*

It is completely and entirely in accord with Jewish destiny that Jewish professors are being hunted out of German, Austrian and Czech universities, that Jewish writers, doctors and intellectuals are being driven from their homes and must look all over the world for new places in which to settle and continue their activity and earn their living. It is the Jewish destiny. But the full depth and sacredness of Jewish destiny will be understood only if we realise that every small businessman and every petty official from Germany, Austrian and Czechoslovakia who has been deprived of his livelihood is not merely a dispossessed citizen but a man who is suffering for the sake of God. The man who suffers for the sake of God has a priestly destiny. Jewish wandering is the priestly road. The Jew beats at the doors of the world and his enquiry 'Can I come to live here?'

coincides with the priestly query to mankind: have you heard that the message of the kingdom of God will be on earth, the kingdom of justice and peace?

Every place where this message is unknown or is actually repudiated, he must leave and go further. This is the fate of the Jew. It is his holy fate. I have been saying all along in these sermons that I have been delivering in London, as a refugee to Jewish refugees: take the consolation that our religion offers us. We are, indeed, sufferers in need of consolation. I have urged you to trust and hope. But today I call upon you also to be proud. The soldier shows his wounds – see, this is how I fought. I was at the front. God will bless these scars as he blesses all that is brave and true. The Jew too is always at the front. The Jew shows his road through the world and God sees the stations of his journeys of suffering. Our suffering is endured for the sake of God. That is our pride, our consolation and our hope.

Source: Ignaz Maybaum, *Man and Catastrophe*, p. 15.

COMMENT: *Maybaum seeks to lift the morale of each individual by suggesting that their suffering is not only a terrible personal experience but an important messianic destiny. Taken collectively, Jewish suffering is a rebuke to the ungodly nations of the world and a badge of honour in God's eyes. Some might question the value of this honour or become angry at the theology behind it; but it may have helped alleviate the misery of some of his listeners, making them feel part of a cosmic drama in which their suffering held some meaning.*

## 24.4 Albert Friedlander on the Experience of Suffering (1974)

*As a child, Rabbi Dr Friedlander walked the streets of Berlin during Kristallnacht to escape being rounded up by the Gestapo. Much of his later writings dealt with aspects of the Holocaust and how to give religious meaning to life after Auschwitz.*

Experiencing suffering in this world, Israel has always placed primary stress upon the fact that this world should not be the place of suffering.

The reminder that we were slaves in the land of Egypt is placed into the Sabbath commandment. And it is the Sabbath which can be seen as a concrete example of the Jewish approach to suffering. It is a fore-taste of the messianic time, the recognition that there are values in the world which do not accept the self-centred, materialistic approach of our times. The independence of every human being – no matter if soci-ety has assigned him the role of servant – becomes clear on the Sabbath. Human beings are ends in themselves, not means to an end. They have rights. They should not suffer . . . The Garden of Eden is the story of human existence. We are expelled from the womb into a world of pain. There are dolorous stages along the road which we must walk . . . But where we accept the actuality of suffering, we challenge the proposition that suffering is inevitable, and that the conditions of existence cannot be changed. The messianic dream which appears in so much of the Hebrew Scriptures is not a picture of a world beyond time: it is the anticipation of what the world will be. And the concerted efforts of mankind help bring about the age of brotherhood. Suffering need not be the permanent con-dition of man.

. . . The Jewish people, reflecting upon their past, still assert that it is better to be among the hunted than to be the hunter – but do not feel that there is a privilege or virtue in being a victim. Other insights arising from this experience: we too often note the silence of God and ignore the silence of man. Suffering rises out of human imperfections – apathy, self-ishness, greed, coldness of heart and mind. It rises out of the complexi-ties of modern existence, where men can hide behind machines, send trains to concentration camps . . . which makes us cry out, asserting the reality of God which ultimately does not condone suffering but demands the creation of a better world through human efforts.

Not all suffering can be alleviated through human efforts. Earthquakes and avalanches, water and fire, illness and death can come at any time. Judaism, together with other religions, can offer the comfort of prayer and the help of friends. This is not inconsiderable. The shared hopes and concerns of the religious life give an inner dimension to the Jewish home which sustain the individual in his time of suffering. Yet Judaism does not claim to have the full answer to the question: 'Why do I suffer?' Suffering rises out of the world as it is constituted. We are a 'this-worldly' religion. Pain and suffering are part of it. Rebelling, questioning, changing and improving the world, we yet come to the point of where we accept the reality of suffering and seek the best response to it. This holds true in the life of the individual Jew, and in the life of the community.

Source: Albert Friedlander, *Suffering: A Jewish View*, pp. 4–5, 14–16.

COMMENT: *As with previous writers, Friedlander is more concerned with the response to suffering than the reasons for it. He holds out the hope that it is not a permanent condition, but emphasizes that human effort is the only way to help conquer it. It implies that those who do suffer should react to their situation not with despair but with increased vigour – a conclusion that is demanding but uplifting .*

## A Final Thought . . .

When I was a student I hitch-hiked back from my first term at university to visit my parents. I arrived home just as they were going out to a party. They took me to a house full of people aged in their thirties and forties who were drinking cups of tea, and chatting about mortgages and house prices, rewiring and children's education. I was eighteen, long-haired and bearded. No one was talking about the meaning of life or the overthrow of political tyranny! It was all about plumbing and the cost of school uniforms. Rabbi Hugo Gryn was also there. He came to me as I sat in a corner and asked me 'What do you think of the party?' I said 'Nice people but it is a little boring.' 'Don't you know who these people are?' asked Hugo. 'No' I replied. 'These are the people your parents looked after following the war; everyone of them has a story. Ask your parents.' I asked my parents. During the war they had a home for children who arrived as *kinderstransport* children, and after the war they looked after people from the camps. This party was a reunion. My mother told me about them: 'Twenty years ago that woman was a child who could never be left alone because she was suicidal, while that man over there had to sleep alone because he screamed so much throughout the night that he kept everyone else awake.' These people had all been through the most profound physical and psychological difficulties when they were children; and now here they were, and the fact that they could discuss schools and homes was wonderful. It was a miracle. The fact that they were living ordinary lives was extraordinary. These ordinary people were moral giants. They were keeping the story alive. They were living life and living it well.

Source: Daniel Smith, *Lechayyim: Learning for Life*, pp. 5–6.

# 25

# WOMEN

The fact that a separate section has been devoted to the subject of women could be taken as unnecessary or even discriminatory. However, this is an indication of how radically the position of women in Judaism has changed. Initially in Reform synagogues, there was separate seating for men and women, while the latter had no active role in religious services or communal leadership. Today, women participate fully alongside men, are lay leaders in Reform congregations, and serve as rabbis. What led to such changes, what difficulties had to be overcome, and what was the reaction to the transition?

## 25.1 David Woolf Marks on the Neglect of Women (1842)

*In his 'Introductory Discourse' – a sermon delivered at the consecration of the West London Synagogue – Reverend Professor Marks sought to justify the need for radical reforms to Jewish worship. He lambasted the failure of Orthodox services to inspire interest, and bemoaned the fact that synagogues that were once full were now poorly attended, especially by women.*

In endeavouring to trace the causes which have produced this painful contrast, we shall not discover them in the insufficiency of our holy religion, for that is eternal and immutable as its Almighty Father; but in the abuses engendered by ages of darkness, superstition and intolerance. Eastern customs totally at variance with the habits and dispositions of an enlightened people have been associated with our religious practices. Woman, created by God as a 'help meet for man', and in every way his equal; woman, endowed by the same parental care, as man, with wondrous perceptions, that she might participate (as it may be inferred from holy Writ, that she was intended to participate) in full discharge of every moral and religious obligation, has been degraded below her proper station. The power of exercising these exalted virtues that appertain to her sex has been withheld from her; and since equality has been denied to her in other things, as a natural consequence, it has not been permitted to her in the duties and delights of religion. It is true that education has done much to remedy this injustice in other respects; yet does its memory live in the indifference manifested for the religious instruction of females.

It cannot be doubted that this indifference is one of the fruitful sources of the laxity in the Jewish religion, which we so much deplore. The duties to be performed by women lie at the very foundation of human life; for as upon them depends the earliest education of the great body of mankind, and as the mind is ever powerfully influenced by the lessons received in infancy, it is as hopeless to expect a truly pious community, where proper religious instruction is withheld from females, as to look for effect without cause.

Source: David Woolf Marks, *Lectures & Sermons*, Vol. I, pp. 18–19.

COMMENT: *Marks has no hesitation in championing the cause of females and demanding that they deserve the same equality as men. However, it could be argued that he was more interested in using the neglect of women as a stick with which to beat the Orthodox than as a cause in its own right. A few minor changes were introduced at West London – such as confirmation of girls at the age of thirteen – but women still sat apart from men and had a secondary role in synagogue services.*

## 25.2 Morris Joseph on Women's Influence (1893)

*By the end of the nineteenth century, the role of women in synagogue life had still changed little, even though it coincided with the growth of the Suffragette movement. The increasing calls for female rights in all aspects of*

*society raised the issue of their Jewish rights too, and Reverend Joseph felt*
*obliged to address the subject.*

Women who complain that they have no power forget that rule often
belongs less to the hands that actually hold the sceptre than to the power
behind the throne, that the mind which inspires actions, whether they be
done in public or private, is far more truly their author than the agent that
actually performs them. And this is woman's part – the part for which
Nature clearly destined her. Unsuited for the rough work of the world,
ill-adapted to battle with men for supremacy in the political field, she
yet wields immeasurable power in the quiet influence she exerts over her
husband and her sons. Let her not talk of women's rights, for those are
not rights which have to be won by wrong; and it is a wrong to drive men
out of their own sphere, nay, to deface the feminine character, gentle,
placid, equable with the dust of political warfare. No; woman must look
elsewhere for her vocation. Her sphere is that of lofty suggestion. Nobly
aspiring, she must imbue man with her ideals, and act through him.

What cannot a strong woman do to deepen the good instincts of her
husband, to fortify the weak points in his moral armour, to throw the
decisive weight into the scale when he is oscillating between right and
wrong. What may she not do to make him a God-fearing man, towards
turning his indifference to religion into unpretending, yet genuine piety.

. . . She has tasted the sweets of power – power far transcending in
joyousness the might of the king on his throne – the power of one soul
to imbue another with its own strength and to lift it by magnetic force
from earth to heaven.

Source: Morris Joseph, *The Ideal in Judaism*, pp.166–8, 171–4.

COMMENT: *Joseph's depiction of women was intended to be a lofty con-*
*cept and highly complimentary, but is far less acceptable to modern readers*
*with its rigid separation of roles, and the limitations placed on women.*
*Moreover, he fails to address the point that if women have such powerful*
*control already, why not give it formal recognition; or that if their influence*
*is so beneficial, what is there to fear from giving them rights. This refusal to*
*acknowledge women in civil spheres mirrored the unwillingness to enhance*
*their role in religious life either.*

## 25.3 Aryeh Dorfler on the Neglect of Female Equality (1967)

*By the 1960s, the progress in women's rights in the secular world had been matched to a certain extent inside Reform synagogues: men and women now sat together, while girls had 'confirmation' – a coming of age ceremony, but which, unlike barmitzvah, was a collective event and did not involve reading from the Torah. Some considered these to be sufficient advances, given the fact that Orthodox Judaism had made no concessions at all to women's involvement in services. Others felt that far too little had been done, including Rabbi Dr Dorfler.*

We are realising in our time the grand biblical idea of equality of all human beings, encouraging idealistic enthusiasm to remove the barriers between classes and nations, and to abolish discrimination against colour and religion. We see women active in all spheres, social, political and professional – mastering the most complex modern studies. Can we, on the basis of the arguments of female levity, vanity, lack of authority and serious devotion to study, and some newly-invented petty arguments, bar or discourage the modern Jewish woman from studying Judaism? Is it not time to dispel courageously these prejudicial notions, which cannot withstand the elementary facts of present-day life?

Progressive Judaism has failed pathetically in the last hundred years, both in having neglected the intensive education of women in Judaism, in not having attracted them to the deeper study of Jewish sources, and in not having attracted them to the Ministry as a spearhead in the drive to invigorate Judaism within and without the Jewish home. Let us open the gates now, and after the destruction of our great, learned European Jewry, strengthen our ranks by recruiting gifted Jewish women to the institutes of higher learning. This would indeed be in the spirit of those Sages who said: 'For the merits of the righteous women were the children of Israel redeemed from Egypt.'

Source: Aryeh Dorfler, 'Open the Gates', *Living Judaism*, Vol. 1, No. 3, p. 81.

COMMENT: *Dorfler was not the first to issue a call for women rabbis, but none had expressed as forcefully his criticism of the way in which the cause of women's equality had been allowed to stagnate. He also supple-*

*ments his argument out of principle by an appeal to practical needs, citing the loss of leadership following the devastation caused by the Holocaust.*

## 25.4 Jonathan Magonet on the Challenge of Change (1985)

*The first woman rabbi in Britain was ordained in 1975, but there was a curious gap between the rights accorded to women who were rabbis and to women among the laity. The former functioned fully as rabbis, but the latter were often barred in individual Reform synagogues from performing certain roles in the services. It was a source of frustration for many, both those who considered matters were changing too slowly or too fast. Rabbi Professor Magonet analysed the inner struggle that often lay behind the battle for equality.*

In these new understandings of male and female roles, women may be ahead of the game in many ways – at least in terms of an awareness of what must change, within themselves and within society. Men have been slower to understand, probably because we recognise, somewhere along the line, that we are being forced to give up privileges that we are reluctant to lose. Women may be frightened to give up their dependence on men and take a chance on their own inner resources. But men are equally frightened of losing their self-image of authority and significance before possibly their last captive audience. We are all reluctant revolutionaries – but there is no way back to where we were before.

What is the religious dimension to all of this? On a formal level, the demand for equal rights has legitimately entered the world of the synagogue. In a religious tradition where public ritual is dominated by male practices, a woman is forced to try them out, however reluctantly or uncomfortably – and, of course, at the risk of being ridiculed. Nothing is as conservative as a religious congregation.

But a synagogue is a living congregation not a cemetery. A woman who is called up to the *Torah*, or who wears a *kippah* or *tallit*, or who lays *tefillin*, is actually entering into her legitimate heritage. There are no *halachic* objections to any of these practices. It is only convention that is being upset. Perhaps what makes people nervous is the implications of such a slight action for their own lives. Men feel uncomfortable because another bastion of male identity and independence seems to be falling. Or perhaps we are challenged to examine things we have taken for granted.

Perhaps for women they can be even more disturbing – because when another woman puts on a tallit, it questions the whole basis of an upbringing and a traditional role in life. But if it does feel threatening that suggests that the questions are already there. And the more nervous the response, the more deep the questioning must be going. Neither masters nor slaves ask questions. One who asks has taken the first painful steps to self-understanding and emancipation.

Source: Jonathan Magonet, 'Every Wolf Whistle is an Assault upon a Woman's Self-Respect', *Manna*, 6, pp. 5–6.

COMMENT: *Magonet digs beneath the surface issues of what is or is not permissible according to Jewish law and examines the personal and emotional implications for changes in the role of women; although unspoken, these may have far greater impact than other factors. They certainly influence the way in which traditional texts are interpreted and whether those doing so are looking for ways in which to be permissive or restrictive.*

## 25.5 Sheila Shulman on the Impact of Women in the Rabbinate (1992)

*By the 1990s there were a considerable number of female rabbis, and they had changed from being isolated individuals to a strong group, each different in character but with a shared sense of rediscovering the female role within Judaism both for themselves and for others. Although there was little opposition to their entry to the rabbinical college, many found difficulties once they emerged into congregations, along with the overall problem of pioneering a new path in Jewish life. It was a problem that Rabbi Shulman knew well from her own personal experience.*

Hundreds of thousands of men have been rabbis for two millennia; a handful of women for two decades. Men, not women have created what we now understand to be Judaism. So when a woman, now, decides to become a rabbi, she is necessarily making a more unusual decision, to say the least, than any man in the same circumstances. We have two choices; either we become, so to speak, honorary men, which is to a large degree what is required of us, or, in the entire absence of role models, we struggle to invent ourselves, often with pain, at considerable cost, amid the bewildered incomprehension and occasionally the hostility of our colleagues and teachers.

It is profoundly difficult and paradoxical to study, intensively, the texts of a tradition which you love but in which you apparently do not exist, a history which is yours but in which you nowhere appear, a legal system in which your status is that of a chattel or a minor, and a theology in which how you are part of the Covenant is a moot point. Having done all that, to emerge with your love of Judaism intact, not to mention your integrity as a woman, and then go out to teach, to share that love with other Jews, half of whom are women, to suggest to them that they claim a centrality within Judaism that you know is theirs by right but which has not been part of your own education . . . well, it seems we have to be some sort of spiritual and intellectual acrobats, as indeed we are.

[A] crucial value that women rabbis share, or at least that those of us who perceive ourselves as in any way 'agents for change' share, is empowerment. We conceive our work as Jewishly empowering our congregants, seeing to it that they become more knowledgeable, more capable of living as fully responsible Jews, more capable of themselves becoming teachers, more in love with Judaism and with living Jewishly. That is in contrast to either the priestly model, or the hierarchical model of a strong rabbi in authority in control at the top, or the surrogate Jew model. Many women rabbis are working with, or toward, another, very different model of rabbi as teacher, transmitter of tradition. Our work toward this model, which for the sake of shorthand I will call lateral as opposed to hierarchical, has significantly affected some of our male colleagues, who speak with relieved hope of incorporating these 'feminist' working methods into their own work.

Source: Sheila Shulman, *The Impact of Women in the Rabbinate*, pp. 4–5, 16–18.

COMMENT: *Shulman highlights the conceptual difficulties women rabbis faced, quite apart from practical issues of acceptance. But although*

*women rabbis may have been expected to simply imitate male colleagues,*
*they have developed their own rabbinic style, and that in turn has been wel-*
*comed by some male colleagues as a model for their own ministry.*

## 25.6 Alexandra Wright on the Feminist Revolution (1994)

*The entry of women into the rabbinate raised questions as to what effect*
*this would have not only on the rabbinate, but on Jewish life as a whole.*
*Was it merely extending the rabbinic franchise, or would it have a quali-*
*tative impact on how Judaism developed and carry consequences for both*
*women and men? Rabbi Wright, who was ordained eleven years after the*
*first female rabbi in Britain, felt that it signalled a new era in Judaism.*

Feminist theology, like all theology, begins not with God, but with the
self. How do I see God? What do I believe God wants from me? I am
engaged in a dialectic that wrests from me an understanding of how I
should act in this world, indeed what I should think and believe. I was
brought up in a synagogue that espoused the ideology of classical Reform
Judaism. For all its liberalism, God was still that dominating, transcendent, kingly, authoritarian father figure who demanded moral excellence
from his servants. Man, in the words of the *Yom Kippur* confessional
liturgy, was seen as an arrogant, deceitful, hard-hearted, authoritarian,
lustful, malevolent and ambitious creature . . . I found the image of man
foreign, his sins not necessarily those sins and weaknesses that I found
in myself. I wanted to confess the sins of self-deprecation, of feeling too
much guilt, of failing to acknowledge the validity of my feelings.

It is not difficult to find language to express such prayers, just as it
was not difficult for me to articulate my praise and thanksgiving of new
life when my children were born, though it was a scandal that no ritual
existed to acknowledge and sanctify the miraculous event of birth. It is
more difficult for me to deal with the issue of the language of God. I am
uncomfortable with the constant use of male pronouns and metaphors
in the Hebrew, and yet still loyal to the formulation of an ancient liturgy.
However hard we struggle for a neutral-sounding English word, the patri-
archal, male Hebrew word will remain: God as the 'Commander of the
hosts', Shepherd, King, Father, He, Him. Perhaps what will happen will

be a rejection of patriarchy completely, to be followed by an acceptance of a liturgy enriched by metaphors and phrases that are drawn from both male and female imagery about God [with the latter including a nurturing, caring and loving God].

Why is feminist theology so crucial to Judaism? It has opened up an entirely new dimension of spiritual creativity and thought that can only have a regenerative and renewing influence on Judaism. The Judaism that survives the feminist revolution will be a truly strong Judaism for the future. And above all, it will be a Judaism that honours completely the prophetic ideal of a broken society renewed and made whole through the vision and action of humanity in partnership with God.

Source: Alexandra Wright, 'An Approach to Jewish Feminist Theology', in Sybil Sheridan (ed.), *Hear Our Voice: Women Rabbis Tell Their Stories*, pp. 159–61.

COMMENT: *The major achievement of women in the rabbinate was not so much allowing women to have greater rights of participation, although that was important enough in itself, but in giving voice to a different perspective of Judaism and Jewish spirituality. Wright both highlights this and is herself an example of it.*

## A Final Thought ...

About eight years ago, through a series of events and apparent coincidences I cannot attribute entirely to chance, I became friends with a Benedictine nun. Though she was in her seventies, she was in many ways younger in spirit and tougher of mind than I could ever hope to be. She was rather astringent, but I found myself talking to her easily, and explaining to this woman in a full habit that I was a radical feminist, and a lesbian, and what that meant to me. I said that we were, together, on the one hand slowly extricating ourselves from a millennial oppression, an enslavement which denied not only our participation in the world as agents, but our very being as persons, and that we were on the other hand working towards an unprecedented, but imagined, longed-for, wholeness. Naturally I didn't speak so abstractly to Sister Jane, but rather with all the concrete detail I could muster. She didn't say much, only asked some hard questions. Eventually, after she had been so quiet for a while that I thought surely she was outraged and would throw me out of the house, she said, 'Yes, I see. You're in a prophetic position.' At first I'd thought she'd said 'pathetic'. That was the first word of validation for who I was, for the self-understanding that came from my experience, spoken to me by anyone outside my own feminist circles. Jane's words came to me across what I then perceived to be an unbridgeable chasm, and from the most unlikely of all possible quarters. I did not know what to do with her words then, though something in me responded with a sort of shock. I recognized, however, that I'd been given a bit of ground to stand on. Jane's statement, connecting me squarely with my tradition, was, somehow, in the remarkable Hebrew idiom, an idea that 'had feet'.

Source: Sheila Shulman, 'Some Thoughts on Biblical Prophecy and Feminist Vision', in Sybil Sheridan (ed.), *Hear Our Voice: Women Rabbis Tell Their Stories*, pp. 55–6.

# 26

# WORSHIP

The desire for a form of Jewish worship that was both 'intelligible' and 'elevating' was the founding hallmark of the first Reform congregation in Britain. The early reformers desired a service that they felt was more decorous and meaningful than the ones to which they were accustomed. It needed to hold the interest of those who, like themselves, were as much at home in wider society as in the synagogue. Equally important was that it should be of sufficient appeal to their children, who were even more integrated into the outside world, so that they would maintain their Jewish heritage. What shape would such reforms take? Could centuries of tradition be changed without losing its coherence? Would the revised format become a new orthodoxy or, once started, would change become on-going process?

## 26.1 David Woolf Marks on Reforming the Service (1842)

*Reverend Professor Marks was the person most responsible for composing the new Reform liturgy. He had previously served as rabbi to an Orthodox congregation, where his reforming tendencies had already become apparent. When invited to become the first minister of the West London Synagogue, he was able to express his principles without constraint and he had no hesitation in explaining the need for radical change.*

The Synagogue in olden days inspired [its worshippers]; alas! for the change that has come over us! Where is the devotion that was wont to reign in the house of God? where are the sacred fires that animated our fathers? Does the service now impress us, do we leave the Synagogue better in mind or in spirit than we entered it? With a bitter heart and a mournful spirit we are compelled to reply, 'No!', to these important questions. Who can reflect on the Synagogue of olden days, and not arrive at the painful conviction of the degeneracy of our modern houses of prayer – when we find the men's Synagogue but partially attended, the women's gallery almost solitary, the pulpit mute, and religious instruction totally exiled.

Another serious evil may be discovered in the extreme length of the prayers, and in the blending with them of heterogeneous opinions with metaphysical disquisitions, that can have no affinity with prayer. This renders it impossible to command the unwearied attention of the congregation during the entire service, and defeats every effort to excite devotion. An over-fondness for opinions of bye-gone times, and a veneration for every custom and observance that claims antiquity, have been equally detrimental to the interests of Judaism, [such as] the several Chaldaic compositions scattered through the liturgy, introduced with the laudable intention of making the prayers intelligible, but clung to at a time when, it must be acknowledged, that Chaldee has become obsolete. Also the observance of double festivals [i.e. additional days] – a practice which originated before the astronomical calculation of the calendar was introduced – has, nevertheless, been rigorously upheld in days when we are enabled to determine the months even to a fraction of a minute.

If, in addition to these grave abuses, we consider the unseasonable hour at which the morning service commences, the levity occasioned by the blessings during the reading of the Law, the sale and distribution of the honours, and the want of pulpit instruction, we shall have arrived at the principal causes that have depressed Judaism and separated so many in Israel from their God. It is to remedy these glaring evils that this synagogue has been formed, and the improvements that we have determined to introduce therein will, I trust in God, prove most effectual in restoring the house of worship to a state so pure that the presence of God may abide there:

The time appointed for divine service is such as to enable the entire congregation to assemble prior to the commencement of prayer. The prayers will be read aloud by the minister only; appropriate psalms and hymns will be chanted by the choir, and responses made by the congregation. The reading of the Law will not be interrupted by the *aliyah*. As prayer will be offered up in Hebrew only, and as it is indispensable that that every Israelite should perfectly understand the supplications he addresses to the Supreme Being, I confidently hope that the sacred language will be generally cultivated by both sexes of this congregation.

Source: David Woolf Marks, *Lectures & Sermons*, Vol. I, pp. 17–21.

COMMENT: *Marks cites the lack of inspiration – and lack of attendance – as the justification for change, and lists a variety of faults that he perceives to be the cause. In some instances, these are customs that have arisen – such as the lack of decorum or the absence of sermons; in other cases, they are changes that were introduced by previous generations that Marks declares have outlived their original purpose and can now be discarded – such as additional days of festivals and prayers in Chaldee. This in itself is indication that the liturgy has been subject to change in the past, and therefore can continue to be adapted. Nevertheless, the reforms Marks announces led to a dramatic change in the dynamics of the service, with the role of the minister being greatly enhanced and the participation of the congregation being greatly reduced. Moreover, the abolition of the extra days of festivals was more than a change in custom, but a challenge to the authority of rabbinic law, and it was this aspect that aroused the condemnation of Orthodox authorities.*

## 26.2 Morris Joseph on Praying in the Vernacular (1903)

*The founders of Reform Judaism had assumed the right to instigate changes in worship appropriate to their needs. It was inevitable, therefore, that succeeding generations would feel able to introduce further reforms which they considered essential for their time too.*

*The high hopes that Reverend Professor Marks had expressed above for all Jews to be familiar with Hebrew – in which all services were conducted – had not been realized. Reverend Joseph argued that this necessitated another radical change.*

Let it be said here once for all that to know Hebrew, the language in which the divine oracles have been given, the language of the lawgiver and Prophet and Psalmist, is one of the primary duties of the Jew . . . [Some argue that] even if Hebrew were as diligently studied by Jews as it deserves to be, it would still not be the proper language of prayer in these times. The most learned Hebrew scholar does not think in Hebrew; he thinks in his mother-tongue. The mother-tongue, then, is the language naturally designated as the language of prayer. May we not go even as step further and plead that the language most fitted to express the devotional feeling of the individual is necessarily the proper language in which to conduct public worship?

It is true that Jewish public worship is essentially the devotional act of collective Israel, and not the collective act of individual Jews. It is also true that any congregant is at liberty during the service to give expression to his personal needs and feelings in silent prayer in his mother-tongue. But in spite of this, there are important reasons why the ancient custom of retaining Hebrew as the sole language of public worship should be modified. The present age seems to be marked by a decline in the practice of private prayer. People seem to pray less commonly than of old in their homes, and to be less inclined to pray independently in the House of God. We must try to mend the evil if we can. And the only way to mend it is so to alter the form of public worship as to ensure it some of the attributes of private prayer . . . [Some of the service] should be in the language of the country, and it should consist of prayers interpreting the religious ideas and the spiritual wants of living men and women. Each congregant should be able to feel that, no longer a mere spectator, he is a sharer in the service; that so far as he personally is concerned, public worship is the service of the heart.

Two changes, then, are necessary to give effect to these ideas – the use of the vernacular, and the addition to the service of new prayers embodying the special thoughts and aspirations of each age. Neither would be an innovation. Each would be merely a return to ancient practice. Two thousand years ago the Greek-speaking Jews of Alexandria offered public prayers in Greek, and somewhat later in Babylonia certain parts of the service were rendered in Aramaic . . . New prayers, to correspond to new wants, have from time to time been added to the Jewish Prayer Book. The history of our liturgy is the history of continuous growth from the time of the early Rabbins to a late period in the Middle Ages. The cessation, historians tell us, marked the beginning of the dark age in Judaism. But that age has now come to an end. A better era is dawning, an era of increased spiritual energy and wider religious thought.

Source: Morris Joseph, *Judaism as Creed and Life*, pp. 289–93.

COMMENT: *Joseph argues for the introduction of prayers in English not just as a practical remedy for the decline in Hebrew knowledge, but also out of principle, as the most effective method of individuals communing with God. The historical precedents to which he refers are only partially applicable: in Babylon just a handful of Aramaic prayers were introduced, compared with major parts of the service being conducted in English, while the Greek-speaking Jews who abandoned Hebrew, are a dubious example as they eventually lost their Jewish identity. Joseph is on firmer ground when citing the addition of new prayers over the ages. Here Reform is reviving a tradition that came to a halt for no pressing reason.*

### 26.3  Harold Reinhart on the Power of Prayer (1938)

*'Prayer, charity and good deeds' is a frequent refrain in the traditional High Holy Day liturgy. However, Orthodox Judaism was often seen as putting too much emphasis on mechanically fulfilling commandments and devoting attention to minutiae, rather than expressing the spiritual aspects of Judaism. Rabbi Reinhart was renowned for his energy in matters of practical organization, but always regarded his ministry, and the purpose of Judaism in general, as founded upon the power of prayer.*

Man needs strength. All about him mighty forces rage tumultuously. Man needs courage. The daily round of deed and thought must be faced with each recurring sun. Man needs faith. Events are topsy-turvy, dreams decay, and effort loses purpose . . . Prayer is one ever-present answer to man's ever-present need. Prayer brings strength and courage, faith and chastening, enlightenment, imagination and comfort. Prayer is not the only answer; study and valiant deed are answers too, and they react, each on the other. But prayer is one – and a necessary one: in the long run, without it the others will not avail.

Prayer is the channel through which man draws from the universal Power new vigour for the struggle of life. In prayer the individual soul faces the Soul of all creation, and in the fleeting experience of that vast Being finds something of the secret of his own reality and his own resources. Prayer is the token of kinship between the power of man and the power of God, and as such is the guarantee of human dignity and human purpose, the high possessions which are the secret of the daring life. Man dares in good and holy ways because he feels himself at one with truth. Prayer is the token that truth is real and living and available for man, and that man should believe and not despair. That same touch with truth which strengthens the human spirit struggling to live, also purifies it from thoughts and acts which cannot stand the light of truth. To pray is to assay godliness. To look to God is to focus life's energies upon the universal and the good, and so to grow in enlightenment and understanding. Most of all, to pray is to give rein freely and expansively, to human warmth and tenderness claiming its place in the universal order. Individual love and yearning asserts itself in the face of All-being, and claims answer from the universal Love. It thus makes the leap from earth to heaven; and in so doing hurls the ladder up which the thoughts of man may rise to give incentive to fresh and eager living, and down which may descend the angels of the peace and companionship of fellowship with God.

None of this is the reason for prayer. Man prays because it is his destiny to pray. He is the son of the spirit, and when heaven and earth shall have wasted away, God will still be praised. But through prayer man does win strengths that he may establish and hallow his life on earth.

Source: Harold Reinhart, 'Fulfilment', *The Synagogue Review*, Vol. XII, No. 6, pp. 79–80.

COMMENT: *It was said of Reinhart that he never led his congregation in prayer, but prayed in front of his congregation. The passage is illustration both of this characteristic of his, and of the importance attached to prayer as much as ritual observance as a vehicle to God in Reform Judaism.*

## 26.4 Lionel Blue on the Need for Modern English (1969)

*The three decades following the last revision of the prayer book – in 1931*
*– saw massive political upheavals in the Jewish world at large, as well as*
*major social changes in British life. There were calls for modernization*
*within all religions, with, for example, the Catholic Church experiencing*
*Vatican II. Rabbi Blue was asked to co-edit a new Reform prayer book suit-*
*able for the changing religious needs. One key issue he faced was a radical*
*revision of the English translation of the Hebrew passages. It aroused much*
*controversy and he sought to address those fearful of the innovation.*

I have heard that a member of a Reform congregation wept when she
heard that the translation of the Prayer Book was to be changed. Understandably one cannot help having affection for the words used in one's
childhood, but one must also grow up. There are many things in the
world that deserve our tears, let us not waste them on 'Thou' and 'Thee'
and 17th century grammar. We are not dressed in doublet and hose, and
God does not ask us to masquerade as our forefathers. Some feel that
the old forms should be kept as a sign of respect when addressing the
Lord. Respect, however, is shown naturally in other ways. The God who
walked with Enoch, bargained with Abraham, and spoke to the prophets
required no artifice.

The beauty of Judaism is that it has the power to take the humdrum
small activities of ordinary people and make them glorious. It starts off
from our own experience of life. Perhaps such direct contact with the
holy is frightening; many people wish to meet God yet fear the encounter
at the same time. As a result, they make the words long and unconsciously
push back the presence of God. Redemption is not the bread and butter
of my existence. I am not even sure that I know what the terms mean
theologically. But I do know what it is to be helped, to be rescued, to be
given safety, as do you who live through troubled times. We have tried
to be loyal to the text, and loyal to you. Let me give you an example. At
the end of the Book of Proverbs, there is a description of the 'woman of
valour', read in the home on a Friday night. Times have changed, as has
the social position of women. I have not met many woman of valour, but
I have met true and loyal wives, working selflessly for their husbands and
children, for the poor, for the aged and the lonely.

... I have also tried to be true to you in my use of words. I have known many congregations and met there many misguided people, many foolish people, many who caused harm, often unintentionally. But I have never met in my life a truly wicked person. Therefore our translation speaks of refraining from causing hurt and telling lies, rather than stopping being wicked and evil. We may think of each other as misguided, but I don't think we are wicked.

... The word of God endures forever, but it is almost untranslatable in its fullness. The words in which we express the word of God change. In a future generation someone will pick up this Prayer Book and find it wanting. This is good, for the living word can never be imprisoned in any time or any style.

Source: Lionel Blue, 'A New Translation of the Prayer Book', *Living Judaism*, Vol. 3, No. 4, pp. 104–6.

COMMENT: *Blue highlights the need for the prayers to ring true to the lives of those who use them. The fact that he was obliged to go to such lengths indicates how easy it is for reforming faiths to loose their radicalism and sink into a new orthodoxy. His final paragraph is a timely reminder that the essence of faith is God, not the way in which God is described.*

## 26.5 Jonathan Magonet on Creating New Liturgy (1977)

*Rabbi Professor Magonet was co-editor of the new Reform prayer book with Rabbi Blue. When it was published, it proved to be markedly different from its predecessor, not only in its translation but in the assumptions it made about Jewish life in general and the religious life of individual Jews. Was it true that modern Jews were less sure of their identity and more questioning about their heritage? Magonet explained what had motivated the editors.*

The Jewish liturgy is a highly complex blending of materials created, gathered and prayed by Jews in every period of our history, in every country where communities have settled. To seek to renew the liturgy, from within and without, is thus a challenge facing every generation. In our troubled times, such a renewal amounts to a grave responsibility.

For we are a generation of orphans – in both a physical and spiritual sense. A generation of Jews was all but destroyed – with its teachers, leaders and rabbis. And with them not only the bridge to the great traditional resources of East European Jewry, but also the thinkers and creative teachers of the West who shouldered the task of finding a new Jewish spirituality in our time. We are estranged from God and estranged from our spiritual heritage in a world of bewildering challenges and terrifying contradictions. The last link with our real, inner identity is the prayerbook. It must speak to us clearly, with the directness, and even bluntness, that characterised the great classical prayers. It must speak to the needs of our times – clarifying our confusion, indicating a path, challenging us to rediscover God in the reality of our lives.

. . . The traditional prayerbook assumed a community which prayed its private and public prayers at the very least out of a sense of duty, at best out of a real awareness of the closeness of God to the daily life of the individual and community. Such an assumption is no longer valid – at least not in the same way as formerly. The need and desire to pray remain part of human nature; the feeling of identification with Judaism, for any number of conscious and unconscious reasons, is still in evidence; and even a longing for a framework for existence, a sense of order and significance, has many private and public expressions. But the prayerbook, in the apparent remoteness of its language or its concepts, is not the place to which a Jew turns to find a voice that responds to his inner needs. Where once we learnt to pray by growing up with the prayer book – now we are lucky if we learn to pray at all, and only then can find in the liturgy the prayers that might match the reality of our experience.

. . . Early Reform shared with the nineteenth century a belief in the mastery of reason, and an optimistic assessment of its ultimate success in ushering in the messianic age. Two world wars and untold suffering have reminded us that there are layers of irrationality in man that must be granted their part in his make-up, and that for man to mature these layers must also be reached and tamed. A religion of intellect or of aesthetics alone is no adequate answer to these problems – the confrontation with the truth of our own fear and prejudice, our own irrationality and potential destructiveness must also be part of prayer life.

Source: Jonathan Magonet, *New Reform Prayer Book*, pp. 1–2, 6.

COMMENT: *Magonet analyses the new religious world which many modern Jews inhabit – in which prayer is no longer automatic, traditional concepts can no longer be taken for granted, and confusion is rife. It is a powerful justification for a new prayer book that can attempt to address such a reluctant readership. Whether the new prayer book would be able to fulfil that task is a separate issue, but the need for it is not in doubt.*

## 26.6 Rachel Montagu on Inclusive Language (1994)

*If there had been much controversy in the 1960s and 1970s over the use of modern English in the prayer book, there was a similarly forceful debate over gender-inclusive language in the 1980s and 1990s. Was it a modern fad that would pass and should therefore be ignored, or was it a significant development that would henceforth be a permanent feature of religious life and needed to be accepted? Rachel Montagu explains how her own attitude had changed decisively.*

'Man should always be in awe of heaven, in private as well as in public. He should tell the truth and speak it in his heart.' Once upon a time and not so long ago, I used to read statements like this in the prayer book quite happily. Then I began to wonder. Man should be in awe of heaven – very true. But gradually, instead of feeling included in this admirable sentiment, I began to wonder what I, and every other Jewish woman should do while men kept their minds on heaven. Reform Judaism recognizes the equality of men and women, allows women to become rabbis, yet still uses a prayer book which either leaves women to watch from the outside a description of male experience, or to describe themselves as men while they pray – and neither of these is a good idea. Prayer is supposed to be one of the most honest and true forms of communication, even more than the conversations we have with those closest to us. The language of prayer should enable us all to say the words of every prayer sincerely and without half of us being forced to describe ourselves as something we are not.

. . . What gender do we believe God to be? All too often I have heard people say without a trace of irony, 'God is neither male or female – He is beyond gender.' He is, is He? . . . Does it matter what names we use for

God, providing we have the sense to know that God is not an old man up in the sky? I think it does. I feel the continual use of masculine language for God is why many children of *Bar* or *Bat Mitzvah* age do think that is just who God is, as I have been alarmed to discover while teaching. By the age of thirteen, boys and girls have both been conditioned by the prayer book to think of men as more in the image of God than women. We should consider why we tell our children that no, God is not an old man in the sky, yet we never bother telling them that God is not an old woman in the sky. We don't need to, because we think it so unlikely that anyone should be under such a delusion.

But even if we are to pray to God in language that is neither male nor female, that does not mean we cannot use analogies which use both male and female images to say what God is like; though God is not limited to human roles, and we must guard against making God in our human image by the language we use for God. We can find human images useful about God – and we only gain if we follow the biblical example and use both masculine and feminine metaphors for God. The prophet Isaiah is quite happy to say 'Just as a mother comforts a child, so will I comfort you, says the Eternal God'. If we talk of God comforting like a mother, instead of only protecting like a father, this does not mean we believe in two Gods, a male and a female God. We know that our God is one. Also, if we use both male and female language, we make it clear that neither is wholly accurate or adequate, and we do not fall into the trap of creating a prayer book that is so carefully neutral that it creates a sense of distance from God. That would be wholly alien to the Jewish tradition of prayer which, while marvelling at the infinite greatness of the transcendent God, has always tried to convey to us a sense of our closeness to God manifest in the world.

. . . This is a subject which touches people on a very deep level. Both men and women dislike changes in our prayer books. It is difficult to change the praying habits of a lifetime. But once one has bitten the apple of awareness there is no spitting it out again. I was much happier with our liturgy before I realized that its masculine language is inappropriate. Now I realize that we must, for our own sakes and for the sake of our children, change it so that all members of the congregation, men and women, boys and girls, can pray in words which make it clear that we are all part of the praying community and are all in the image of God.

Source: Rachel Montagu, 'Inclusive Language in the Liturgy', in Sybil Sheridan (ed.), *Hear Our Voice: Women Rabbis Tell Their Stories*, pp. 161–9.

COMMENT: *Montagu argues the case for inclusive language very cogently and epitomizes the growing awareness among both men and women of its importance. It was a trend that led to the use of gender-neutral terminology in the next edition of the Reform prayer book, both in the description of people – such as 'ancestors' rather than 'fathers' – and in the descriptions of God – such as 'sovereign' rather than 'king'.*

## 26.7 Jonathan Magonet on New Liturgical Issues (1995)

*The Reform movement in Britain is an organization which links autonomous synagogues, and so it lacks the centralized control of many other religious bodies. Individual Reform synagogues share a broadly similar theology, but there can still be significant variations in the application of religious practices. One of the unifying features is the prayer book which is edited centrally and used throughout the movement, and therefore has an important influence in shaping its religious character. The publication of the third prayer book in the trilogy co-edited by Rabbi Professor Magonet and Rabbi Blue – Daily and Sabbath, High Holy Days and Pilgrim Festivals – was a suitable occasion for reflecting on the movement's identity and direction.*

Recent years have seen the need to explore in religious terms certain fundamental questions that affect the whole of our society. They include: the growth of the pluralistic society, with a greater challenge to share in a new inter-religious and inter-cultural dialogue; an awareness of the fragility of the natural environment and the limited resources available on our planet; the questions to conventional social and religious attitudes raised by the emergence of the women's movement; the growth of new 'fundamentalist' religious movements worldwide and the challenges these pose to 'liberal' religions of all kinds. As Reform Jews we are called on to clarify and exercise the values of reason and tolerance that have been at the heart of our movement, while at the same time exploring for ourselves the emotional and spiritual dimensions of religion that we have to some extent neglected in the past.

... If these are the general background factors in the creation of this prayerbook, it is also important to note some local ones. The prayerbooks of the Reform Synagogues of Great Britain have a particular quality that could probably only develop in this country. They are more traditional than their counterparts in America, but at the same time quite radical in the range of Jewish voices that echo through the study and anthology passages. In this way they acknowledge the great divides that exist today in the Jewish world but suggest that it is religiously important to live with them rather than settle for a bland middle ground or conventional religiosity. The willingness to do this may stem from certain qualities of British life; a respect for tradition combined with a determined independence of spirit; a readiness to honour the collective but equal respect for the individual voice; a commonsense practicality and a quiet spirituality, bordering on mysticism; an ability to express serious theological issues in a lucid, direct and accessible way. These are some of the elements that give British Reform Judaism its distinctive voice in the Jewish world. We would be the poorer if we failed to acknowledge them.

Source: Lionel Blue and Jonathan Magonet (eds), *Forms of Prayer for Jewish Worship: Prayers for the Pilgrim Festivals*, pp. ix–xi.

COMMENT: *Magonet provides a reminder that rather than just concentrate on the timeless aspects of Judaism – God, faith, covenant – it is in the nature of Reform liturgy to consider contemporary issues important too, and actively to seek to address them. It is axiomatic that its liturgy has constantly to evolve as different generations face different concerns. His analysis of the key features of British Reform explains why it has been able to maintain its dynamic character: meeting new social and religious developments, but integrating them into a strongly Jewish context.*

## 26.8 Sylvia Rothschild on Composing Liturgy for Modern Needs (1997)

*The process of modernizing the liturgy led to a growing realization that it was not enough to make changes to the translation or gender-equality of the existing prayers. It was also important to introduce prayers for personal situations that most ordinary Jews faced at some point in their lives but which were not reflected in the prayer book. Rabbi Rothschild, who had composed prayers for special occasions of her own accord, issued a call for a much more systematic approach to cater for such needs.*

Progressive Judaism began with the challenge of articulating meaning to our sometimes mute existence as Jews, forcing us to stand at Sinai in each and every generation and find a way to bring Jewish meaning into our life as Jews in the contemporary world. To continue that challenge we must be prepared to be iconoclastic, to shatter some of the behaviours or the stories that hide the theophany at Sinai. We must be prepared to at least lift the layers and see what they protect or express. Everyone who sits around a *seder* table is enjoined to remember that they must act out of the understanding that they were there at the Exodus. The stories they must tell must have themselves as the central characters. It was our experience because we are Jews. We participate and locate ourselves in the particular history of our people. In the same way we need to be telling new stories about ourselves, create new rituals and liturgies to address situations and experiences in our life which our tradition does not yet satisfactorily consider, finds ways to constantly tie ourselves back to peoplehood.

. . . Sing to the Lord a new song. Our lives are full of experiences that are different from those of our ancestors and which need the support of Jewish articulation and structure. Our context today has expectations and perceptions that are radically changed from even the recent generations before us. For example, we expect to live a long time in good physical condition. We expect all pregnancies to end in healthy babies, we expect to use our skills to increase our value in the workplace, we expect our work to give us identity. [Yet] we have no liturgy for coming to terms with divorce, with redundancy, with loss of children, with loss of ability, with entry into a home for the aged, with long-term decline.

We have barely any liturgy to celebrate impressive lengths of marriage, entry into the community of the proselyte, going on *aliyah* [emigration to Israel], undertaking higher education, setting up a home outside of the traditional pattern of *chuppah* [Jewish marriage]. Jews want Judaism to reflect what is going on, to make it coherent and take the threads of real life into the tapestry of Jewish expression.

I know of private ceremonial to mark miscarried children, to celebrate menarche and menopause, to enter a daughter into the covenant, to grieve for unacknowledged parents and children . . . All Jews tell the same story but over the generations we tell it differently, accenting different aspects of the story, dwelling on those that are most relevant at the time. Our story is about Creation and Exodus, about the existence of the unique and universal God outside of all rules of space and time, who yet makes a relationship of mutual obligation with Jews as part of the completion process of creation. As Jews it is our single duty to keep telling the story. As Progressive Jews, it is a self-imposed challenge to tell the story the most relevant way we can for our generation and for the generations who will come after us. If that means writing more liturgy, sanctifying some events our ancestors didn't know about, discarding some dates from our traditional calendar, that is our task. Blessed are you, our Sovereign God who rules over the world, who is continually giving us *Torah.*

Source: Sylvia Rothschild, 'Renewing Jewish Celebration', *Manna*, 57, Theology Supplement.

COMMENT: *Rothschild's advocacy of new types of liturgy is a reflection both of her own personal interest and of a small but growing trend among Jews – both rabbis and lay members – to fill the perceived vacuum in appropriate prayers through their own efforts. In most, but not all, cases it is Jewish women who have been at the forefront of such attempts, as many life-cycle events specific to them have previously lacked any Jewish structure or validation. She is careful to insist that any new liturgy should not only articulate modern realities, but also be linked to Jewish tradition, so that alongside its contemporary relevance it still has strong Jewish resonances.*

## A Final Thought...

One of the difficulties in prayer is that we are not at home with God or with our own religion. We have lost one form of innocence with our enlightenment, and we have not recovered another. Religiously we are like adolescents at that awkward in-between age. The view from the pulpit is revealing. I watched a lady once at High Holy Days sitting stiffly in her seat trying to mouth the unfamiliar Hebrew vowels. Her clothes were unfamiliar too, for they were her best and not broken in. I watched her as she dropped her handbag and lost her place in the book, turning the pages the wrong way, and with a slight creak from her corsets she suddenly leaned back and her lips said 'damn!' That was the first prayerful word she had said, because it was the first honest word. She could now pray because she was not on her best behaviour but starting off from where she was.

Source: Lionel Blue, *Prayer for a Worldly Society*, p. 10.

# BIOGRAPHICAL NOTES

Below are brief career details of the rabbis quoted in the book. A list of their main publications can be found in the Bibliography. All are English-born unless stated otherwise. All the synagogues are in London unless stated otherwise. The Hochschule fuer die Wissenschaft des Judentums in Berlin was the main Progressive rabbinic seminary in pre-war Germany, while the Leo Baeck College in London was established in 1956 as a continuation of the work of the latter, which had been destroyed by the Nazis. The Hebrew Union College is its American equivalent.

Hillel Avidan (1933–). He worked as an art teacher in Australia before changing career and being ordained by the Leo Baeck College (1966). He served as minister of Glasgow New Synagogue, and then held pulpits in Wimbledon, Manchester and Ealing before becoming rabbi of Bet David, Johannesburg.

Tony Bayfield (1946–). Ordained by the Leo Baeck College (1972). After serving as rabbi of North West Surrey Synagogue, he became Director of the Sternberg Centre for Judaism, and in 1994 was appointed Chief Executive of the Reform Synagogues of Great Britain. He is also editor of the journal *Manna*.

Leo Baeck (1873–1956). Born in Lissa, Germany, he studied at the Jewish Theological Seminary in Breslau and then the Hochschule. After holding pulpits in Oppeln and Duesseldorf, he went to serve in Berlin. In 1933 he became President of the Reichsvertretung, the representative body of German Jewry. He refused opportunities to emigrate and was deported to Theresienstadt concentration camp. After the war he settled in England, although travelling and teaching widely. He was President of the Reform Synagogues of Great Britain (1951–56), as well as the World Union for Progressive Judaism. The rabbinic college established in London just before his death was renamed in his memory.

Charles Berg (1911–79). Born in Berlin (as Karl Rautenberg), his rabbinic studies at the Hochschule were interrupted by the war, and he came to England. During the war he served in the Pioneer Corps and afterwards became minister of Bournemouth Reform Synagogue. He was ordained by Leo Baeck in London and was minister of Wimbledon Synagogue from 1953 till his retirement in 1974.

Lionel Blue (1930–). He was one of the first two ordinees of the Leo Baeck College, along with Michael Leigh in 1958. He assisted small communities in Europe on behalf of the World Union for Progressive Judaism, and then served as minister to the Settlement Synagogue and Middlesex New Synagogue. He became Convener of the Beth Din of the Reform Synagogues of Great Britain, as well as achieving national fame for his religious broadcasts on radio and television. In 1993 he won the Templeton Prize.

Barbara Borts (1953–). Born in California, she later studied in England and was ordained by the Leo Baeck College (1981). She was minister of Hampstead Reform Community and then Radlett & Bushey Reform Synagogue, before returning to the United States and occupying various posts, including Dean of the Reconstructionist Rabbinical College in Philadelphia and is currently serving a congregation in New Hampshire.

Michael Boyden (1946–). Ordained by the Leo Baeck College (1972). He was minister of Menorah Synagogue, Manchester until he emigrated to Israel in 1985 where he served various rabbinic roles within the Israel Movement for Progressive Judaism, including convener of its Beth Din and minister of Ra'anana Congregation.

Howard Cooper (1953–). Ordained by the Leo Baeck College (1980). He served congregations in Buckhurst Hill and Finchley, but now works primarily as a psychoanalytical psychotherapist, as well as writing and lecturing on Jewish and psychological themes.

Aryeh Dorfler (1898–1968). Born in Germany, he was ordained at the Hochschule. He came to England in 1938, where he had a series of teaching posts, including lecturer in rabbinics at the Leo Baeck College.

Albert Friedlander (1927–). Born in Berlin, he emigrated with his family to the United States and was ordained at the Hebrew Union College in

Cincinnati. After serving rabbinic positions in the United States, he came to England to be minister of Wembley Progressive Synagogue and later Westminster Synagogue, while also acting as Dean of Leo Baeck College.

Percy Selvin Goldberg (1917–81). He was ordained at Jews College and initially served Orthodox congregations in London before changing to Reform Judaism. He was minister of the Manchester Congregation of British Jews from 1940 till 1975 and then went to the United States to become rabbi in Hot Springs, Arkansas.

Henry Goldstein (1936–). Ordained by the Leo Baeck College (1967). He was minister of Finchley Reform Synagogue and then South West Essex Reform Synagogue. He also served as a prison chaplain.

Michael Goulston (1932–72). After his ordination at the Hebrew Union College in Cincinnati, he returned to England and became minister at Middlesex New Synagogue and then associate minister at the West London Synagogue. He was founding editor of *European Judaism*. The Michael Goulston Educational Foundation was launched in his memory to continue his work and ideas.

Gerhard Graf (1912–86). Born in Berlin, he was ordained at the Hochschule and served the Berlin community. He came to England in 1939 and held pulpits in Bradford and Leeds before becoming the first minister of Cardiff New Synagogue in 1949, where he served until his retirement in 1980.

Hugo Gryn (1930–96). Born in Czechoslovakia, he was later deported to Auschwitz as a teenager. After the war he emigrated to the United States and was ordained at the Hebrew Union College in Cincinnati. After serving rabbinic positions in Bombay and New York, he came to England in 1964 to be Senior Minister of West London Synagogue. He became known nationally both as a broadcaster and for his inter-faith work. He was President of the Reform Synagogues of Great Britain (1990–96).

Arthur Herman (1928–). He worked as a potter and then in the airline industry, before being ordained by the Leo Baeck College (1966). He was minister of Southgate Reform Synagogue, and then specialized as a therapist helping survivors of the Holocaust in Holland.

Michael Hilton (1951–). Ordained by the Leo Baeck College (1987). He served as minister of Menorah Synagogue, Manchester and North London Progressive Synagogue before becoming rabbi at Kol Chai-Hatch End.

Morris Joseph (1848–1930). He was ordained at Jews College and initially served Orthodox congregations in London and Liverpool before becoming Reform. He was minister of West London Synagogue from 1893 till 1925.

Arthur Katz (1908–96). Born in Czechoslovakia, he was trained as an Orthodox rabbi and served in Sobieslav until the war. He came to England in 1939 and assisted at West London Synagogue before becoming the first minister of Hendon Reform Synagogue, which he served from 1949 till 1982.

David Kunin (1961–). Born in the United States, he was ordained at the Hebrew Union College. He came to England and served as minister to Glasgow New Synagogue before returning to the United States.

Michael Leigh (1928–2000). He was one of the first two ordinees of the Leo Baeck College, along with Lionel Blue in 1958. He was assistant minister at West London Synagogue and then served as Senior Minister of Edgware Reform Synagogue from 1963 till 1990.

Jonathan Magonet (1942–). He qualified as a physician before being ordained by the Leo Baeck College in 1971. He later returned as a lecturer, becoming Head of the Bible Department and then Principal in 1985. He helped found and organize both the annual Bible Week at Bendorf, Germany and the Standing Conference of Jews, Christians, Muslims.

David Woolf Marks (1811–1909). He initially served Orthodox congregations in London and Liverpool. In 1840 he was appointed as the first minister of West London Synagogue, which he served until he retired in 1893.

Dow Marmur (1935–). Born in Poland and educated in Sweden, he was ordained by the Leo Baeck College in 1962. He served as minister of South West Essex Reform Synagogue and North Western Reform Synagogue before becoming Senior Minister of Holy Blossom Temple, Montreal. On retirement, he moved to Israel and also acted as Executive Director of the World Union for Progressive Judaism.

Ignaz Maybaum (1897–1976). Born in Vienna, he was ordained at the Hochschule. After holding pulpits in Bingen-on-the-Rhine and Frankfurt-on-the-Oder, he went to serve in Berlin. In 1939 he came to England. In 1948 he became minister of Edgware Reform Synagogue, a position he occupied until he retired in 1963.

Alan Miller (1929–). He was ordained by the Leo Baeck College in 1960. He served as assistant minister of West London Synagogue and then minister of South West Essex Reform Synagogue before going to New York as the spiritual leader of the Reconstructionist synagogue there. After many years he retired from the ministry and became a therapist.

Rachel Montagu (1956–). She was ordained by the Leo Baeck College in 1984. She served as minister of Cardiff New Synagogue and then assistant minister of North Western Reform Synagogue before becoming Education Director of the Council of Christians and Jews.

Jeffrey Newman (1941–). He was ordained by the Leo Baeck College in 1970. He served as minister of Menorah Synagogue, Manchester and then Finchley Reform Synagogue from 1973 until 2000. He was a co-founder of the Israel Palestine Centre for Research and Information. He is now Director of the Rabbinic Development Foundation for the Assembly of Rabbis.

Roger Pavey (1939–). He was ordained by the Leo Baeck College in 1967. He served as minister of Southend Reform Synagogue and then emigrated to Canada to serve pulpits there. He currently teaches at Saskatoon University.

Harold Reinhart (1891–1969). Born in Oregon, he was ordained at the Hebrew Union College, Cincinnati. He served pulpits in Gary, Indiana and Baton Rouge, Louisiana before moving to Sacramento, California. He came to England and served as Senior Minister to West London Synagogue from 1929 till 1957. He became founder minister of Westminster Synagogue, which he served from 1957 until his death.

Jonathan Romain (1954–). He was ordained by the Leo Baeck College in 1980. He has served as minister of Maidenhead Synagogue since then.

Sylvia Rothschild (1957–). She worked as a psychiatric social worker before being ordained by the Leo Baeck College in 1987. She served as minister to Bromley and District Reform Synagogue and then became rabbi at Wimbledon and District Synagogue.

Elizabeth Tikvah Sarah (1955–). She spent several years in feminist research and writing before being ordained by the Leo Baeck College in 1989. She has served as minister to Buckhurst Hill Reform Synagogue and Leicester Progressive Congregation, as well as Director of the Programmes Division of the Reform Synagogues of Great Britain. She is now rabbi of Brighton Progressive Synagogue.

Sheila Shulman (1936–). Born in New York, she worked as an academic and editor before being ordained by the Leo Baeck College in 1989. She is founder minister of Beit Klal Yisrael Synagogue and associate minister of Finchley Reform Synagogue.

Vivian Simmons (1886–1961). He served as assistant minister at West London Synagogue from 1914 till 1940 and then transferred to the Liberal movement, where he served pulpits in Birmingham and London.

Daniel Smith (1949–). Born in Israel and educated in England, he was ordained by the Leo Baeck College in 1977. He served as associate minister at West London Synagogue, and then as minister to Wimbledon Synagogue and now leads Edgware Reform Synagogue. He helped found the Raphael Centre Jewish Counselling Service.

Solomon Starrels (1901–76). Born in the United States, he was ordained by the Hebrew Union College, Cincinnati. After serving pulpits in New Orleans and Nebraska, he came to England in 1928 to assist at the Liberal Jewish Synagogue. In 1933 he became the first minister of North Western Reform Synagogue. He returned to the United States in 1938 and served pulpits in Albuquerque, New Mexico and Savannah, Georgia.

Jacqueline Tabick (1948–). Born in Dublin and educated in England, she was the first female rabbi to be ordained by the Leo Baeck College in 1977. She served as associate minister at West London Synagogue, and is now minister of North West Surrey Synagogue

Andre Ungar (1929–). Born in Budapest, he was ordained by the Leo Baeck College in 1961. He was associate minister at West London Synagogue, went to serve Port Elizabeth, South Africa, returned to London to serve the

Settlement Synagogue and then took up the pulpit of Temple Emmanuel, New Jersey.

Werner van der Zyl (1902–84). Born in Schwerte, Germany, he was ordained at the Hochschule. After holding pulpits in Berlin, he emigrated to England in 1939. He was minister of North Western Reform Synagogue from 1943 till 1958, and then Senior Minister of West London Synagogue until he retired in 1968. He was the first Director of Studies at the Leo Baeck College, and was President of the Reform Synagogues of Great Britain (1973–1984)

Alexandra Wright (1956–). She worked as a secondary school teacher before changing career and being ordained by the Leo Baeck College in 1986. She served as associate minister of the Liberal Jewish Synagogue (LJS) and then as minister of Radlett & Bushey Reform Synagogue. She is now the Senior Minister of the LJS.

# GLOSSARY

This glossary does not include words or phrases used only once, which are explained in the main text itself. All are Hebrew terms unless indicated otherwise.

*Aggadah* – non-legal rabbinic literature, often parables and anecdotes.

*Aliyah* – a person being called up to recite the blessings over the scrolls during a service.

*Amidah* – central prayer in all daily, Sabbath and festival services.

*Barmitzvah* – ceremony for boys aged thirteen in which they read from the Torah to mark the beginning of Jewish adulthood.

*Beth Din* – rabbinic court, nowadays primarily concerned with supervising status issues, such as conversion and divorce.

*Bubbe* – grandmother (Yiddish).

*Cohen* – a descendant of the High Priest Aaron, and still having a priestly role in Orthodox synagogues today.

*Halacha* (*also* halachah/halakhah; *adj.* halachic/halakhic) – Jewish law as derived from the Bible and rabbinic literature.

*Hanukkah* – Festival of Dedication, celebrating the survival of the Jewish faith despite attempts to destroy it.

*Havdalah* – ceremony that marks the end of the Sabbath and festivals.

*Kashrut* – dietary laws concerning permitted and forbidden foods.

*Kippah* – head-covering worn during prayer.

*Mamzer* – a person born of an incestuous or adulterous relationship.

*Matza* – unleavened bread eaten during Passover.

*Menorah* – candelabra, often associated with the festival of Hanukkah.

*Mitsvah/mitzvah* (*pl.* mitzvot) – one of the 613 commandments; also a good deed.

*Prosbul* – legal formula to override the ban on claiming debts after the Sabbatical Year; enacted by Hillel in the first century.

*Purim* – Festival of Lots, celebrating the deliverance of the Jews of Persia from attempts to kill them.

*Rosh Hashannah* – the Jewish New Year, a time of renewal.

*Seder* – the service surrounding the Passover meal.

*Shabbat* – the Sabbath, a time of rest lasting from sunset on Friday evening till after dark on Saturday.

*Shatnez* – clothing containing a mixture of wool and linen, banned according to Leviticus 19.19.

*Shema* – prayer recited at all morning and evening services stressing the unity of God.

*Shiva* – the seven days of mourning after the loss of a close relative.

*Shulchan Aruch* – code by Joseph Caro (d. 1575) summarizing the main practices of Jewish Law, which became recognized as a definitive statement and served to standardize divergent customs.

*Simchat Torah* – Festival of the Rejoicing of the Law, celebrating a new cycle of public readings in synagogue from the Torah.

*Tallit* – prayer shawl, worn mainly during morning prayers.

*Tefillin* – leather boxes containing the Shema worn on the head and arm.

*Torah* – the five books of Moses; also used to refer to the entirety of Jewish teaching.

*Yom Kippur* – the Day of Atonement, a time of prayer, fasting and repentance.

# BIBLIOGRAPHY

The following list includes sources quoted in the book, as well as other publications consulted in its preparation. Where authors have written more than one work, they are listed in order of the original date of publication.

The abbreviation RSGB refers to the Reform Synagogues of Great Britain.

## Books

Baeck, Leo, *Essence of Judaism*, Berlin, 1905; 1st translated 1936; New York: Schocken, 1970.

Baeck, Leo, *God and Man in Judaism*, Bonn, 1929; translated 1931; London: Vallentine Mitchell, 1958.

Baeck, Leo, *The Pharisees and other Essays*, New York: Schocken, 1947.

Baeck, Leo, *This People Israel*, Berlin: 1955; translated, Philadelphia: Jewish Publication Society of America, 1965.

Baeck, Leo, *Judaism and Christianity*, 1958; translated, Philadelphia: Jewish Publication Society of America, 1960.

Bayfield, Tony and Braybrooke, Marcus (eds), *Dialogue with a Difference*, London: SCM Press, 1992.

Bayfield, Tony, Brichto, Sidney and Fisher, Eugene (eds), *He Kissed Him and They Wept*, London: SCM Press, 2001.

Blue, Lionel, *To Heaven with Scribes and Pharisees*, London: Darton, Longman & Todd, 1975.

Blue, Lionel, *Backdoor to Heaven*, London: Darton, Longman & Todd, 1979.

Blue, Lionel, *Bright Blue*, London: BBC, 1985.

Blue, Lionel, *Bolts from the Blue*, London: Hodder & Stoughton, 1986.

Blue, Lionel, *Blue Heaven*, London: Hodder & Stoughton, 1987.

Blue, Lionel, *My Affair with Christianity*, London: Hodder & Stoughton, 1988.

Blue, Lionel, *Blue Horizons*, London: Hodder & Stoughton, 1989.

Blue, Lionel and Magonet, Jonathan (eds), *Forms of Prayer for Jewish Worship: Daily, Sabbath and Occasional Prayers*, London: RSGB, 1977.

Blue, Lionel and Magonet, Jonathan (eds), *Forms of Prayer for Jewish Worship: Prayers for the High Holy Days*, London: RSGB, 1985.

Blue, Lionel and Magonet, Jonathan (eds), *Forms of Prayer for Jewish Worship: Prayers for the Pilgrim Festivals*, London: RSGB, 1995.

Blue, Lionel and Magonet, Jonathan, *Blue Guide to the Here and Hereafter*, London: Collins, 1988.

Blue, Lionel and Magonet, Jonathan, *How to Get Up When Life Gets You Down*, London: HarperCollins, 1992.

Blue, Lionel and Magonet, Jonathan, *Sun, Sand and Soul*, London: Hodder & Stoughton, 1999.

Blue, Lionel and Rose, June, *A Taste of Heaven*, London: Darton, Longman & Todd, 1977.

Cooper, Howard (ed.), *Soul Searching: Studies in Judaism and Psychotherapy*, London: SCM Press, 1996.

Cooper, Howard and Morris, Paul, *Sense of Belonging*, London: Weidenfeld & Nicolson, 1991.

de Lange, Nicholas (ed.), *Ignaz Maybaum: A Reader*, New York & Oxford: Berghahan Books, 2001.

Friedlander, Albert, *Leo Baeck: Teacher of Theresienstadt*, London: Routledge & Kegan Paul, 1973.

Friedlander, Albert, *Riders Towards the Dawn*, London: Constable, 1993.

Friedlander, Albert (ed.), *Out of the Whirlwind*, 2nd edn, New York: UAHC Press, 1999.

Friedlander, Albert and Wiesel, Elie, *The Six Days of Destruction*, Oxford: Pergamon Press, 1988.

Golden, Lewis and Jacqueline, *Harold Reinhart: A Memorial Volume*, London: Westminster Synagogue, 1980.

Gryn, Hugo, *Chasing Shadows*, London: Viking, 2000.

Hilton, Michael, *The Christian Effect on Jewish Life*, London: SCM Press, 1994.

Hilton, Michael and Marshall, Gordian, *The Gospels and Rabbinic Judaism*, London: SCM Press, 1988.

Homolka, Walter, Jacob, Walter and Seidel, Esther (eds), *Not By Birth Alone*, London: Cassell, 1997.

*In Spirit and Truth: Aspects of Judaism and Christianity*, London: The Society of Jews and Christians, 1934.

Joseph, Morris, *The Ideal in Judaism*, London: David Nutt, 1893.

Joseph, Morris, *Judaism as Creed and Life* (1903), 4th edn, London: Routledge & Kegan Paul, 1958.

Joseph, Morris, *The Message of Judaism*, London: George Routledge, 1907.

Joseph, Morris, *The Spirit of Judaism*, London: George Routledge, 1930.

Kershen, Anne and Romain, Jonathan, *Tradition and Change: A History of Reform Judaism in Britain 1840–1995*, London: Vallentine Mitchell, 1995.

Magonet, Jonathan (ed.), *Returning*, London: RSGB, 1975.

Magonet, Jonathan, *A Rabbi's Bible*, London: SCM Press, 1991.

Magonet, Jonathan, *Bible Lives*, London: SCM Press, 1992.

Magonet, Jonathan, *A Rabbi Reads the Psalms*, London: SCM Press, 1994.

Magonet, Jonathan (ed.), *Jewish Explorations of Sexuality*, New York & Oxford: Berghahn Books, 1995.

Magonet, Jonathan, *The Subversive Bible*, London: SCM Press, 1997.

Magonet, Jonathan, *The Explorer's Guide to Judaism*, London: Hodder & Stoughton, 1998.

Magonet, Jonathan, *Talking to the Other*, London: I. B. Tauris, 2003.

Marks, David Woolf, *Lectures & Sermons*, London: R. Groonbridge & Sons, 1851 (Vol. I), 1862 (Vol. II), 1884 (Vol. III).

Marmur, Dow (ed.), *Reform Judaism*, London: RSGB, 1973.

Marmur, Dow (ed.), *A Genuine Search*, London: RSGB, 1979.

Marmur, Dow, *Beyond Survival*, London: Darton, Longman & Todd, 1982.

Maybaum, Ignaz, *Man and Catastrophe*, London: Allenson & Co, 1941.

Maybaum, Ignaz, *The Jewish Home*, London: James Clarke, 1945.

Maybaum, Ignaz, *The Jewish Mission*, London: James Clarke, 1949.

Maybaum, Ignaz, *Jewish Existence*, London: Vallentine Mitchell, 1960.

Maybaum, Ignaz, *The Faith of the Jewish Diaspora*, London: Vision, 1962.

Maybaum, Ignaz, *The Face of God after Auschwitz*, Amsterdam: Polak & Van Gennep, 1965.

Maybaum, Ignaz, *Creation and Guilt*, London: Vallentine Mitchell, 1969.

Maybaum, Ignaz, *Trialogue between Jew, Christian and Muslim*, London: Routledge & Kegan Paul, 1973.

Maybaum, Ignaz, *Happiness Outside the State*, Stocksfield: Oriel Press, 1980.

Romain, Jonathan, *Faith and Practice: A Guide to Reform Judaism Today*, London: RSGB, 1991.

Romain, Jonathan, *Till Faith Us Do Part: Couples Who Fall in Love Across the Religious Divide*, London: HarperCollins, 1996.

Romain, Jonathan (ed.), *Renewing the Vision: Rabbis Speak Out on Modern Jewish Issues*, London: SCM Press, 1996.

Romain, Jonathan, *Your God Shall be My God: Religious Conversion in Britain Today*, London: SCM Press, 2000.

Rothschild, Sylvia and Sheridan, Sybil (eds), *Taking Up the Timbrel: The Challenge of Creating Ritual for Jewish Women Today*, London: SCM Press, 2000.

Sheridan, Sybil (ed.), *Hear Our Voice: Women Rabbis Tell Their Stories*, London: SCM Press, 1994.

Williams, Bill, *The Making of Manchester Jewry*, Manchester: Manchester University Press, 1985.

Wolff, William (ed.), *Werner van der Zyl: Master Builder*, London: RSGB, 1994.

## Pamphlets

The following were all published by the RSGB (London) unless stated otherwise:

Baeck, Leo, *The Law in Judaism*, 1950.

Bayfield, Tony, *God's Demands and Israel's Needs*, 1981.

Bayfield, Tony, *Sinai, Law and Responsible Autonomy*, 1993.

Bayfield, Tony, *Reform Judaism is Living Judaism*, 2001.

Bayfield, Tony, *What is Reform Judaism?*, 2002.

Berg, Charles, *The Way We Worship*, 1949.

Blue, Lionel, *Prayer for a Worldly Society*, London: Leo Baeck College, 1982.

Borts, Barbara, *Abortion – A Jewish Response*, 1984.

Borts, Barbara, Chiat, Sheila and Joseph, Vicky, *Do Not Destroy My World*, Parts I and II, 1989.

Borts, Barbara and Eimer, Dee and others, *Women and Tallit*, 1988.

Eimer, Colin, *Progressive Judaism: Vision and Reality*, lecture, 1990.

Friedlander, Albert, *The Jews and God*, London: Jewish Information Service, 1972.

Friedlander, Albert, *Suffering: A Jewish View*, London: Jewish Information Service, 1974.

Goldberg, Percy Selvin, *The Idea of Development in Judaism*, 1950.

Goldberg, Percy Selvin, *My Guide to Reform Jewish Practice*, 1963.

Graf, Gerhard, *The Jewish Home*, 1954.

Golby, Amanda, *Conversion to Judaism*, 1991.

Golby, Amanda, *Women in Reform Judaism*, 1991.

Gryn, Hugo, *A Moral and Spiritual Index*, London: Jewish Council for Racial Equality, 1996.

Hilton, Michael, *Kashrut for Pesach*, 1999.

Kershen, Anne, *150 Years of Progressive Judaism in Britain*, 1990.

Leigh, Michael, *Jewish Religious Education*, 1962.

Leigh, Michael, *Aspects of Kashrut*, 1973.

Leigh, Michael, *Halacha in a Changing Society*, lecture, 1981.

Leigh, Michael, *Remember the Sabbath Day*, 1983.

Magonet, Jonathan, *New Reform Prayer Book*, 1977.

Magonet, Jonathan, *One People*, lecture, London: Hillel House, 1991.

Magonet, Jonathan, *Pilgrim Festivals Prayer Book*, 1995.

Maybaum, Ignaz, *The Office of a Chief Rabbi*, 1964.

Marmur, Dow, *Intermarriage*, 1973.

Marmur, Dow, *The Jewish Family Today and Tomorrow*, 1983.

Montagu, Rachel, *Marriage*, 2001.

Reinhart, Harold, *Our Jewish Task*, 1952.

Romain, Jonathan, *I'm Jewish, My Partner Isn't*, 1993.

Romain, Jonathan, *Mixed-Faith Burials*, 1999.

Rothschild, Walter, *Cremation*, 1991.

Shulman, Sheila, *The Impact of Women in the Rabbinate*, 1992.

Silverman, Reuven, *Tevilah – The Use of a Mikveh for Conversion*, 1992.

Smith, Daniel, *Lechayyim – Learning for Life*, 1998.

Tabick, Larry, Bulka, Colin and Miller, Steve, *The Plight of the Homeless – A Jewish Response*, 1989.

Ungar, Andre, *Living Judaism*, 1958.

van der Zyl, Werner, *Judaism as a Way of Life*, 1948.

van der Zyl, Werner, *Jewish Law in the Modern World*, 1953.

*World Union for Progressive Judaism Report*, Sixth International Conference, London, 1949.

## Periodicals

*A Rabbi's Journal* (1975–79, Assembly of Rabbis, RSGB).

*Common Ground* (Council of Christians and Jews, London).

*European Judaism* (1966ff., London).

*Living Judaism* (1966–81, RSGB).

*Manna* (1983ff., RSGB).

*The Journal of Progressive Judaism* (1993–99, Leo Baeck College, London).

*The Synagogue Review* (1934–66, RSGB).

*The West London Synagogue Magazine* (1924–34, West London Synagogue).

# ACKNOWLEDGEMENTS

I am grateful to the following who permitted me to use copyrighted material:

Schocken Books, a division of Random House Inc, for the material in extracts 4.3, 8.1, 11.3, 13.3, 15.2, 17.1, 18.3, 19.2 and 24.2. *From The Essence of Judaism* by Leo Baeck, copyright © 1961 by Leo Baeck. Used by permission of Schocken Books, a division of Random House, Inc.

James Clarke & Co. Ltd for the material in extracts 4.5, 5.4 and 7.2.

Berghahn Books for the material in extract 4.8.

The Jewish Publication Society of America for the material in extract 7.3. Reprinted from *Judaism and Christianity* © 1958, Leo Baeck, The Jewish Publication Society, with the permission of the publisher, The Jewish Publication Society.

Hodder and Stoughton Ltd for the material in Chapter 10, A Final Thought, and 17.4.

Penguin Books Ltd for the material in extracts 16.8, 20.3, and Chapter 23, A Final Thought.

The access to material under the auspices of the Leo Baeck College, Reform Synagogues of Great Britain, and West London Synagogue of British Jews is also appreciated.